The Oral Torah

The Sacred Books of Judaism

An Introduction

JACOB NEUSNER

1817

Harper & Row, Publishers, San Francisco

Cambridge, Hagerstown, New York, Philadelphia
London, Mexico City, São Paulo, Singapore, Sydney

FIRST EDITION

Library of Congress Cataloging-in-Publication Data

Neusner, Jacob.
  The oral Torah.

  Bibliography: p.
  Includes index.
  1. Mishnah—Evidences, authority, etc. 2. Rabbinical litera-
ture—History and criticism. 3. Tradition (Judaism) I. Title.
BM497.8.N485 1985   296.1′2061   85-42788
ISBN 0-06-066103-8

86 87 88 89 90 RRD 10 9 8 7 6 5 4 3 2 1

To

The director, editors, and the entire staff of
The University of Chicago Press who, with
honor and integrity, stand behind honest
scholarship in the face of abuse and
obscurantist, deranged hatreds. They bring
honor to the calling of publisher of academic
learning and glory to their university.

Contents

Acknowledgments

Matthew Chanoff at Harper & Row made not only many valuable proposals for improvement but a still more important contribution. He saw, more clearly than I, what lay at the heart of matters and made suggestions about the reorganization of my discussion that produced a far better manuscript than I had originally written. By his clear vision of the whole, he guided me to a correct perception of what comes first and what takes second place. For me his editorial work was ideal, and I am deeply grateful for the real devotion and critical acumen that he lavished on my work.

I wrote this book at the suggestion of my student and friend, Paul Flesher (soon to complete his doctoral degree in History of Judaism at Brown University). He saw the need to put together, in a single sustained account, the results of my work on most of the principal documents of the canon of Judaism in late antiquity. In insisting that I see these documents as a whole, he focused my attention on the questions that ultimately defined the center of my work. It is the fortunate teacher who is taught by his students, as I have been in the past and am instructed today.

Winnie Bell typed the manuscript with that good cheer and cameraderie that, in our home, we refer to as "the typical Rhode Island experience." She joined conscientious and hard work with good humor and good will, and she claims to have not only typed my work but also to have learned from it. Since she gave me more than a few excellent suggestions on matters of style and clarity, I know she is right.

Preface

What is the Oral Torah?

Judaism has always maintained that God revealed a dual Torah to Moses at Sinai: One Torah was to be transmitted to the people of Israel through the medium of writing; the other was to be handed down orally, memorized by successive sages. These words of God were specifically formulated to be memorized, and the formula was repeated to Moses. Moses repeated the formula to Joshua, Joshua handed it on to his disciples, and so on through the ages. The written Torah and the oral Torah together constitute a single whole Torah—the full and exhaustive statement of God's will for Israel and humanity. This fundamental teaching is stated as follows: "Moses received Torah at Sinai and handed it on to Joshua, Joshua to elders, elders to prophets, and prophets handed it on to the men of the Great Assembly." (Mishnah-tractate Avot 1:1). This book is about the documents that comprise the principal parts of this first full statement, in writing, of that originally memorized Torah.

The writing down of the oral Torah began with the Mishnah, a philosophical law code, at ca. 200 C.E. It concluded with the closure of the Talmud of Babylonia, a sustained exposition of both the Mishnah and Scripture, at ca. 600 C.E. Between these two dates, a period of four hundred years, a sizable variety of books, some of them devoted to the exposition of the Mishnah, others to the amplification and explanation of Scripture, took shape. Sayings in these documents derive from sages who flourished from somewhat before the first century C.E. to the conclusion of the Talmud of Babylonia, hence over a period of more than six hundred years—a longer span of time than separates us from Columbus.

It is easy to become confused, and think that the written Torah goes back to Sinai, while the oral Torah derives from a much later period in the early centuries C.E. In fact the Torah, God's revelation to Moses at Sinai, is one. Viewed from the perspective of Judaic faith, the teachings of the named sages of late antiquity—the rabbis of the Mishnah, Talmuds, and *midrash*-compilations—preserve principles, teachings handed on by tradition from Sinai. These teachings of Sinai in concrete detail become associated only later on with the names of particular authorities of the age of the writing down of the oral Torah.

When, therefore, the Sayings of the Founders (Pirqe Avot) assigns to the authorities listed in its chain of tradition one saying after another, the implication is clear. What a given sage tells us *now* derives from what God told Moses *then*. The sage has given his own name, standing, and authority to a small part of the great tradition of Sinai. Now the list of the founders, beginning with Sinai, ends up right in the middle of names of authorities prominent in the Mishnah and related writings. The claim of the Sayings of the Founders becomes crystal clear. The oral tradition of Sinai takes shape in the Mishnah and in other documents that bear the names and authority of the memorized Torah of Sinai. Thus the Mishnah and successive documents present Torah from Sinai, the part that comes down through the medium of memory. What aspect of that Torah? The principles of Sinai in the application of the Mishnah and subsequent documents as sages centuries after Sinai spell them out. So the detail proves contingent upon time and circumstances. But the principle stands for eternity.

When you confront the documents at hand, you will form a quite different impression. The received, memorized, oral tradition of Sinai in the writings of the sages of late antiquity takes the form of arguments among various sages (who are called by the title of honor "rabbi," which simply means "my lord" or, as we would say, "Mister"). So the oral part of the Torah looks suspiciously like nothing more than transcriptions of conflicting opinions about a shared program of rules, regulations, and scriptural interpretations. This superficial impression then produces the picture not of one Torah, part of a still larger Torah revealed by one God to Moses, but of something rather more secular and academic —a mere library of conflicting viewpoints. In this book I argue that that collection—a "mere library"— does, in fact, cohere. Indeed, from the beginning to the end of the process of the unfolding of the authoritative books—the "Judaism" of the ancient sages, the Judaism of "the one whole Torah of Moses, our rabbi"—the books comprise a cogent, sustained composition, single and whole, (if in diverse components) of holy books: Authoritative writings that say a single harmonious truth constitute not a library, but a canon. The canon of Judaism, made up of the authoritative books, so constitutes not merely a collection of writings but a coherent and harmonious statement, that is, *torah,* or instruction. In fact, then, the books at hand form part of *the* Torah, once more—but now for our reasons—"the one whole Torah of Moses, our rabbi."

At stake in this book is the integrity of Judaism. Why? The Judaic religion stands or falls on the claim of the unity and cogency of the one whole Torah, oral and written, of Sinai. If I make my point stick, then I provide the key to living and believing as an informed Jew. If I do not, then I contribute merely a useful source of information about some books. So much more matters, in the pages that follow, than mere questions of detail. Specifically, details flow together into a single, whole, and cogent proposition. In literary and logical terms, sentences—that is, individual units of thought— compose paragraphs; paragraphs, chapters; chapters, a book; books, a canonical proposition. *That* proposition constitutes the faith of Israel in God's Word and Will at Sinai. So, framed descriptively, the argument of this book concerns how books form a canon. To state my claim theologically, it is how the writings of the ancient sages present, in written form, the oral part of that cogent and one whole Torah of Sinai that defines the way of life and worldview of Israel, the Jewish people, the people of the God who revealed the Torah to Moses at Sinai.

In the Introduction I restate matters in a somewhat more secular framework, so that readers who are not concerned with the nurture of the faith of Judaism, but only with the nature of Judaism as learning people, may join in the argument as full and equal partners. For my hope is both to introduce Jews to the unity of the Torah and its literature, and interested people to the authentic and classical literature of Judaism. I write as a believing and (imperfectly) practicing Jew who also, and at the same time, and always, is a humanistic scholar of Judaism: a teacher about Judaism, and not solely a practitioner of Judaism. But I do stand among Israel, the people whom God first loved and everyday still chooses.

Abbreviations

A.Z.	Tractate Abodah Zarah
B.	Babylonian Talmud
B.C.E.	Before the Common Era = B.C.
Ber.	Tractate Berakhot
B.M.	Tractate Baba Mesiah
C.E.	Common Era = A.D.
Chr.	Chronicles
Deut.	Deuteronomy
Ex.	Exodus
Ez.	Ezekiel
Gen.	Genesis
Hag.	Tractate Hagigah
Hos.	Hosea
Is.	Isaiah
Kgs.	Kings
Lev.	Leviticus
M.	Mishnah
Neh.	Nehemiah
Num.	Numbers
Prov.	Proverbs
Ps.	Psalms
Qoh.	Qohelet = Ecclesiastes
Sam.	Samuel
San.	Sanhedrin
T.	Tosefta
Tr.	Tractate
Ta.	Taanit
Y.	Yerushalmi, Palestinian Talmud
Zech.	Zechariah

Introduction:
The Argument of This Book
and How It Unfolds

This book argues that the several important documents produced by Judaism in late antiquity form a connected statement. I propose to show that from the beginning of the writing down of the oral Torah in the Mishnah, ca. 200 C.E., to the conclusion of the work in the Talmud of Babylonia, ca. 600 C.E. the successive generations' labors were characterized by a certain logic and proportion, an orderly progression. When we grasp the problems of logic and of literature that were confronted as the documents took shape in sequence, we shall see the inner connections between each book, especially the way in which one set the issue for the next.

Consequently, we shall grasp the whole not as a library, not as diverse items, written one by one for a purpose no one can now tell; but as a canon. A canon presents the entirety of the faith, all of its holy literature, as one harmonious statement. The documents speak as a whole. Because each item makes a contribution to the one cogent message of the whole, the books of the ancient rabbis comprise such a canon: in all, the Torah.

A book about the oral Torah could easily provide an occasion for a learned game of show-and-tell, bibliography disguised as scholarship. Instead, I want this book to stake an important claim and make it stick. If I succeed, I shall demonstrate the inner cogency and intellectual coherence of a number of the principal parts of the oral Torah—some, the Mishnah and Talmuds, critical; others, such as Sifra and Leviticus Rabbah, exemplary. If I fail, I shall have left matters where they were before: a literature perceived as a collection of this and that; sayings and stories good for rabbis' sermons; some wise apophthegms; and a lot of erudite nonsense to be learned by scholars as an exercise not of intellect, but merely of academic ritual. So that is what is at stake: One whole Torah in two forms, in writing and in memory, facing the world with a single cogent address in the person of "our sages of blessed memory," or (from a secular perspective) a valuable collection of information about Jews in olden times.

What then is this Torah? The religion that the world calls "Judaism" calls itself "Torah." That is to say, the Torah defines the faith and the generative symbolic and mythic structure, the worldview and way of life, of all Judaists (or practitioners of Judaism). This is a book about one-half of the Torah, that substantial component called the oral Torah. Until the early centuries of the Common Era, the oral Torah (in Hebrew *Torah she-be'al peh,* the Torah that is memorized) in substance was indeed handed down orally, alongside the written Torah. My purpose here is to give readers access to several of the principal parts of the oral Torah—to explain what these documents are, to provide suggestive samples of their literary character, and to make possible further inquiry into this critical and definitive aspect of Torah.

In particular, I want to show how each document carried forward its predecessor's program in some important way. Why does this matter? Because, in so far as Judaism is more than the religion of the Hebrew Scriptures, the oral Torah defines that other part. The oral Torah is what makes Judaism different from Christianity and Islam, which also appeal to the Hebrew Bible as revelation. So a fair step across the outer frontiers of Judaism and inward towards its heart carries us into the territory of that memorized and oral part of the Torah, of what talmudic sources call "the one whole Torah of Moses, our rabbi." And that is the part of the Torah that most people interested in Judaism will find unfamiliar. For people know Judaism through its scriptural evidence in what Christians call the Old Testament, but often do not realize that Judaism reads the Hebrew Scriptures in a distinctive way.

That distinctive way is set forth and explained in this book. It is the approach to the Hebrew Scriptures taken by the great sages, or rabbis, of late antiquity. Those sages wrote the Mishnah and the Talmuds as well as other books so as to express their system, their way of life and worldview, addressed to Israel, the Jewish people. The central question at hand is a simple one. *What is the standing of the great rabbinic writings of ancient times in relationship to the Torah revealed by God to Moses at Mount Sinai?* The answer to that question, given by Judaism from ancient times to the present day, is that those writings—the Mishnah and the documents that were precipitated by the appearance of the Mishnah—constitute part of the Torah. So the concrete problem worked out in this book is exactly *how* the Mishnah is part of the Torah, and precisely how the documents that flowed from the Mishnah and explained it addressed the fundamental question made urgent by the appearance of the Mishnah, the question of the meaning and definition of the Torah.

Let me now explain exactly what happens in this book. We are going to take up in succession the main documents that, all together, comprise the oral Torah. Because each document is autonomous, we have to look upon and describe each piece of writing on its own. We want to see each document in three dimensions: first, by itself; second, in relationship to others; and third, as part of the whole. Each writing is connected to the others, fore and aft: so we must ask which question has been left open by an earlier writing and then answered by the following one. Each composition is continuous with all the others; we therefore will look upon all of the components and constituents of the oral Torah at one time.

We start with the first and most important document of the memorized Torah, the Mishnah, a philosophical law code that defined everything that followed. The Mishnah's closest neighbors are the Tosefta, a collection of supplements to the Mishnah, and Pirqe Avot, a somewhat later collection of wise teachings on how to conduct one's life. To these we turn in Chapters 2 and 3, respectively. In both cases we want to know how the successors to the Mishnah carry forward the fundamental enterprise begun by the framers of the Mishnah. In what way do the later writings join together with the first document of the oral Torah to form a larger, yet single, Torah?

One critical question, addressed to the Mishnah as soon as it came forward as the code of conduct for Israel in the Land of Israel, concerned the written Torah. People had to figure out how the written Torah and the oral Torah joined together, just as we wish to ask that basic question. Accordingly, in Chapter 4, we turn to two documents that address that issue. The first is a commentary to the biblical book of Leviticus; the second is a commentary to the Mishnah produced in the Land of Israel and therefore called the Talmud of the Land of Israel. The writers of both documents prove that statements in the Mishnah depend point by point upon the authority and meaning of the written Torah.

Chapter 5 turns in a new direction to meet a very different document from the Mishnah and its successors in the Tosefta and the Talmud of the Land of Israel. It is a long and interesting work called Leviticus Rabbah; devoted to certain verses in the book of Leviticus. This composition follows the modes of thought of the Mishnah and so turns a book of Scripture into a kind of Mishnah-tractate (or, more accurately, thirty-seven tractates). What is this mode of thought? It is a systematic inquiry into a given topic or problem. The Mishnah's authors take up a theme or a problem and assemble information to work out that problem. Through what they collect and how they arrange that information, the authors of the Mishnah lay down certain basic propositions about their subject. So, by making lists of facts, the writers of the Mishnah make important points about the theme under analysis. In Leviticus Rabbah, this same mode of thought—logic and proposition, based on collections of facts appropriately drawn together into syllogistic lists—comes to grips with a book of the Hebrew Scriptures. To state the matter simply, Leviticus Rabbah turns matters around and treats the written Torah exactly as if it were part of the oral Torah, right along with the Mishnah. So they accomplish an amazing reversal.

At the end comes the Talmud of Babylonia, called the Bavli.

Here we want to know precisely what we have asked of each prior document: exactly how do the authors at hand relate the Mishnah to Scripture, or, in the language of Judaism, the oral to the written Torah? In other words, we want to know in what way the authors of the Bavli regard the writings of the oral Torah as complementary to the written Torah. To begin with, therefore, we ask about harmony and union by addressing the simplest question at hand, the one with which we started.

Chapter 7 draws together what we have learned into a clear and simple picture of how the entire set of books explains the conception of the oral Torah. Exactly how do the ancient sages portray the process of oral formulation and oral transmission of teachings of the Torah from Sinai to their own day? We see two things. First, we get a clear notion of where and when people framed the fundamental conviction of two Torahs and the dual media of their tradition. So we grasp, fully and finally, precisely what the word "tradition" means in Judaism. Second, we realize that there is something more at issue: the figure of the sage himself.* So there really were *three* media for the formulation and transmission of the Torah of God to Moses at Sinai: the written, the oral, and the living. The sage was that living Torah. What the dual Torah means and why it defines the true character of Judaism form the program of the concluding chapter.

The plan of the book is simple and flows from a single line of inquiry into the three principal parts, written, oral, incarnate, of the "one whole Torah of Moses, our rabbi." I mean in this way to describe the oral Torah and to explain how and why within the logic of the system itself and the necessary unfolding of its thought on its central symbol the Torah—the writings of the oral Torah took shape and so made Judaism what it now is.

In introducing the books at hand, I wish only to provide first

---

*In our day, happily, women become rabbis and hence sages; but that is an achievement of our own country and our own generation. In the history of Judaism, however the notion of the sage as a woman was unheard of. In this book we must speak about the facts as they were in the times which we study, hence the sage is referred to throughout in the masculine gender.

access to what now is little known or understood only in a vague and confused way. The oral Torah tends to be treated as a source of stunning sayings. I promise to straighten out a few facts, to show how several documents actually relate to one another and to the entire Torah of Judaism, and in that one, simple way to introduce them. If I succeed in this venture, then later on, in other books, readers may pursue other aspects of the literature of the oral Torah that they find interesting.

I approach the writings at hand—the written version of what was originally an oral, memorized Torah—with respect for their sanctity. I hold sacred the sanctity of the Torah and of the people who believe that God speaks in these writings, as much as in the Hebrew Scriptures. I am one of those people. So in these pages I pursue no secular or historical program, but one of logic and religious literature.

In all, I ask simple questions, important to both secular and religious readers, to both gentiles and Jews, as well as Judaists, the faithful of Judaism. Just what are the principal parts of the oral Torah? How do they speak? What message do they lay forth? Above all, how do they relate to one another and form a whole—a canon, not a library?

In the interstices between one document and the next, I wish to listen to enduring echoes of holy Israel's unique encounter with the living God. My hope is that, in these pages, no one will find reason to take offense. I pray that many people will discover clear and ready access to books that, in the past, were unknown altogether or closed and incomprehensible, confused and indistinct.

1. The Oral Torah Written Down: The Mishnah

The first and most important component of the **oral Torah*** is the **Mishnah.** What, exactly, is the Mishnah? What topics does it cover? Why is it important?

The Mishnah is a fanciful code of laws, some of them relevant to the times of the authors of the document, ca. 200 C.E., but most of them pertinent only to a distant age. It is a utopian document that speaks of nowhere and no time in particular, and to whomever it may concern. The laws that applied and could be kept, which concerned aspects of civil life and family affairs, occupy only one-third of the whole in volume. The laws that aimed at a distant future, the other two-thirds, deal with such subjects as the conduct of the *Temple in Jerusalem,* which lay in ruins from 70 C.E. onward (about 130 years before the Mishnah came into existence); the cultic taboos that protected the Temple and its sacrificial process; the offerings to be made in the Temple on various holy days as well as on an everyday basis; the feeding and maintenance of the Temple priests; the government of the **Land of Israel** by a king and a high priest; and on and on. This curt catalogue points toward the character of the Mishnah as a whole: a work of extraordinary imaginative power, a design of a utopia for an Israel that did not exist when the design was made up, and which would never come into existence.

This Mishnah, this code of laws that embodies in rules for petty details of life some rather profound philosophical conceptions,

---

*Words set in boldface type are defined in the glossary on page 226.

stands at the head of a long line of writings, which all together comprise the oral Torah. That simple statement demands a metaphor. If Alexander Hamilton and James Madison had retired to the backwoods of western Virginia and made up a constitution based on the life of ancient Athens, referring to the conditions of life prevailing not when and where they lived but somewhere else altogether; and if their constitution for nowhere in particular and for no special time then came to be adopted as the basic law of the United States, we should have a remote parallel to the astounding fate of the Mishnah.

How so? **Galilean sages** wrote about a fantasy of a Jerusalem rebuilt and a dream of a Temple restored. They knew neither and made it up in their minds, just as Plato did in his *Republic*. The one thing the Mishnah's authors never indicate is what they expected to happen with the wonderful vision they embodied in their fanciful document. And the one thing they could not have thought is that, within a brief time of their concluding the work, without divine or messianic intervention, their vision would in some measure frame the workaday world. An Israel organized around the Temple in Jerusalem, neatly arrayed in lines of order and structure emanating from that center, like Israel in the wilderness, governed under king and priest, engaged in serving God by killing lambs from day to day and bulls on weekends—that fantasy is not what the Mishnah's heirs brought into being. But it is what the Mishnah offered as an ideal for the Israel that adopted the Mishnah and made it its fundamental law. So the Mishnah was turned from a Jewish counterpart of Plato's *Republic* to a Jewish counterpart of the Institutes of Gaius. For in its character at its inception no law code in history ever gave so little promise of the influence that the Mishnah would enjoy. And it is difficult to imagine that the original authors expected what in fact happened to their book. What exactly did they offer Israel?

THE SIX DIVISIONS OF THE MISHNAH

When we turn to the topical program of the Mishnah, our work of description is made easy by the beautifully organized plan of the

Mishnah itself. The authors lay out their ideas in terms of well-defined subjects and say what they wish about each topic in accord with a rigorously logical program of exposition. The Mishnah comprises six divisions (in Hebrew, Seder[im]), and each division is made up of tractates. Sixty-two (of sixty-three) tractates exhibit the same literary characteristics and participate in the single topical program of the document as a whole. (We shall deal with the sixty-third tractate, **Pirque Avot,** in chapter 3.) If we had the occasion merely to outline the divisions in the order of their tractates and the chapters of those tractates, we would come up with a cogent and easily followed topical scheme. For the present purpose, we require only an account of the main points of the six divisions.

THE DIVISION OF AGRICULTURE

The Division of Agriculture treats two topics: first, producing crops in accord with the scriptural rules on the subject; second, paying the required offerings and tithes to the priests, **Levites,** and poor. The principal point of this division is that the land is holy, because God has a claim both on it and upon what it produces. God's claim must be honored by setting aside a portion of the produce for those for whom God has designated it. God's ownership must be acknowledged by observing the rules God has laid down for use of the land. In sum, this division is divided along these lines: (1) rules for producing crops in a state of holiness —tractates Kilayim, Shebiit, Orlah; (2) rules for disposing of crops in accord with the rules of holiness—tractates Peah, Demai, Terumot, Maaserot, Maaser Sheni, Hallah, Bikkurim, Berakhot.

THE DIVISION OF APPOINTED TIMES

The Mishnaic Division of Appointed Times forms a system in which the advent of a holy day, such as the Sabbath of creation, sanctifies the life of the Israelite village by imposing on the village rules on the model of those of the Temple. The purpose of the system, therefore, is to bring into alignment the moment of sanctification of the village and the life of the home with the moment of sanctification of the Temple on those same occasions of appointed times. The underlying and generative theory of the system is that the village is the mirror image of the Temple. If things are done in one way in the Temple, they will be done in the opposite way in the village. Together the village and the Temple on the occasion of the holy day therefore form a single continuum, a completed creation, thus awaiting sanctification.

The village is made like the Temple in that on appointed times one may not freely cross the lines that distinguish the village from the rest of the world, just as one may not freely cross the lines that distinguish the Temple from the world. But the village is a mirror image of the Temple. As the boundary lines prevent free entry into the Temple, they also restrict free egress from the village. On the holy day what one may do in the Temple is precisely what one may *not* do in the village. So the advent of the holy day affects the village by bringing it into sacred symmetry in such a way as to effect a system of opposites; each is holy, in a way precisely the opposite of the other. Because of the underlying conception of perfection attained through the union of opposites, the village is not represented as conforming to the model of the cult, but of constituting its antithesis.

The world thus regains perfection when on the holy day heaven and earth are united, the whole completed and done: the heaven, the earth, and all their hosts. This moment of perfection renders the events of ordinary time, of "history," essentially irrelevant. For what really matters in time is that moment in which sacred time intervenes and effects the perfection formed of the union of heaven and earth, of Temple, in the model of the former, and Israel, its complement. It is not a return to a perfect time but a recovery of perfect being, a fulfillment of creation, which explains the essentially ahistorical character of the Mishnah's Division of Appointed Times. Sanctification constitutes an ontological category and is effected by the creator. This explains why the division in its rich detail is composed of two quite distinct sets of materials. First, it addresses what one does in the sacred space of the Temple on the occasion of sacred time, as distinct from what one does in that same sacred space on ordinary, undifferentiated days, which is a subject worked out in The Division of Holy Things. Second, the division defines how for the occasion of the holy day one creates a corresponding space in one's own circumstance, and what one does, within that space, during sacred time. The issue of the Temple and cult on the special occasion of festivals is treated in tractates Pesahim, Sheqalim, Yoma, Sukkah, and Hagigah. Three further tractates, Rosh Hashshanah, Taanit, and Megillah, are necessary to complete the discussion. The matter of the rigid definition of the outlines in the village, of a sacred space, delineated by the limits within which one may and may not do within that space in sacred time, are specified in Shabbat, Erubin, Besah, and Moed Qatan.

While the twelve tractates of the division appear to fall into two distinct groups, joined merely by a common theme, in fact they relate through a shared, generative metaphor. It is the comparison, in the context of sacred time, of the spatial life of the Temple to the spatial life of the village, with activities and restrictions to be specified for each, upon the common occasion of the Sabbath or festival. The Mishnah's purpose therefore is to correlate the sanctity of the Temple, as defined by the holy day, with the restrictions of space and of action which make the life of the village different and holy, as defined by the holy day.

THE DIVISION OF WOMEN

The Mishnaic Division of Women defines the position of women in the social economy of Israel's supernatural and natural reality. That position acquires definition wholly in relationship to men, who impart form to the Israelite social economy. It is effected through both supernatural and natural, this-worldly action. What man and woman do on earth provokes a response in heaven, and the correspondences are perfect. So the position of women is defined and secured both in heaven and here on earth, and that position is always and invariably relative to men.

The principal interest for the Mishnah is the point at which a woman becomes, and ceases to be, holy to a particular man—

when she enters and leaves the marital union. These transfers of women are the dangerous and disorderly points in the relationship of woman to man, and therefore to society as well. Five of the seven tractates of the Division of Women are devoted to the formation and dissolution of the marital bond. Of them, three (Qiddushin, Ketubot, and Gittin) treat what is done by man here on earth: formation of a marital bond through betrothal and marriage contract, and dissolution through divorce and its consequences. One of them, Sotah, is devoted to what is done by woman here on earth. And Yebamot, greatest of the seven in size and in formal and substantive brilliance, deals with the corresponding heavenly intervention into the formation and end of a marriage: the effect of death upon both the formation of the marital bond and its dissolution through death. The other two tractates, Nedarim and Nazir, draw into one the two realms of reality, heaven and earth, as they work out the effects of vows (perhaps because vows taken by women and subject to the confirmation or abrogation of the father or husband make a deep impact upon the marital life of the woman who has taken them). So, in sum, this division and its system delineate the natural and supernatural character of the women's role in the social economy framed by man: the beginning, end, and middle of the relationship.

The Mishnaic Division of Women thus focuses upon the two crucial stages in the transfer of women and of property from one domain to another: the leaving of the father's house in the formation of a marriage, and the return to the father's house at its dissolution through divorce or the husband's death. There is yet a third point of interest, however (though it is clearly much less important than these first two stages): the duration of the marriage. Finally, included within this division and at a few points relevant to women in particular, are rules of vows and of the special vow to be a **Nazir**. The former is included because, in the scriptural treatment of the theme, the rights of the father or husband to annul the vows of a daughter or wife form the central problematic. The latter is included for no very clear reason except that it is a species of which the vow is the genus.

There is in the Division of Women a clearly defined and neatly conceived system of laws, not about women in general, but concerning what is *important* about women to the framers of the Mishnah. This is the transfer of women and property associated with that same transfer from one domain, the father's, to another, the husband's, and back. The whole constitutes a significant part of the Mishnah's encompassing system of sanctification, because heaven confirms what men do on earth. A correctly prepared writ of divorce on earth changes the status of the woman to whom it is given, so that in heaven she is available for sanctification to some other man; without the same writ, in heaven's view, if she were to go to some other man she would be liable to be put to death. The earthly deed and the heavenly perspective correlate. That is indeed very much part of a larger system, which says the same thing over and over again.

The formation of the marriage comes under discussion in Qiddushin and Ketubot, as well as in Yebamot. The rules for the duration of the marriage are scattered throughout, but derive especially from parts of Ketubot, Nedarim, and Nazir on the one side, and the paramount unit of Sotah on the other. The dissolution of the marriage is dealt with in Gittin, as well as in Yebamot. We see very clearly, therefore, that important overall are issues of the transfer of property, along with women (covered in Ketubot and to some measure in Qiddushin), and the proper documentation of the transfer of women and property (treated in Ketubot and Gittin). The critical issues therefore turn upon legal documents— writs of divorce, for example—and legal recognition of changes in the ownership of property (e.g., through the collection of the settlement of a marriage contract by a widow, through the provision of a dowry, or through the disposition of the property of a woman during the period in which she is married). Within this orderly world of documentary and procedural concerns a place is made for the disorderly conception of the marriage not formed by human volition, but decreed in heaven, the **levirate** connection. Yebamot states that supernature sanctifies a woman to a man (under the conditions of the levirate connection). What it says by indirection is that man sanctifies too: Man, like God, can sanctify that relationship between a man and a woman, and can also effect the cessation of the sanctity of that same relationship.

To the message and the purpose of the Division of Women, woman is essential and central. But she is not critical. She sets the stage for the processes of the sacred. It is she who can be made sacred to man. It is she who ceases to stand within a man's sacred circle. But God and man, the latter through the documentary expression of his will and intention, possess the active power of sanctification. Like the holy Land of Agriculture, the holy Temple of Holy Things, and the potentially holy realm of the clean of Purities, women for the Division of Women define a principal part of the Mishnah's orderly conception of reality. Women form a chief component of the six-part realm of the sacred. It is their position in the social economy of the Israelite reality, natural and supernatural, which is the subject of the division and its tractates. But the whole—the six-part realm—is always important in *relationship* to man on earth and God in Heaven. Man and God effect the transaction. Sanctification is effected through process and through relationship. The center of logical tension is at critical relationship. The relationship—that is, the process or transaction—is what makes holy or marks as profane. God and the man shape that process. Food grown from the earth, women, cult, and the cult-like realm of the clean—these foci of the sacred form that inert matter made holy or marked as profane by the will and deed of God and of man, who is like God.

At issue in the Division of Women is not whether or not a woman may have sexual relations, but with whom she may have them and with what consequence. It is assumed that, from long before the advent of puberty, a girl may be married and, in any event, is a candidate for sexuality. From puberty onward she will be married. But selected for intense and continuing concern is the question of with whom she may legitimately marry, and with what economic and social effect. There is no sexual deed without public consequence, and without transfer of property from one hand to another. So what is anomalous in the Mishnah's system is the woman's sexuality, which is treated in a way wholly different from man's. And the goal of the Mishnah's Division of Women is to bring under control and force into stasis all of the wild and unruly potentialities of sexuality, with their dreadful threat of uncontrolled shifts in personal status and material possession alike.

The Mishnah thus invokes heaven's interest in the most critical moment—whether Appointed Times or harvest-time or the woman's hymeneal season—for individual and society alike. Its conception is that what is rightly done on earth is confirmed in heaven. A married woman who has sexual relations with a man other than her husband has not merely committed a crime on earth. She has sinned against heaven. It follows that when a married woman receives a writ of divorce and so is free to enter into relationships with any man of her choosing, heaven's perceptions of that woman are affected just as much as are those of man on earth. What was previously a crime and a sin, is afterward holy. The woman may contract a new marriage on earth which heaven, for its part, will oversee and sanctify. What is stated in these simple propositions is that those crucial and critical turnings at which a woman changes hands produce concern and response in heaven above as much as on earth below. And the reason, as I suggested at the beginning, is that heaven is invoked specifically at those times, and in those circumstances, in which Mishnah confronts a situation of anomaly, changes, or disorder, and proposes to effect suitable regulation and besought order.

THE DIVISION OF DAMAGES

The Division of Damages comprises two subsystems, which fit together in a logical way. One part presents rules for the normal conduct of civil society. These cover commerce, trade, real estate, and other matters of everyday intercourse; as well as mishaps, such as damages by chattels and person, fraud, overcharge, interest, and the like, in that same context of everyday social life. The other part describes the institutions governing the normal conduct of civil society, that is, courts of administration, and the penalties at the disposal of the government for the enforcement of the law.

The two subjects form a single tight and systematic dissertation on the nature of Israelite society and its economic, social, and political relationships, as the Mishnah envisages them.

The main point of the first of the two parts of this division is expressed in the sustained unfolding of the three Babas, Baba Qamma, Baba Mesia, and Baba Batra. It is that the task of society is to maintain perfect stasis, to preserve the prevailing situation, and to secure the stability of all relationships. To this end, in the interchanges of buying and selling, giving and taking, borrowing and lending, it is important that there be an essential equality of exchange. No party in the end should have more than what he had at the outset, and none should be the victim of a sizable shift in fortune and circumstance. All parties' rights to, and in, this stable and unchanging economy of society are to be preserved. When the condition of a person is violated, so far as possible the law will secure the restoration of the antecedent status.

An appropriate appendix to the Babas is at Abodah Zarah, which deals with the orderly governance of transactions and relationships between Israelite society and the outside world, the realm of idolatry, relationships which are subject to certain special considerations. These are generated by the fact that Israelites may not derive benefit (e.g., through commercial transactions) from anything that has served in the worship of an idol. Consequently, commercial transactions suffer limitations on account of extrinsic considerations of cultic taboos. While these cover both special occasions (e.g., fairs and festivals of idolatry) and general matters (e.g., what Israelites may buy and sell, the main practical illustrations of the principles of the matter pertain to wine). The Mishnah supposes that gentiles routinely make use, for a libation, of a drop of any sort of wine to which they have access. It therefore is taken for granted that wine over which gentiles have had control is forbidden for Israelite use, and also that such wine is prohibited for Israelites to buy and sell. This other matter—ordinary everyday relationships with the gentile world, with special reference to trade and commerce—concludes what the Mishnah has to say about all those matters of civil and criminal law that together define everyday relationships within the Israelite nation and between that nation and all others in the world among whom, in Palestine as abroad, they lived side by side.

The other part of this division describes the institutions of Israelite government and politics. This is in two main aspects: first, description of the institutions and their jurisdiction, with reference to courts, conceived as both judicial and administrative agencies; and, second, extensive discussion of criminal penalties. The penalties are three: death, banishment, and flogging. There are four ways by which a person convicted of a capital crime may be put to death. The Mishnah organizes a vast amount of information (alleged to derive from Scripture) on what sorts of capital crimes are punishable by which of the four modes of execution. But the facts are many, and the relevant verses few. What the Mishnah clearly contributes to this exercise is a first-rate piece of organization and elucidation of available facts. Where the facts come from we do not know. Mishnah-tractate Sanhedrin further describes the way in which trials are conducted in both monetary and capital cases, and pays attention to the possibilities of perjury. The matter of banishment brings the Mishnah to a rather routine restatement by flogging and application of that mode of punishment conclude the discussion.

These matters, worked out at Sanhedrin-Makkot, are supplemented in two tractates, Shebuot and Horayot, both emerging from Scripture. Leviticus 5 and 6 refer to various oaths which apply mainly, though not exclusively, in courts. Leviticus 4 deals with errors of judgment inadvertently made and carried out by the high priest, the ruler, and the people; the Mishnah knows that these considerations also apply to Israelite courts. What for Leviticus draws the chapters together is their common interest in the guilt offering, which is owing for violation of the rather diverse matters under discussion. Now in tractates Shebuot and Horayot the materials of Leviticus 5–6 and 4, respectively, are worked out. But here in the Mishnah it is from the viewpoint of the oath or erroneous instruction, rather than the cultic penalty. In Shebuot the discussion is intellectually imaginative and thorough; in Horayot, routine. The relevance of both to the issues of Sanhedrin and Makkot is obvious. For the matter of oaths in the main enriches the discussion of the conduct of the courts. The possibility of error is principally in the courts and other political institutions. So the four tractates on institutions and their functioning form a remarkably unified and cogent set.

The goal of the system of civil law is the recovery of the prevailing order and balance, the preservation of the established wholeness of the social economy. This idea is powerfully expressed in the organization of the three tractates of civil law, the Babas, which treat first abnormal and then normal transactions. The framers deal in the former category with damages done by chattels and by human beings, thefts, and other sorts of malfeasance against the property of others. The Babas in both aspects pay closest attention to how the property and person of the injured party so far as possible are restored to their prior condition, that is, a state of normality. So attention to torts focuses upon penalties paid by the malefactor to the victim, rather than upon penalties inflicted by the court on the malefactor for what he has done. When speaking of damages, the Mishnah thus takes as its principal concern the restoration of the fortunes of victims of assault or robbery. Then the framers take up the complementary and corresponding set of topics, the regulation of normal transactions. When we rapidly survey the kinds of transactions of special interest, we see from the topics selected for discussion what we have already uncovered in the deepest structure of organization and articulation of the basic theme.

The other half of this same unit of three tractates presents laws governing normal and routine transactions, many of them of the same sort as those dealt with in the first half. Bailments, for example, occur in both wings of the triple tractate: first, bailments subjected to misappropriation, or accusation thereof, by the bailiff; then, bailments transacted under normal circumstances. Under the rubric of routine transactions are those of workers and householders, that is, the purchase and sale of labor; rentals and bailments; real estate transactions; and inheritances and estates. Of the lot, the one involving real estate transactions is the most fully articulated and covers the widest range of problems and topics. The Babas all together thus provide a complete account of the orderly governance of balanced transactions unchanging civil relationships within Israelite society under ordinary conditions.

The character and interests of the Division of Damages present probative evidence of the larger program of the philosophers of the Mishnah. Their intention is to create nothing less than a full-scale Israelite government, subject to the administration of sages. This government is fully supplied with a constitution and bylaws (Sanhedrin, Makkot). It makes provision for a court system and procedures (Shebuot, Sanhedrin, Makkot), as well as a full set of laws governing civil society (Baba Qamma, Baba Mesia, Baba Batra) and criminal justice (Sanhedrin, Makkot). This government, moreover, mediates between its own community and the outside ("pagan") world. Through its system of laws it expresses its judgment of the others and at the same time defines, protects, and defends its own society and social frontiers (Abodah Zarah). It even makes provision of procedures of remission, to expiate its own errors (Horayot).

The (then-nonexistent) Israelite government imagined by the second-century philosophers centers upon the (then-nonexistent) Temple, and the (then-forbidden) city, Jerusalem. For the Temple is one principal focus. There the highest court is in session; there the high priest reigns. The penalties for law infringement are of four kinds, one of which involves sacrifice in the Temple (the others are compensation, physical punishment, and death). The basic conception of punishment, moreover, is that unintentional violation of the rules of society, whether "religious" or otherwise, is not penalized, but rather expiated through an offering in the Temple. If a member of the people of Israel intentionally infringes against the law, to be sure, that one must be removed from society and is put to death. And if there is a claim of one member of the people against another, that must be righted, so that the prior, prevailing status may be restored. Offerings in the Temple are thus given up to appease heaven and restore a whole bond between heaven and Israel, specifically on those occasions on which without malice or ill will an Israelite has disturbed the relationship. Israelite civil society without a Temple is not stable or normal, and not to be imagined. And the Mishnah is above all an act of imagination in defiance of reality.

The plan for the government involves a clear-cut philosophy of society, a philosophy that defines the purpose of the government and ensures that its task is not merely to perpetuate its own power. Within the Mishnaic fantasy, the Israelite government is supposed to preserve that state of perfection which, within the same fantasy, the society of Israel everywhere attains and expresses. This is in at least five aspects.

First of all, one of the ongoing principles of the law, expressed in one tractate after another, is that people are to follow and maintain the prevailing practice of their locale. Second, the purpose of civil penalties is to restore the injured party to his prior condition, so far as this is possible, rather than merely to penalize the aggressor. Third, there is the conception of true value, meaning that a given object has an intrinsic worth, which, in the course of a transaction, must be paid. In this way the seller does not leave the transaction any richer than when he entered it, or the buyer any poorer (parallel to penalties for damages). Fourth, there can be no usury, a biblical prohibition adopted and vastly enriched in the Mishnaic thought, for money ("coins") remains always the same. Any pretense that money has become worth more than what it originally had been in its way violates the conception of true and fixed value. Fifth, when real estate is divided, it must be done with full attention to the rights of all concerned, so that, once more, one party does not gain at the expense of the other. In these and many other aspects the law expresses its obsession with the perfect stasis of Israelite society. Its paramount purpose is to preserve and ensure that the perfection of the division of this world is kept inviolate, or is restored to its true status when violated.

THE DIVISION OF HOLY THINGS

Let us first review the tractates and then consider their message when they are seen whole. Viewed from a distance the tractates divide themselves up into the following groups (in parentheses are tractates containing relevant materials): (1) rules for the altar and the praxis of the cult—Zebahim Menahot, Hullin, Keritot, Tamid, Qinnim (Bekhorot, Meilah); (2) rules for the altar and the animals set aside for the cult—Arakhin, Temurah, Meilah (Bekhorot); and (3) rules for the altar and support of the Temple staff and buildings —Bekhorot, Middot (Hullin, Arakhin, Meilah, Tamid). In a word, this division speaks of the sacrificial cult and the sanctuary in which the cult is conducted. The law pays special attention to the matter of the status of the property of the altar and of the sanctuary, both materials to be utilized in the actual sacrificial rites; and property, the value of which supports the cult and sanctuary in general. Both are deemed to be sanctified, that is: *qodoshim*, "holy things."

The division prefers not to deal with the special offerings (e.g., those designated for particular days of the week or seasons of the year), which are treated in the Division of Appointed Times; with other than animal fees for the priesthood, specifically omitting reference to agricultural dues paid over in their support, dealt with in the Division of Agriculture; or with that matrix of cleanness in which the cult is to be carried on, expounded in the Division of Purities. Those three areas of the law pertinent to the cult are only alluded to here.

By "holy things" we refer specifically to the altar and animals and cereals offered on the altar or belonging to the altar, and to property and goods belonging to the altar or to the sanctuary. Within these two categories, we find a place for the whole of the thematic repertoire of the fifth division or, at the very least, account for the inclusion of each and every one of its significant topics. The division is content to leave over for use in other divisions materials pertinent to the altar and the sanctuary.

The Division of Holy Things centers upon the everyday and rules always applicable to the cult: the daily whole offering, the sin offering and guilt offering which one may bring any time under ordinary circumstances; the right sequence of diverse offerings; the way in which the rites of the whole, sin, and guilt offerings are carried out; what sorts of animals are acceptable; the accompanying cereal offerings; the support and provision of animals for the cult and of meat for the priesthood; the support and material maintenance of the cult and its building. We have a system before us: the system of the cult of the Jerusalem Temple, seen as an ordinary and everyday affair, a continuing and routine operation. That is why special rules for the cult, both in respect to the altar and in regard to the maintenance of the buildings, personnel, and even the holy city, will be elsewhere, in Appointed Times and Agriculture. But from the perspective of Holy Things, those divisions intersect by supplying special rules and raising extraordinary (Agriculture: land-bound; Appointed Times: time-bound) considerations for that theme which Holy Things claims to set forth in its most general and unexceptional way: the cult as something permanent and everyday.

The order of Holy Things thus, in a concrete way, maps out the cosmology of the sanctuary and its sacrificial system, that is, the world of the Temple, which had been the cosmic center of Israelite life. A later saying states matters as follows:

Just as the navel is found at the center of a human being, so the land of Israel is found at the center of the world . . . and it is the foundation of the world. Jerusalem is at the center of the land of Israel, the Temple is at the center of Jerusalem, the Holy of Holies is at the center of the Temple, the Ark is at the center of the Holy of Holies, and the Foundation Stone is in front of the Ark, which spot is the foundation of the world. (Tanhuma Qedoshim 10)

THE DIVISION OF PURITIES

The Division of Purities is a very simple system of three principal parts: sources of uncleanness, objects and substances susceptible to uncleanness, and modes of purification from uncleanness. It tells the story of what makes what unclean, and what makes what clean. The tractates on these several topics are as follows: (1) sources of uncleanness—Ohalot, Negaim, Niddah, Makhshirin, Zabim, Tebul Yom; (2) objects and substances susceptible to uncleanness—Kelim, Tohorot, Uqsin; and (3) modes of purification—Parah, Miqvaot, Yadayim.

Before we consider the details of the Division of Purities, the reader must wonder why the Mishnah devotes so much attention to the matter—in volume, this division encompasses about one-fourth of the Mishnah. Let us now digress to consider the meaning of purity in biblical Israel and the role purity came to play in the Mishnah.

When we speak of "clean" or "unclean," we are far from a concern with the physical presence of dirt. We are rather confronted with the legacy of concerns left over from pre-Mosaic Israelite culture. That culture, like many others, regarded some things as taboo, therefore to be kept out of the holy community. Various crucial periods in life—childbirth, or the menstrual period—were regarded as dangerous. Various diseases, especially leprosy, were particularly feared, regarded as the mark of the presence of an evil spirit or demon. Mildew, which mysteriously appeared on walls, was also feared.

When we reach the biblical legislation contained in the books of Leviticus and Numbers, we enter a world in which demons (who can do things independent of the will of God) or terrors outside the divine power are unknown. The biblical law comes long after the revolution effected by the concept of one, unique, all-powerful God, transcendent over the world, not subject to any of its laws. It cannot take account, therefore, of evil forces, demons, which work their will outside of God's purpose. But the law must and does take account of the archaic remains of those old conceptions —the taboos associated with certain animals, periods of life, and natural phenomena. These are neutralized, first by being subsumed under the Torah's laws, therefore made to express the Will of God. The laws that designate as impure certain animals, excretions, or diseases know nothing of these as malignant enemies operating independent of the divine will. Uncleanness is merely hateful to God and must be avoided by all who have anything to do with the divinity.

The treatment of purity in the biblical laws, made by priests, accomplishes a purpose. The priestly laws take for granted that whatever its cause, impurity has one constant effect: *You cannot go to the Temple.* Purity functions mainly as the requirement of entering into and participating in the cult. The multiform world of impurities thus is homogenized. While treating purity primarily in the context of the cult may not seem so imaginative as regarding it as a metaphor for moral uprightness, in fact the force of the consequent limitation of the fear of impurity as a cause or mark of evil is enhanced. For if purity and impurity are made relative to the cult, they are limited in the locus of that power's effects. One who is impure is not everywhere a bearer of a malevolent, autonomous power. The menstruating woman or the leper is not dangerous outside of the cult. These people are unclean—which means that they cannot come to the Temple until purified. Focusing the matter upon the Temple therefore begins to convert purity into a matter of relationship or status. It eventually will remove from impurity any sort of independent, material, uncontingent significance.

The reason we have had to review these facts is that one central issue of the Mishnah concerns purity in the ritualistic sense in which we have just treated it. Specifically, the laws at hand take for granted that cleanness matters not only in the Temple, but also in the home. The meal that people eat at home is to be conducted in those same conditions of cultic cleanneess as is the meal that priests eat in the Temple. The participants—ordinary folk—are not priests.

But the sages of the Mishnah at its origin believe that the ordinary meal of an ordinary person in his own home has to be eaten *as if* he were a priest, as if his home were the Temple, and as if he were engaged in the act of sacrifice to God. It is not merely that his food has to conform to the biblical laws of what may or may not be eaten. The man himself, his wife and family and all present, also must be in a state of purity in accord with the requirements of the biblical code of the priesthood in the Temple eating a share of God's food on the altar. The utensils with which he eats, the pots and pans in which the food is prepared, have likewise to conform to those requirements.

On what basis do the Mishnah's authors incorporate the Temple purity laws into the meal? What lies behind the rules, everywhere taken for granted, that you eat your meal like a priest in the Temple—free of contact with a corpse, or with a creeping thing, or with a woman in her menstrual period, careful not to touch unclean objects, thoughtful about what you have done all day long and about what has been done to your food and your dishes? This is a far cry from the biblical priests' interpretation of purity, which limited purity to the Temple. For the Mishnah's Division of Purities rule raises purity to a level of consciousness and importance without parallel in the ordinary life of Jewry in pre-Talmudic times, introduces purity and impurity into every aspect of the common life, and above all into the everyday meal.

The answer is that the Mishnah's philosophers are heirs of the Pharisaic group, which flourished 150 years before the destruction of the Temple in 70 C.E. The Pharisees' interest in purity was one significant part of their legacy to the post-70 rabbis, their continuators. The Pharisees before the destruction were Jews who believed that one must keep the purity laws outside of the Temple. Other Jews, following the plain sense of Leviticus, supposed that purity laws were to be kept only in the Temple, where the priests had to enter a state of cultic purity in order to carry out the requirements of the cult, such as animal sacrifice. They also had to eat their Temple food in a state of cultic purity, but lay people did not. To be sure, everyone who went to the Temple had to be cultically pure. But outside of the Temple the laws of cultic purity were not observed, for it was not required that noncultic activities be conducted in a state of Levitical cleanness.

The Pharisees held, to the contrary, that even outside of the Temple—in one's own home—one had to follow the laws of cultic purity in the only circumstance in which they might effectively apply, namely, at the table. They therefore held that you must eat secular food—ordinary, everyday meals—in a state of cultic purity *as if you were a Temple priest.* The Pharisees thus arrogated to themselves—and to all Jews equally—the status of the Temple priests, and did the things that priests must do on account of that status. The table of every Jew in his home was seen to be like the table of the Lord in the Jerusalem Temple. The commandment, "You shall be a kingdom of priests and a holy people," was taken literally. The whole country was holy. The table of every man possessed the same order of sanctity as the table of the Temple cult. But at this time, before 70, only the Pharisees held such a viewpoint, and eating unconsecrated food as if one were a Temple priest at the Lord's table thus signified that a Jew was a Pharisee. Now that the background and meaning of the laws of purity have become clear, let us turn to the division itself.

Viewed as a whole, the Mishnah's Division of Purities treats the interplay of people, food, and liquids. Dry inanimate objects or food are not susceptible to uncleanness. What is wet is susceptible. So liquids activate the system. What is unclean, moreover, emerges from uncleanness through the operation of liquids, specifically through immersion in fit water of requisite volume in its natural condition. Liquids thus deactivate the system. Therefore water in its *natural* condition concludes the process by removing uncleanness. Water in its *unnatural* condition, that is, water deliberately affected by human agency, imparts susceptibility to uncleanness to begin with. The uncleanness of people, furthermore, is signified by body liquids or flux in the case of the menstruating woman (Niddah) and the *zab* (Zabim) (a person described at Lev. 15:1–31). Corpse uncleanness is conceived to be a kind of effluent, a viscous gas, which flows like a liquid. Utensils for their part receive uncleanness when they form receptacles able to contain liquid.

In sum, we have a system in which the invisible flow of fluidlike substances or powers serves to put food, drink, and receptacles into the status of uncleanness and to remove those things from that status. Whether or not we call the system "metaphysical," it certainly has no material base, but is conditioned upon highly abstract notions. Thus in material terms, the effect of liquid is upon food, drink, utensils, and people. The consequence has to do with who may eat and drink what food and liquid, and what food and drink may be consumed in which pots and pans. These loci are specified by tractates on utensils (Kelim) and on food and drink (Tohorot and Uqsin).

The human being is ambivalent. That is to say, people fall in the middle, between sources and loci of uncleanness. They are both: They serve as sources of uncleanness; they also become unclean. The *zab,* the menstruating woman, the woman after childbirth, the *tebul yom,* and the person afflicted with *nega* (the ailment of Leviticus 13–14)—all are sources of uncleanness. But being unclean, they fall within the system's loci, its program of consequences. So they make other things unclean and are subject to penalties because they *are* unclean. Unambiguous sources of uncleanness never constitute loci affected by uncleanness. They always are unclean and never can become clean: the corpse, the dead creeping thing, and things like them. Inanimate sources of uncleanness and inanimate objects are affected by uncleanness. Systematically unique, man and liquids have the capacity to inaugurate the processes of uncleanness (as sources) and also are subject to the same processes (as objects of uncleanness).

THE MISHNAH AS A WHOLE: THE MESSAGE OF THE ORAL TORAH

From these specific topics treated by the six divisions of the Mishnah, let us now turn to the general points characteristic of the system as a whole. What in fact is the oral Torah, as written down in the Mishnah?

The Judaism shaped by the Mishnah consists of a coherent worldview and comprehensive way of living. It is a worldview that speaks of transcendent things, a way of life in response to the supernatural meaning of what is done, a heightened perception of the sanctification of Israel in deed and in deliberation. Sanctification means two things: First, distinguishing Israel in all its dimensions from the world in all its ways; second, establishing the stability, order, regularity, predictability, and reliability of Israel at moments and in contexts of danger. Danger means irregularity, uncertainty, and betrayal. Each topic of the system as a whole takes up a critical and indispensable moment or context of social being. Through what is said in regard to each of the Mishnah's principal topics, what the system as a whole wishes to declare is fully expressed. Yet if the parts severally and jointly give the message of the whole, the whole cannot exist without all of the parts, so well joined and carefully crafted are they all together.

The critical issue in economic life—which means in farming—is in two parts. First, Israel, as tenant of God's holy land, maintains the property in the ways God requires, keeping the rules that mark the land and its crops as holy. Next, the hour at which the sanctification of the land comes to form a critical mass, namely, in the ripened crops, is the moment ponderous with danger and heightened holiness. Israel's will so affects the crops as to mark a part of them as holy, the rest of them as available from common use. The human will is determinative in the process of sanctification. Second, what happens in the land at certain times, at "appointed times," marks off spaces of the land as holy in yet another way. The center of the land and the focus of its sanctification is the Temple. There the produce of the land is received and given back to God, the one who created and sanctified the land. At these unusual moments of sanctification, the inhabitants of the land in their social being in villages enter a state of spatial sanctification. That is to say, the village boundaries mark off holy space. This is expressed in two ways. First, the Temple itself observes and expresses the special, recurring holy time. Second, the villages of the land are brought into alignment with the Temple, forming a complement and completion to the Temple's sacred being. The advent of the appointed times precipitates a spatial reordering of the land, so that the boundaries of the sacred are matched and mirrored in village and in Temple. At the heightened holiness marked by these moments of appointed times, therefore, the occasion for an effective sanctification is worked out. Like the harvest, the advent of an appointed time such as a pilgrim festival is also a sacred season and is made to express that regular, orderly, and predictable sort of sanctification for Israel that the system as a whole seeks.

If we now leap over the next two divisions, we come to the counterpart of the Divisions of Agriculture and Appointed Times, at Holy Things and Purities; namely, dealing with the everyday and the ordinary, as against the special moments of harvest, on the one side, and special time or season, on the other. Here what is to be said hardly needs specification. The Temple, the locus of sanctification, is conducted in a wholly routine and trustworthy, punctilious manner. The one thing that may unsettle matters is the intention and will of the human actor. This is subjected to carefully prescribed limitations and remedies. The Division of Holy Things generates its companion, the division on cultic cleanness, Purities. The relationship between the two is like that between Agriculture and Appointed Times—the former locative, the latter utopian, the former dealing with the fields, the latter with the interplay between fields and altar. Here, too, once we speak of the one place of the Temple, we also address the cleanness that pertains to every place. A system of cleanness, taking into account what imparts uncleanness and how this is done, what is subject to uncleanness, and how that state is overcome—that system is fully expressed, once more, in response to the participation of the human will. Without the wish and act of a human being, the system does not function. It is inert. Sources of uncleanness, which come naturally and not by volition, and modes of purification, which work naturally and not by human intervention, remain inert until human will has imparted susceptibility to uncleanness—has introduced into the system that food and drink, that bed, pot, chair, and pan, which to begin with form the focus of the system. The movement from sanctification to uncleanness takes place when human will and work precipitate it.

The third and fourth divisions, Women and Damages, take their place in the structure of the whole by showing the congruence, within the larger framework of regularity and order, of human concerns of family and farm, politics and workaday transactions among ordinary people. For without attending to these matters, the Mishnah's system does not encompass what, at its foundations, it is meant to comprehend and order. So what is at issue is fully cogent with the rest. In the case of Women, attention focuses upon the point of disorder marked by the transfer of that disordering anomaly—woman—from the regular status provided by one man, to the equally trustworthy status provided by another. That is the point at which the Mishnah's interests are aroused: Once more, predictably, at the moment of disorder. In the case of Damages, there are two important concerns. First, there is the paramount interest in preventing, as far as possible, the disorderly rise of one person and fall of another, and in sustaining the status quo of the economy of Israel, the holy society in stasis. Second, there is the necessary concomitant in the provision of a system of political institutions to carry out the laws that preserve the balance and steady state of people.

The two divisions which take up topics of concrete and material concern, the formation and dissolution of families and the transfer of property in that connection, the transactions, both through torts and through commerce, which lead to exchanges of property and the potential dislocation of the state of families in society, are locative and utopian at the same time. They deal with the concrete locations in which people make their lives, household and street and field, the sexual and commercial exchanges of a given village. but they pertain to the life of all Israel, both in the Land and otherwise. These two divisions, together with the household tractates of Appointed Times, constitute the sole opening outward toward the life of utopian Israel, that diaspora in the far reaches of the ancient world, in the endless span of time. This community from the Mishnah's perspective is not only in exile but unaccounted for, outside the system; for the Mishnah declines to recognize and take into account the lives of Israelites who dwell in the land of (unclean) death instead of in the land. They simply fall outside the range of (holy) life.

The Mishnah's principal message, which makes the Judaism of this document and of its social components distinctive and cogent, is that man is at the center of creation, the head of all creatures upon earth, corresponding to God in heaven, in whose image man is made. The way in which the Mishnah makes this simple and fundamental statement is to impute power to man to inaugurate and initiate those corresponding processes, sanctification and uncleanness, which play so critical a role in the Mishnah's account of reality. The will of man, expressed through the deed of man, is the active power in the world. Will and deed constitute those actors of creation that work upon neutral realms, subject to either sanctification or uncleanness. These are the Temple and table, the field and family, the altar and hearth, woman, time, space, transactions in the material world and in the world above as well. An object, a substance, a transaction, even a phrase or a sentence is inert, but may be made holy—when the interplay of the will and deed of man arouses or generates the potential to be sanctified. Each object may be treated as ordinary or (where relevant) made unclean by the neglect of the will and inattentive act of man. The entire system of uncleanness and holiness awaits the intervention of man, which imparts the capacity to become unclean upon what was formerly inert, or which removed the capacity to impart cleanness from what was formerly in its natural and puissant condition. So too in the other ranges of reality man is at the center on earth, just as is God in heaven. Man is counterpart and partner in creation in that, like God, he has power over the status and condition of creation, putting everything in its proper place, calling everything by its rightful name.

So, stated briefly, the question taken up by the Mishnah is, What can a man do? And the answer laid down by the Mishnah is, Man, through will and deed, is master of this world, the measure of all things. Since when the Mishnah thinks of man, it means the Israelite, who is the subject and actor of its system, the statement is clear. This man is Israel, who can what he wills. In the aftermath of the last two wars, A.D. 66–70 and 132–135, the message of the Mishnah cannot have proved more pertinent—or poignant and tragic.

The Mishnah presents a Judaism which, at its foundations and through all of its parts, deals with a single fundamental question: What can a man do? The evidence of the Mishnah points to a

Judaism that answers this question simply: Man, like God, makes the world work. If man wills it, nothing is impossible. When man wills it, all things fall subject to that web of intangible status and incorporeal reality, with a right place for all things, each after its kind, all bearing their proper names, described by the simple word "sanctification." The world is inert and neutral. Man, by his word and will, initiates the processes that force things to find their rightful place on one side or the other of the frontier, the definitive category, holiness. That is the substance of the Judaism of the Mishnah, that is to say, of the oral Torah.

Having dealt with the text of the Mishnah and its intellectual context, we proceed to address the important question, How does the Mishnah fit into the oral Torah? In the present setting we must begin by asking why people should have thought it important to relate the Mishnah to the **Torah** at all.

The lines of structure emanating from the Mishnah led to the formation of a vast and unprecedented literature of Judaism. The explosive force of the return to Zion, in the time of Ezra, had produced the formation of the Torah-book and much else. The extraordinary impact of the person and message of Jesus (among other things) had led to the creation of an unprecedented kind of writing in yet another sector of Israel's life. So too would be the case with the Mishnah, Israel's response to the disaster wrought by **Bar Kokhba**'s calamity.

For the advent of the Mishnah around 200 demanded that people explain the status and authority of the new document. The reason the Mishnah presented a stunning challenge to its age and heirs is simple. It was because of the Mishnah's sponsorship in Israel's politics. To begin with, the Mishnah enjoyed the sponsorship of *Judah the Patriarch,* the man Rome had made autonomous ruler of the Jewish nation in the Land of Israel. The result was that the Mishnah served for purposes other than simply learning and speculative thought. Whatever had been intended at its very beginnings, the Mishnah was turned by Judah's government into an authoritative law code, the constitution, along with Scripture, of Israel in its land. Those who served in the government learned the

Mishnah. Accordingly, when completed, the Mishnah emerged from the schoolhouse and forthwith made its move into the politics, courts, and bureaus of the Jewish government of the Land of Israel. Men (never women, until our own day) who mastered the Mishnah thereby qualified themselves as judges and administrators in the government of Judah the Patriarch, as well as in the government of the Jewish community of Babylonia. Over the next four hundred years, the Mishnah served as the foundation for both the Talmuds' formation of the system of law and theology we now know as Judaism.

The vast system constituted by the Mishnah therefore demanded explanation: What is this book? How does it relate to the *written Torah* revealed to Moses at Mount Sinai? Under whose auspices, and by what authority, does the law of the Mishnah govern the life of Israel? These questions bear both political and theological implications. But to begin with, the answers emerge out of an enterprise of **exegesis,** of literature. People explained the Mishnah phrase by phrase and the rest followed. The reception of the Mishnah followed several distinct lines, each of them symbolized by a particular sort of book. Each book, in turn, offered its theory of the origin, character, and authority of the Mishnah. For the next four centuries these theories would occupy the attention of the best minds of Israel, the authorities of the two Talmuds and the numerous other works of the age of the seed-time of Judaism.

One line from the Mishnah stretched through the **Tosefta,** a supplement to the Mishnah, and the two Talmuds, one formed in the Land of Israel, thus, the **Yerushalmi,** the other in Babylonia, the **Bavli,** both serving as exegesis and amplification of the Mishnah. The second line stretched from the Mishnah to compilations of biblical exegesis of three different sorts. First, there were exegetical collections framed in relationship to the Mishnah, in particular **Sifra,** on Leviticus, **Sifre** on Numbers, and **Sifre** on Deuteronomy. Second, exegetical collections were organized in relationship to Scripture, with special reference to Genesis and Leviticus, thus **Genesis Rabbah** and **Leviticus Rabbah.** Third, exegetical collections focused on constructing abstract discourse out of diverse verses of Scripture but on a single theme or problem, represented by Pesikta de Rab Kahana.

This simple catalogue of the types, range, and volume of creative writing over the four hundred years from the closure of the Mishnah indicates an obvious fact. The Mishnah stands at the beginning of a new and stunningly original epoch in the formation of Judaism. Like such generative crises as the return to Zion in the sixth century B.C.E. which provoked the writing down of the Torah, the Mishnah ignited in Israel a great burst of intellectual energy. The extraordinary power of the Mishnah, moreover, is seen in its very lonely position in Israelite holy literature of its time and afterward. The entire subsequent literature of Judaism refers back to the Mishnah or stands in some clearcut hermeneutical relationship to it. But for its part, the Mishnah refers to nothing prior to itself, except (and then, mostly implicitly and by indirection) to Scripture. So from the Mishnah back to the revelation of God to Moses at Sinai, in the view of the Mishnah, there lies a vast desert. But from the Mishnah forward stretches a fertile plain.

2. The Mishnah and the Tosefta

The three dimensions of each text dictate our approach to taking the measure of the oral Torah. We ask first about a text by itself, its character as a document on its own. We inquire next into the text in context, moving outward from the text by itself to points of relationship to its larger setting. Finally, we investigate the larger matrix in which the text, as part of its proximate context, finds its place and meaning. These successive sets of questions correspond to the dimensions I specified as the premises at hand: autonomy, connection, and continuity.

For the purpose of this study of principal parts of the oral Torah, we take up a sample of the text at hand, for example, a complete chapter. We proceed to take a few, sometimes uncertain steps, out from the *text* to the *context* suggested by traits of the text. Finally, we raise that question of *matrix* that concerns us here: How a given text, viewed in its context, finds a place in the matrix of the oral Torah of which that text constitutes a principal part.

So, to state matters simply: We look at a concrete text. We ask about its points of emphasis and insistence. We inquire into its position in, and purpose for, the oral Torah as a whole.

A CHAPTER FROM THE MISHNAH

I have chosen this particular chapter of the Mishnah because its subject matter presents few complications. The passage speaks of fasting and praying when rain fails. Specifically, the liturgy assumed in the passage introduces a prayer for rain on the occasion of the Festival of Tabernacles (Sukkot). That festival commonly marks the beginning of the rainy season in the Land of Israel. The first paragraph deals with the question of what point in the festival the community should commence the recitation of a prayer for rain. The second paragraph discusses at what time in the spring, when the rains cease, the community should stop reciting the prayer. The opening two paragraphs (marked M., for Mishnah; 1, for the chapter number; and 1, for the paragraph number, with letters affixed to each distinct **stich** of thought in a given paragraph), complete that topic.

The next four paragraphs, M. 1:3–7, proceed to confront the possibility of calamity. So we move from regular to irregular. If the rain has not fallen by the beginning of Marheshvan (November), the month following Tishre (October) in which the Festival of Tabernacles falls, people get worried. They commence the process of prayer and fasting. In M. 1:3–7 this process is described. Within the set, marked off by Roman numerals, are a number of matched paragraphs, a triplet of three. A common mnemonic in the Mishnah (a highly disciplined and formalized document) is to present patterns of three entries of the same type, with the third slightly varying the established form. Patterns assist memorization. We see such a set at M. 1:4, 5, and 6. These are marked at the left side with Roman numerals.

I have chosen to present, in the very context of the Mishnah, the relevant passages of a complementary text, the Tosefta. The Tosefta, or supplement, contains numerous sayings arranged in accord with the topical outline of the Mishnah and meant to complement and complete the Mishnah's version of the law. Where these saying are attributed, the persons named occur also in the Mishnah, for Tosefta-sayings mostly are attributed to figures who occur in the Mishnah. It is important, when encountering the components of the oral Torah, to take account not only of the base-documents, but also of secondary writings, composed by the authorities of late antiquity to draw together and preserve important materials not selected for the principal texts. My presentation of the Tosefta's pertinent passages shows us how the Mishnah, even at the beginnings and early stages in its formation and transmission, precipitated efforts to expand and clarify its main points. In the case of the Tosefta, what we find is simply a corpus of complementary statements. Tosefta's contribution is indicated with indentation and each passage is marked with T.

The chapter thus addresses the matter of declaring fasts in order to pray for rain. M. 1:1, 2, begin with the time that the simple sentence "He causes rain to fall" is added to the prayer on the eve of the rainy season, at the Festival. This serves as a prologue to the immense and exquisite construction formed of M. 1:3–7, six, or five, stages in the process of fasting, running on from the end of Tishre and the beginning of Marheshvan, at which the rains are expected but have not come, into the end of Kislev. Thirteen fasts, in several sequences of increasing strictness, are specified for the two months. The unitary construction is unusually clear and bears whatever exegesis is needed beyond the simple statements of each of the stichs.

Mishnah Taanit 1:1

    A. When do they include the mention of *the powers of rain* [in the Prayer]?

    B. R. Eliezer says, "On the first day of the Festival [of Tabernacles]."

    C. R. Joshua says, "On the last day of the Festival."

    D. Said to him R. Joshua, "Since rain is only a sign of a curse when it comes on the Festival itself, why should one mention it?"

    E. Said to him R. Eliezer, "I too have said so not for the purpose of asking [for rain], but only of mentioning 'restoring the wind and bringing down the rain,' [that is,] in its due season."

    F. He said to him, "If so, one should always make mention of it."

                               M.1:1

At issue is the time at which is included the sentence, "He causes rain to fall and wind to blow." The debate, D–F, fully explores the issue of the dispute.

Mishnah Taanit 1:2

   A. They ask for rain only near [the time of] rain.
   B. R. Judah says, "He who passes before the ark on the last day of the Festival—
   C. "the latter person [at the Additional Service] makes mention [of rain], the former one [at the Morning Service] does not mention [of rain].
   D. "On the first day of Passover, the former person makes mention of rain, the latter person does not make mention of rain."
   E. Up to what time do they ask for rain?
   F. R. Judah says, "Until Passover is passed."
   G. R. Meir says, "Until the end of Nisan,
   H. "since it says, *And he causes to come down for you the rain, the former rain and the latter rain in the first* [month] (Joel 2:23)."

Judah takes up Joshua's position, M. 1:1B = M. 1:2C, and refines it. The one who says the Additional Service includes the prayer. E–H are separate from the foregoing. The Tosefta's complement is as follows:

   A. *"They ask for rain until Nisan is over, since it says, And he causes the rain to come down for you, the former rain and the latter rain, in the first [month]* (Joel 2:23)," the words of R. Meir [= M. 1:2G–H].
   B. And sages say, '*The former rain* is in Marheshvan, and *the latter rain* is in Nisan."
   C. Said to them R. Meir, "Now we find that a fruit-tree bears fruit in twelve months, while a crop ripens in six months.
   D. "Just as we find stated with regard to a fruit tree, *[And on the banks, on both sides of the river, there will grow all kinds of trees for food. Their leaves will not wither, nor their fruit fail,] but they will bear fresh fruit every month, [because the water for them flows from the sanctuary]* (Ez. 47:12),
   E. "so does the crop bear fruit for fifteen days.
   F. "Thus you have learned that the former rain and the latter rain come in Nisan."

Tosefta Taanit 1:1 (= Lieberman ed., *Tosefta* p. 322, Is. 1–5)

At issue is the exegesis of Meir's proof-text.

A. From what time do they ask for rain [cf. M. 1:2E]?

B. Once the time for the former rain has come.

C. "If the year was lacking [not intercalated], they assign it that which it lacks, and if not, they follow the proper order [of the months]," the words of Rabbi.

D. Rabban Simeon b. Gamaliel says, "Under all circumstances they follow the proper order [of the months].

E. "If the year was intercalated, they assign it its intercalated month."

T. 1:2 (Lieberman ed., p. 322, ls. 5–8)

A. What is *the former rainfall* [cf. M. 1:2H]?

B. R. Meir says, "The first of it falls on the third [of Marheshvan], the intermediate on the seventh, and the late on the seventeenth."

C. R. Judah says, "The first of it falls on the seventh, the intermediate on the seventeenth, and the last on the twenty-third."

D. R. Yose says, "The first of it falls on the seventeenth, the intermediate on the twenty-third, and the last on the new moon of Kislev [December]."

E. And so did R. Yose say, "Individuals do not begin to fast before the new moon [of Kislev]" [cf. M. 1:4A].

T. 1:3 (Lieberman ed., p. 323, ls. 9–13)

A. What is the latter rain?

B. "Once the time for the early rain has come," the words of R. Meir.

C. And sages say, "Once the second rain will fall."

D. R. Yose says, "Whatever depends upon the former rain—once the former rain falls; and whatever does not depend upon the former rain—once the time of the second rain shall come."

F. Rabban Simeon b. Gamaliel says, "Rains which fall on seven successive days without ceasing constitute the second rainfall."

G. How much rain must fall to contain the first rainfall?

H. "Enough to fill a utensil three handbreadths in height," the words of R. Meir.

I. R. Judah says, "The first is a handbreadth, the second, two handbreadths, and the final one, three handbreadths."

J. Said R. Simeon b. Eleazar, "You have not got a handbreadth of rain which falls from above, of which the earth does not absorb two handbreadths on its account,

K. "and so it says, *Deep calls unto deep* (Ps. 42:8)."

L. Why is it called *rebi'ah [bearing the sense of sexual relation]? Because it fructifies the ground.*

T. 1:4 (Lieberman ed., pp. 323–324, Is. 13–22)

T. 1:2 complements M. 1:2E. The reference of M. 1:2H to former and latter rain explains the interest of T. 1:2, 4.

Mishnah Taanit 1:3–7

A. On the third of Marheshvan they pray for rain.

B. Rabban Gamaliel says, "On the seventh day of that month, the fifteenth day after the Festival,

C. "so that the last Israelite [returning home] may reach the Euphrates river."

M. 1:3

I. A. [If] the seventeenth day of Marheshvan came and rain did not fall, individuals began to fast a sequence of three fasts [Monday, Thursday, Monday].

B. They eat and drink once it gets dark.

C. And they are permitted to work, bathe, anoint, put on a sandal, and have sexual relations.

M. 1:4

II. A. [Once] the new moon of Kislev has come and rain has not fallen, the court decrees a sequence of three fasts for the whole community.

B. They eat and drink once it gets dark.

C. And they are permitted to work, bathe, anoint, put on a sandal, and have sexual relations.

M. 1:5

III. A. Once these [fasts] have gone by and they have not been answered, the court decrees a sequence of three more fasts for the community.

B. They eat and drink [only] while it is still day [on the day prior to the fast].

C. And they are forbidden [on the fast] to work, bathe, anoint, put on a sandal, and have sexual relations.

D. And they lock the bath-houses.

E. [If] these [further fasts] have passed and they have not been answered, the court decrees a sequence of seven more fasts for them,

F. which then add up to thirteen fasts for the community.

G. Lo, these [further fasts] are still more stringent than the first ones,

H. for on these they sound the *shofar,* and they lock up the stores.

I. On Mondays they partially open [the stores] after dark.

J. And on Thursdays they are permitted [to open them all day long] because of the honor owing to the Sabbath.

M. 1:6

A. [If] these too have passed and they have not been answered, they cut down on commerce, building, planting, the making of betrothals and marriages, and on greeting one another,

B. like people subject to divine displeasure.

C. Individuals go back and fast until the end of Nisan.

D. [Once] Nisan has ended, [if] it then rains, it is a sign of a curse,

E. since it says, *"Is it not wheat harvest today? I will call unto the Lord, that he send thunder and rain, and you shall know and see that great is your wickedness which you have done in the sight of God to ask a king for yourself"* (1 Sam. 12:17).

M. 1:7

The point is, of course, that fasts and prayers for rain are called once the rainy season has come without significant rainfall. M. presents its own exegesis of its materials, both in Gamaliel's gloss, M. 1:3C of M. 13B; and in the contrasts drawn between M. 1:4B–C, M. 1:5B–C, and M. 1:6B–C, D; as well as in its explicit comments at M. 1:6F; and additional materials at M. 1:6G–I. The Tosefta's complement follows.

A. In all instances in which they have said, *They eat and drink while it is still day* [M. 1:6B],

B. *but they are forbidden to work, bathe, anoint, put on a sandal, and have sexual relations* [M. 1:6C]—

C. by day it is prohibited to work, but by night it is permitted.

D. How do we know that the day follows the night?

E. As it is said, *Go, gather all the Jews [to be found in Susa, and hold a fast on my behalf, and neither eat nor drink for three days, night or day]* (Est. 4:16).

T. 1:5 (Lieberman, ed., p. 324, ls. 22–25)

A. In all instances in which they have said, *They eat and drink after it gets dark, and they are permitted to work, bathe, anoint, put on a sandal, and have sexual relations* [M. 1:4B–C],

B. "they continue to eat and drink until the east is lit up," the words of Rabbi.

C. R. Eleazar b. R. Simeon says, "Until the cock crows."

D. [If] one fell asleep and then got up, he is prohibited forthwith [upon rising].

E. In all these instances in which it is said that *one is prohibited to put on a sandal,* [when] one goes forth from town [which is fasting], he puts it on, and [when he] reaches the town, he takes it off.

F. And so is the rule for one who is excommunicated and for one who is in mourning.

T. 1:6 (Lieberman ed., p. 324, ls. 25–29)

Tosefta's author cites and augments M.

A. What is the definition of an individual [a pious person, who begins to fast if it has not rained by the seventeenth of Marheshvan] (M. 1:4A)?

B. R. Simeon b. Eleazar says, "Not everyone who wants to declare himself an 'individual' [for the present purpose] [or] a disciple of a sage may do so, unless a court has appointed him as an authority for the public."

C. R. Simeon b. Gamaliel says, "In a matter involving anguish, he who wants to declare himself an 'individual' may do so.

D. "[And if he wants to declare himself] a disciple of a sage, let him do so and be blessed.

E. "[But if it is] a matter involving gain, not everyone who wants to declare himself an 'individual' [or] a disciple of a sage may do so, unless a court has appointed him as an authority for the public."

F. F. R. Simeon b. Eleazar says in the name of R. Meir, and so did R. Dosa rule in accord with his opinion, "[The second] half of Tishre, Marheshvan, and the first half of Kislev is seed-time.

G. "The second half of Kislev, and the first half of Shebat, are winter.

H. "The second half of Shebat, Adar, and the first half of Nisan are the cold season.

I. "The second half of Iyyar, and the first half of Sivan are the harvest time.

J. "The second half of Sivan, Tammuz, and the first half of Ab are summer.

K. "The second half of Ab, Elul, and the first half of Tishre are the hot season."

L. R. Judah counted from Marheshvan.

M. R. Simeon counted from Tishre.

T. 1:7 (Lieberman ed., pp. 324–325, ls. 29–38)

Tosefta's compiler complements M. at A–E and supplements M.'s overall theme.

THE TOSEFTA

Let us first deal with the Tosefta. The document follows the program of the Mishnah in every detail, so our task is only to show how the materials it contains relate to the ones we find in the Mishnah. Then we may proceed directly to the rhetorical and topical program of the Mishnah, since by definition that program defines, also, the things the Tosefta treats and what issues it regards as important.

DEFINITION, EDITORIAL, AND REDACTIONAL CHARACTER OF THE TOSEFTA

The Tosefta, as we have seen, is a collection of statements to supplement the rules of the Mishnah. The composition came to closure about two centuries after the Mishnah, one may guess at about 400. Accordingly, the Tosefta is a document of exegesis of the Mishnah, much like the Yerushalmi and the Bavli in its basic purpose, as we shall see later on. That is to say, the circles that produced the Yerushalmi, the Talmud of the Land of Israel, a systematic commentary to thirty-nine of the Mishnah's sixty-three tractates, as well as compositions of scriptural exegesis for the Pentateuch, such as the Sifra and the Genesis Rabbah, also stand behind the Tosefta. But, unlike the named sages of the Yerushalmi, all of the authorities appearing in the Tosefta bear the names of figures who also appear in the Mishnah. Accordingly, the Tosefta appears to constitute a document of Mishnaic provenance, in that (if the attributions are to be believed) its materials derive from the same sages who created the Mishnah.

The Tosefta contains three types of materials. Two of them are secondary to, therefore assuredly later than, the Mishnah's materials; the third is autonomous of the Mishnah and therefore possibly derives from the same period as do the sayings compiled in the Mishnah. The first type of materials contains a direct citation of the Mishnah (given in my translation above in italics), followed by secondary discussion of the cited passage. That type of discourse certainly is post-Mishnaic, hence by definition talmudic as much as are sayings of Samuel, Rab Judah, and R. Yohanan, third-century masters whom we meet in the two Talmuds.

The second sort of materials depends for full and exhaustive meaning upon a passage of the Mishnah, although the corresponding discussion probably is post-Mishnaic, but much depends upon our exegesis. Accordingly, we may be less certain of the matter.

The third type of passage in the Tosefta stands completely independent of any corresponding passage of the Mishnah. This is in one of two ways. First, a fully articulated passage in the Tosefta may simply treat materials not discussed in a systematic way, or not discussed at all, in the Mishnah. That kind of **pericope** can as well reach us in the Mishnah as in the Tosefta, so far as the criterion of literary and redactional theory may come to apply. We cannot show it depends upon the Mishnah. Second, a well-constructed passage of the Tosefta may cover a topic treated in the Mishnah, but follow a program of inquiry not dealt with at all in the Mishnah. What the statements of the Tosefta treat, therefore, may prove relevant to the thematic program of the Mishnah, but not to the analytical inquiry of the framers of the Mishnah. Such a passage, like the former sort, also may fit comfortably into the Mishnah. If any components of the received Tosefta derive from the second century, that is, the time of the framing of the Mishnah, it will be those of the third type.

In proportion, a rough guess would place less than one-fifth of the Tosefta into this third type, well over one-third of the whole into the first. In all, therefore, the Tosefta serves precisely as its name suggests, as a corpus of supplements of various kinds to the Mishnah.

The Tosefta depends upon the Mishnah in yet another way. Its whole **redactional** framework, tractates and subdivisions alike, depends upon the Mishnah's. The Mishnah provides the lattice, the Tosefta, the vines. Accordingly, the rule (though with many exceptions) is that the Tosefta's discussion will follow the themes and problems of the Mishnah's program, much as the two Talmuds' treatments of the passage of the Mishnah are laid out along essentially the same lines as those of the Mishnah. The editorial work highlights the exegetical purpose of the framers of both the two Talmuds and the Tosefta. The whole serves as a massive and magnificent amplification of the Mishnah. In this regard, of course, the framers of the Tosefta may claim considerably greater success than those of the two Talmuds, since the Tosefta covers nearly all the tractates of the Mishnah, while neither Talmud treats more than two-thirds of them (and then not the same two-thirds).

But the Tosefta's redactors or arrangers tend to organize materials, within a given tractate, in line with two intersecting principles of arrangement. First, they follow the general outline of the Mishnah's treatment of a topic. Accordingly, if we set up a block of materials in the Tosefta side-by-side with a corresponding block of those of the Mishnah, we should discern roughly the same order of discourse.

Second, however, the Tosefta's arrangers also lay out their materials in accord with their own types. That is to say, they will tend (1) to keep as a group passages that cite and then comment upon the actual words of the Mishnah's base-passage; then (2) to present passages that amplify in the Tosefta's own words opinions fully spelled out only in response to the Mishnah's statements; and, finally, (3) to give at the end, and as a group, wholly independent and autonomous sayings and constructions of such sayings. That is the arrangement we see for M. Taanit 1. That redactional pattern may be shown only to be a tendency, a set of not uncommon policies and preferences, not a fixed rule. But when we ask how the Tosefta's editors arranged their materials, it is not wholly accurate to answer that they follow the plan of the Mishnah's counterparts. There will be some attention, also, to the taxonomic traits of the units of discourse of which the Tosefta itself is constructed. That is why two distinct editorial principles come into play in explaining the arrangement of the whole.

THE CONTENTS OF THE TOSEFTA

When we turn from the definition of the Tosefta and of its editorial and redactional character to the contents of the document as a whole, the Mishnah once more governs the framework of description. For the Tosefta, as is already clear, stands nearly entirely within the circle of the Mishnah's interests, rarely asking questions about topics omitted altogether by the Mishnah's authors, always following the topical decisions on what to discuss as laid down by the founders of the whole. For our part, therefore, we cannot write about the Tosefta's theology or law, as though these constituted systems susceptible of description and interpretation independent of the Mishnah's system. At the same time, we must recognize that the exegetes of the Mishnah in the Tosefta and in the two Talmuds stand apart from, and later than, the authors of the Mishnah itself.

Accordingly, the exegetes behind most of the Tosefta systematically say whatever they wish to say by attaching their ideas to a document earlier than their own, and by making the principal document say what they wish to contribute or impute to it. The system of expressing ideas by reframing those of predecessors preserves the continuity of tradition and establishes a deep stability and order upon the culture framed by that tradition. But it makes the labor of teasing out the ideas of the later generations parlous. Describing what is particular to the Tosefta's exegetes and distinctive to their layer of the continuous enterprise of thought that in the end became the oral Torah demands protracted and subtle inquiry.

THE MISHNAH'S PROGRAM

Through the circuitous route of the Tosefta, we return to the Mishnah. As the foundation-document of the oral Torah, the Mishnah demands more attention than any other component of that Torah. Through the ages the Mishnah, through the Tosefta and the two Talmuds, has defined one of the two foci of the discourse of the oral Torah, the Scripture being the other. So let us dwell on the exposition of the Mishnah's rhetorical program.

RHETORICAL CHARACTER OF THE MISHNAH

The first thing we notice in the rhetorical character of our Mishnah chapter is the high degree of formalization of its sayings. From beginning to end we observe vigorous efforts at attaining verbal balance and order. At M. 1:1, for example, the sayings of the two authorities, Eliezer and Joshua, are strictly balanced with one another. Then each has an appropriate reply to the reasoning of the other, M. 1:1D, E. Next there is a fifth stich, assigning to Joshua a definitive reply. Such a five-stich paragraph is relatively easy to memorize on the fingers of one hand. Once we know (1) the issue (A), (2) the choices (B, C), and (3) the names of the authorities at hand, everything flows. More important, the tripartite exposition at M. 1:4–6 allows no doubt as to the acute formalization at which the authors of the passage aimed. The entirety of the Mishnah, excluding only one important tractate (Pirqe Avot, which we consider in the next chapter) exhibits precisely the same traits of patterned language as we see here.

There is no reason to doubt that, if we asked the tradental-redactional authorities behind the Mishnah the immediate purpose of their formalization, their answer would be, "To facilitate mem-

orization." For that is the proximate effect of the acute formalization of their document. Much in its character can be seen as mnemonic. The Mishnah was meant to be memorized by a distinctive
group of people for an extraordinary purpose. The formal aspects
of the Mishnaic rhetoric are empty of content, which is proved by
the fact that pretty much all themes and conceptions can be reduced to the same few formal patterns of readily remembered syntax. These patterns, moreover, are established by syntactical recur-
rences, as distinct from recurrence of sounds or rhymes. Long
sequences of patterned and disciplined sentences proceed without
repeating the same words. That is, they omit syllabic balance,
rhythm, or sound. Yet such constructions do establish a powerful
claim to order and formulary sophistication and perfection. The
arrangement of words in set grammatical relationships, not their
substance, indicates the mnemonic pattern. Accordingly, while we
have a document composed along what clearly are mnemonic
lines, the Mishnah's susceptibility to memorization rests principally upon the abstraction of recurrent syntactical patterns, rather
than on the concrete repetition of particular words, rhythms, syllabic counts, or sounds.

What do we learn about the aesthetics of the authors? A sense
for the deep, inner logic of word patterns, a grammar and syntax,
rather than for their external similarities, governs the Mishnaic
mnemonic. Even though the Mishnah is meant to be memorized
and handed on orally (hence: oral Torah), it expresses a mode of
thought attuned to abstract relationships, rather than concrete and
substantive forms. The formulaic, not the formal character of the
Mishnaic rhetoric yields a picture of a group which speaks of im-
material and not material things. In this group the relationship,
rather than the thing or person which is related, is primary and
constitutes the principle of reality. The thing itself is less than the
thing in cathexis—in responsive relationship—with other things,
so too the person. The repetition of form is what creates form.
But what here is repeated, I stress, is not external or superficial,
but formulary patterns deep in the structure of cognition. These
patterns are effected through persistent grammatical or syntactical

relationships, and they affect an infinite range of diverse objects and topics. Form and structure emerge not from concrete, formal things; rather, they emerge from abstract and unstated, but ubiquitous and powerful, relationships.

This fact—the creation of pattern through the relationship of syntactical elements, rather than through concrete sounds—tells us that the scribes who memorized the conceptions reduced to these particular forms were capable of extraordinarily abstract perception. Hearing peculiarities of word order in diverse cognitive contexts, their ears and minds perceived regularities of grammatical arrangement, repeated functional variations in the syntactic utilization of diverse words. They then grasped from such subtleties syntactical patterns *not* expressed by recurrent external phenomena and autonomous of particular meanings. It is clear that what they heard were not only abstract relationships, but also principles conveyed along with, and through, these relationships. For what in fact was memorized, we now realize, was a recurrent and fundamental notion, expressed in diverse examples but in recurrent rhetorical-syntactical patterns. Accordingly, what they could and did hear was what lay far beneath the surface of the rule: the unstated principle, the unsounded pattern. This means that their mode of thought was attuned to what lay beneath the surface. Their minds and their ears perceived what was *not* said behind what was said, and *how* it was said. They sought the ineffable and metaphysical reality concealed within, but conveyed through spoken and palpable, materials.

What is the upshot of this kind of speech? It is that social interrelationships within the community of Israel are left behind in the ritual of speech of the Mishnah. That is the aesthetic counterpart to the Mishnah's contents. For, within the laws, natural realities are made to give form and expression to supernatural or metaphysical regularities. The Mishnah speaks of Israel, but the speakers are a group apart. The Mishnah talks of this-worldly things, but the things stand for and speak of another world entirely.

The framers of the Mishnah expect to be understood by remarkably keen ears and active minds. Conveying what is fundamental at the level of grammar autonomous of meaning, they manifest confidence that the listener will put many things together and draw the important conclusions for himself. That means that the authors of the Mishnah assumed they addressed an active intellect, capable of perceiving inferred convention, and a vividly participating audience capable of following what was said with intense concentration. The deep power of mnemonic patterns is now clear. The authors demand that the hearer first memorize the message on the surface, and second perceive the subtle and unarticulated message of the medium of syntax and grammar. The hearer is then assumed to be capable of putting the two together into the still further insight that the pattern exhibited by diverse statements preserves a substantive cogency among those diverse and delimited statements. Superficially various rules, stated in sentences unlike one another on the surface and made up of unlike word choices, in fact say a single thing, as at M. Taanit 1:3–7. None of this possible without anticipating that exegesis of the fixed text will be undertaken by the audience.

The Mishnah thus demands commentary and so requires, to begin with, the Tosefta. For the Mishnah's writers take for granted that the audience is capable of exegesis and proposes to undertake the work. The Mishnah with the Tosefta commands a sophisticated and engaged social and intellectual context within the Israelite world. The Mishnah's lack of specificity on this point should not obscure its quite precise expectation. What the authors do not tell us, but which we have to know, is this: The Mishnah and its supplements *will* be understood. The process of understanding, the character of the Mishnah's language testifies, is complex and difficult. The authors of the Mishnah and the Tosefta pay a high compliment to their audience.

3. The Theory of Tradition of the Oral Torah: Pirqe Avot (Sayings of the Fathers)

Pirqe Avot stands at the margins of the Mishnah. It always finds a place in editions of the Mishnah, but it is different from all the other tractates. The differences characterize both rhetoric and topic.

Rhetorically, Pirqe Avot goes its own way, exhibiting none of the subtle modes of mnemonic formualtion through patterned language that strikes one in the Mishnah. The sole pattern in Pirqe Avot is a sequence of names joined to sayings by the words "says" or "used to say." No effort goes into matching these sayings in substance or in structure, though in some sequences three diverse sayings will be imputed to a single name.

Avot moreover does not present laws. Rather, it catalogues wise sayings. Avot is not organized topically, as are the legal tractates. Rather, it is organized around the names of particular authorities. These are presented in chains, or sequences, and the sequence of names is meant to tell the whole story. The authorities who appear in this tractate, and also in the other sixty-two tractates of the Mishnah, here present sayings (or, are given sayings) without any relationship at all to opinions or general principles ascribed to them elsewhere. Here, the same great minds who speak of rather remote and impractical laws elsewhere, now tell how to live. They express great principles to guide people in small things. In this way, too, Avot is different from all the rest of the

Mishnah. Perhaps framed last, it was meant to stand at the head and introduce the system of the Mishnah as a whole.

In its values, Pirqe Avot stands outside of the framework of the divisions of the Mishnah we reviewed above. The Mishnah presents a paradox. On the one side, it is the first document in the kind of Judaism of which the principal symbol is Torah; the primary rite, learning of Torah; the virtuoso, the rabbi; the emphasis, sanctifying the way of life of ordinary folk; and the point of central interest, the formation of a holy society of Israel. But, on the other side, none of this is worked out in the Mishnah. The foci of the Mishnah are quite other. But all of it is adumbrated in Pirqe Avot. The basic value of emphasis on Torah study, for example, is explicit.

When the Mishnah became the constitution of the Judaism that emerged in its aftermath, Avot thus formed the bridge to what was to come. How so? The concept that along with the written Torah, the revelation of God to Moses at Mount Sinai, another mode of revelation besides writing was set forth also as a medium of the *torah,* clearly appears in Avot. This other medium of the Torah constitutes a coequal part of the Torah revealed to Moses. But, as we shall see in Chapter 8, it would be centuries before documents would reach closure that contain the identification of the Mishnah in particular with that oral medium for the transmission of part of the Torah.

The principal contribution of Pirqe Avot to the unfolding of the oral Torah is in its opening chapter. There we confront the use of the conception of *torah* in what would later be a characteristically rabbinic mode. "Torah" stands not solely for the Scriptures, but for revelation. Why does that matter? What is interesting in the chapter at hand is that successive authorities in a chain of tradition beginning at Sinai are said to teach Torah-sayings. But the Torah that they teach does not consist in citations of verses of Scripture, that is, of the written Torah. Hence, by implication, in what follows we see the Torah in a new frame of reference. Now we hear a clear message that from Sinai there was a revelation other than, in addition to, the revelation of the Hebrew Scriptures or the written Torah.

In what way, then, does Avot contribute to a theory of the oral Torah? The answer is that it makes an explicit claim concerning an aspect of the Torah not contained within the Scriptures, that is, writings that would in time become known as the written Torah. The first chapter of Avot makes explicit the view that from Sinai came *torah*, revelation, received as tradition by Moses and handed on as tradition to Joshua. That *torah* is generic, and other species of *torah*, in addition to written ones, could fit into the genus. Standing at the head of the Mishnah, that allegation also bears an implicit claim concerning the status of the Mishnah.

THE OPENING CHAPTER OF PIRQE AVOT

The opening chapter of Avot, joined to those that follow, indeed makes nearly explicit the claim for the Mishnah as *torah*. How so? The authors quote, in the chain of tradition, the names of the very authorities who also appear in the other sixty-two tractates of the Mishnah. Accordingly, by setting the law-code's authorities in a direct chain to Sinai, the author of Avot lays the claim that what these authorities teach falls into the category of the Torah of Sinai. From that claim to the concrete allegations that the Mishnah is part of the Torah, that the Torah consists of two parts —one oral, the other written—and that Moses received the Torah in these two media, one does not have to take a long journey.

M. Avot 1:1–18

> Moses received Torah at Sinai and handed it on to Joshua, Joshua to elders, and elders to prophets. And prophets handed it on to the men of the great assembly.
> They said three things:
>> Be prudent in judgment.
>> Raise up many disciples.
>> Make a fence for the Torah.

M. Avot 1:1

Simeon the Righteous was one of the last survivors of the great assembly. He would say: On three things does the world stand:

On the Torah,

and on the Temple service,

and on deeds of lovingkindness.

M. Avot 1:2

Antigonus of Sokho received [the Torah] from Simeon the Righteous. He would say:

Do not be like servants who serve the master on condition of receiving a reward,

but [be] like servants who serve the master not on condition of receiving a reward.

And let the fear of Heaven be upon you.

M. Avot 1:3

Yose ben Yoezer of Zeredah and Yose ben Yohanan of Jerusalem received [the Torah] from them. Yose ben Yoezer says:

Let your house be a gathering place for sages.

And wallow in the dust of their feet,

And drink in their words with gusto.

M. Avot 1:4

Yose ben Yohanan of Jerusalem says:

Let your house be open wide.

And seat the poor at your table ["make the poor members of your household"].

And don't talk too much with women.

(He referred to a man's wife, all the more so is the rule to be applied to the wife of one's fellow. In this regard did sages say: So long as a man talks too much with a woman.

he brings trouble on himself,

wastes time better spent on studying Torah,

and ends up an heir of Gehenna.)

M. Avot 1:5

Joshua ben Perahyah and Nittai the Arbelite received [the Torah] from them. Joshua ben Perahyah says:

Set up a master for yourself.

And get yourself a companion-disciple.
And give everybody the benefit of the doubt.

M. Avot 1:6

Nittai the Arbelite says:

Keep away from a bad neighbor.
And don't get involved with a bad person.
And don't give up hope of retribution.

M. Avot 1:7

Judah ben Tabbai and Simeon ben Shetah received [the Torah] from them. Judah ben Tabbai says:

Don't make yourself like one of those who advocate before judges [while you yourself are judging a case].
And when the litigants stand before you, regard them as guilty.
But when they leave you, regard them as acquitted (when they have accepted your judgment).

M. Avot 1:8

Simeon ben Shetah says:

Examine the witnesses with great care.
And watch what you say,
lest they learn from what you say how to lie.

M. Avot 1:9

Shemaiah and Avtalyon received [the Torah] from them. Shemaiah says:

Love work.
Hate authority.
Don't get friendly with the government.

M. Avot 1:10

Avtalyon says:

Sages, watch what you say,
lest you become liable to the punishment of exile,
and go into exile to a place of bad water,
and disciples who follow you drink bad water and die,
and the name of Heaven be thereby profaned.

M. Avot 1:11

Hillel and Shammai received [the Torah] from them. Hillel says:
>Be disciples of Aaron,
>loving people and drawing them near to the Torah.

M. Avot 1:12

He would say [in Aramaic]:
>A name made great is a name destroyed,
>And one who does not add, subtracts.
>And who does not learn is liable to death.
>And the one who uses the crown, passes away.

M. Avot 1:13

He would say:
>If I am not for myself, who is for me?
>And when I am for myself, what am I?
>And if not now, when?

M. Avot 1:14

Shammai says:
>Make your learning of Torah a fixed obligation.
>Say little and do much.
>Greet everybody cheerfully.

M. Avot 1:15

Rabban Gamaliel says:
>Set up a master for yourself.
>Avoid doubt.
>Don't tithe by too much guesswork.

M. Avot 1:16

Simeon his son says:
>All my life I grew up among the sages, and I found
>nothing better for a person [the body] then silence.
>And not the learning is the thing, but the doing.
>And whoever talks too much causes sin.

M. Avot 1:17

Rabban Simeon ben Gamaliel says: On three things does the world stand:

> on justice,
> on truth,
> and on peace.

As it is said, Execute the judgment of truth and peace in your gates.

M. Avot 1:18

LINKS IN THE CHAIN OF THE TORAH

The purpose of the chapter as a whole is to tell how the Torah came from Sinai to the sages of Avot themselves. The figures mentioned, from Hillel onward, are well known. They are the masters and teachers of the authorities of Avot who appear in the Mishnah. The one who formed the list therefore is saying that what we learn from Hillel and Shammai, Gamaliel and Simeon ben Gamaliel, is part of the Torah received by Moses at Sinai. The chain links Jews of the time of Avot to the giving of the Torah at Sinai, the beginnings of the Jewish people.

The word *avot* itself has several meanings. One is "fathers." But a more important meaning—which can apply to both men and women—is "founders." The sayings before us are the heritage of the founders and teachers of the Mishnah. The Mishnah through its authorities therefore is placed squarely and firmly into relationship with the Torah of Moses at Sinai. What the masters of the Mishnah say—so goes the message of our chapter—is part of the Torah. So the Mishnah itself (not only tractate Avot, not only the sayings at hand) is linked to the Torah. The Mishnah is claimed to be part of the Torah. How is this so? It is because of the process, beginning with Moses at Sinai, of sages' receiving and handing on: receiving Torah, handing on Torah.

But what is it that the named sages receive and hand on? Whatever they received (let us assume it is the Torah), Avot represents them actually handing on sayings *not* in the written Torah, three sayings each. Accordingly, the status and standing of these sayings are explained at the outset. What a sage receives and hands on is in the status of Torah. His teacher gave him the Torah, (including three of the teacher's sayings). Then what he received—the Torah, including all the additions of the ones who came before him—and what he hands on are not quite the same. Why not? Because he adds his three sayings too. Accordingly, what he adds, as a sage in the Mishnah, is joined to the Torah, and each link extends the chain and becomes part of the chain as a whole. The message is powerful: What sages in the time of the Mishnah stated forms part of the Torah beginning at Sinai and extending onward through all time.

The chapter thus begins with a stunning statement: Moses received the Torah. The purpose is to introduce the chain by which the Torah passes on from one generation to the next, down to the men of the great assembly, Simeon the Righteous, and Antigonus. Each one of those authorities stands alone and has three sayings. Then come five pairs of names, each one also given three sayings. These run from saying 4 through sayings 12–15. At the end, 16–18, there are three more individual names: Gamaliel, Gamaliel's son, and Simeon ben Gamaliel. Assuming that Gamaliel's son Simeon and Simeon "his son" were the same person, we see that the person who made the construction wanted to have three groups of three sayings, and that is why the name of one of the authorities was repeated. In all, therefore, there are three individuals, five pairs, and three individuals, each one given three sayings (nine, fifteen, and nine). Clearly, someone thought the numbers of triplets or quintuplets of names and of triplets of sayings were important. Obviously, if you have a number, and you want to memorize, it is easy to do it if the number is fixed. The numbers that make memorizing easy are three and five: five because you count on your fingers; three because you establish a fixed pattern only when you reach the third item in a harmonious series. So when we see the construction of the chapter as a whole, we notice how carefully and thoughtfully the person who framed it has put it together.

There is no exceptional pattern, however, in what the various authorities, the links in the chain of tradition, say. There is much repetition. There are some recurring themes, for instance, good advice to judges or to disciples or to householders. But I do not see in the sayings any sort of pattern of ideas or themes to match the remarkably thoughtful pattern in which the components of the chain as a whole are worked out.

Seen as a sequence of names, Pirqe Avot 1 therefore makes a startling point. *Torah at Sinai* is passed on in unbroken chain through Moses to Joshua and onward . . . to the very sages cited in the Mishnah itself. Now since *Torah at Sinai* to others of that age—to the Christians, for example—meant only the written Torah (e.g., the Five Books of Moses, and prophetic books or the Hebrew Scriptures), the intent becomes clear. The Torah comes to Israel not only in the Scriptures. What sages teach in the Mishnah is part of the Torah, too. How do we know it? Because sages in the Mishnah stand in a direct line of Sinai. It follows that the Mishnah, containing their teachings, also forms part of the Torah revealed by God to Moses at Sinai. What sages say was handed on in a chain of transmission and tradition from Moses through the prophets and down to the named authorities who predominate in the Mishnah itself. So tractate Avot serves to explain the origin of the Mishnah and to certify its authority by giving us it genealogy: how Israel received the Mishnah, how the sages received the Torah.

There is yet a second point. The Mishnah rests upon the authority of Judah the Patriarch, who headed the Jewish nation of the Land of Israel and enjoyed Roman recognition of his standing and authority over Israel in its Land. In his day Judah claimed descent from Simeon ben Gamaliel, Gamaliel, and Hillel, which is why he named his sons Gamaliel and Hillel. So the chain of tradition was seen to extend from Sinai through Hillel to the house of the patriarch, the government of Israel in the Land of Israel. Indeed, Hillel also was alleged at the same period to come from the line of David, hence, the household of the Messiah. At the same time, the Mishnah contains sayings of named sages, and so it rests upon the learning of the great sages. They, too, claim a genealogy, extending through the relationship of sage to disciple, an ancient spiritual family in the supernatural world of the Torah. The other side of the way leads to Sinai through the disciples of Yohanan ben Zakkai, backward from him to Simeon ben Gamaliel, and onward also through Hillel, to Sinai.

THE TWO LINES OF THE TORAH

The opening chapter of Avot forms a single extended composition, beginning to end. It furthermore is continued into the second chapter. What is most important to the framers of these chapters is the sequence of names. It presents itself in an inverted Y:

Avot 1:1	Torah at Sinai
	Moses
	Joshua
	Elders
	Prophets
1–3	Men of the great assembly
	Simeon the Righteous
	Antigonus of Sokho
4–15	Yose ben Yoezer and Yose ben Yohanan
	Joshua ben Perahyah and Nittai the Arbelite
	Judah ben Tabbai and Simeon ben Shetah
	Shemaiah and Avtalyon
	Hillel and Shammai
16–18	Gamaliel
	Simeon, his son
	Simeon ben Gamaliel
2:1–7	Rabbi [Judah the Patriarch]
2:8–14	Yohanan ben Zakkai
	Gamaliel, son of Judah the Patriarch
	Eliezer ben Hyrcanus
	Hillel [son of Judah the Patriarch]
	Joshua ben Hananiah
	Yose the Priest
	Simeon ben Nethanel
	Eleazar ben Arakh

The Torah thus comes down in two lines, a double genealogy. First, there is a direct line from Judah the Patriarch and his sons, Gamaliel and Hillel, back to the figure of Simeon ben Gamaliel, Gamaliel, and Hillel of ancient times—250 years earlier. Accordingly, the authority who promulgated the Mishnah, Judah the Patriarch (and his successors), stand in a direct line to Hillel—and back to Moses at Sinai.

Second, there is also a direct line extending from the five disciples of Yohanan ben Zakkai—two of them, Eliezer and Joshua, among the principal sages of the generation after the destruction of the Temple in 70 C.E.—back to Simeon ben Gamaliel, Gamaliel, Hillel (and Shammai). Since among the most commonly cited authorities in several of the divisions of the Mishnah are Hillel and Shammai's houses, or schools, the most important point is this: The paramount sages of the Mishnah, known on nearly every page of the documents, stand in that same chain of tradition as do the authorities behind the Mishnah, Judah the Patriarch and his administration.

The authority of the Mishnah derives from two paths, both emanating from one source. The patriarchs' and the sages' document, the Mishnah, comes from Sinai. The chain of tradition is direct, specific, and, in context, genealogical. Just as priests validate their standing through their family records, so patriarchs and sages validate their standing—their Torah tradition—through the record of who received, and who handed on, that Torah tradition. That is the stunning declaration of the chains of tradition in the opening two chapters of Avot.

THE CONTEXT OF THE MISHNAH

Since the text of Avot has drawn our attention to the issue of the Mishnah's relationship to the Torah, we have to return to the question of the Mishnah as a whole. Through the unfolding of the several successive components of the oral Torah, the relationship of the Mishnah to Scripture, or, in the language we have inherited from the ancient sages, of the oral Torah to the written Torah, predominated. We move then from text to context. As we saw, the text speaks of *torah* and cites not biblical authorities, but the Mishnah's own sages. What is the relationship of their *torah,* that is their authoritative teaching, to *the* Torah? And why, second, did the issue prove urgent and inescapable? To answer these two questions, we take up the description of the matrix, in the oral Torah, in which the Mishnah, now including Pirqe Avot, finds its natural and definitive place.

Let me begin this account of the context by returning to the Mishnah itself. The Mishnah presented such an unprecedented problem to the partriarch's sages, who received the Mishnah, for a simple reason. So far as all prior forms of Judaism were concerned, revelation had been contained in the Tanakh, the written Torah (called by Christians, "the Old Testament"). True, God may have spoken in diverse ways. Other traditions, particular to diverse groups, did circulate. The last of the biblical books had been completed, however (so far as Jews then knew), many centuries before. How then could a new book, the Mishnah, claim standing as holy and as revealed by God? More pressing, the issue of what validated the authority of the people who knew and applied that holy book to Israel's life had to find an answer. The crisis precipitated by the Mishnah came about because of the urgent requirement of explaining, first, just what the Mishnah was in relationship to the Torah of Moses; second, why the sages who claimed to interpret and apply the law of Mishnah to the life of Israel had the authority to do so; and, third, how Israel, in adhering to the rules of the Mishnah, kept the will of God and lived the holy life God wanted them to live.

But it was the Mishnah in particular that presented these critical problems of a social and theological order. That is not to be taken for granted. The Mishnah hardly was the first piece of new writing to confront Israel from the closure of Scripture to the end of the second century. Other books had found a capacious place in the canon composed by groups of Israelites that received new writings and deemed them holy. The canon of some groups, after all, had made room for writings of apocryphal and **pseudepigraphic** provenance so framed as to be deemed holy. The **Essene library at Qumran** encompassed diverse books, surely received as authoritative and so holy, which other Jews did not know within their canon. So, as is clear, we have to stand back and ask why, to the sages who received and realized the Mishnah, that book should have presented special, particularly provocative, problems. That encompasses the issue of why the relationship of the Mishnah to Scripture should have proved so pressing in third-, fourth-, and fifth-centuries' circles of talmudic rabbis. By contrast, we have no evidence that the relationship to the canon of Scripture exhibited by the Manual of Discipline, the Hymns, the War Scroll, or the Damascus covenant perplexed the teacher of righteousness and the other holy priests of the Essene community. To the contrary, those documents at Qumran appear side by side with the ones we now know as canonical Scripture. The high probability is that, to the Essenes, the sectarian books were no less holy and authoritative than Leviticus, Deuteronomy, Nahum, Habakkuk, Isaiah, and the other books of the biblical canon they, among all Israelites, revered.

So the issue, of the relationship to the Torah of the document at hand had to be raised because of the peculiar traits of the Mishnah itself. But the dilemma proved acute, not merely chronic, for a political reason. The particular purpose the Mishnah was meant to serve and the political sponsorship behind the document explain what was at issue. The Mishnah was made to provide Israel's constitution. It was promulgated by the ethnic ruler of the Jewish nation in the land of Israel, Judah the Patriarch, who ruled with Roman support as the fully recognized Jewish authority in the holy land. He and his government appealed to the Mishnah, and so, in time, did his counterpart, the exilarch who ruled the Jews of Iranian Babylonia. So the Mishnah was public, not sectarian; nor merely the idle utopian speculation of a handful of Galilean sages, rabbinical philosophers—though, in structure and content, that is precisely what it was.

Accordingly, the Mishnah emerged as a political document. It demanded assent and conformity to its rules, where they were relevant to the government and court system of the Jewish people in its land. The Mishnah could not be ignored and therefore had to be explained in universally accessible terms. Furthermore, the Mishnah demanded explanation not merely in relationship to the established canon of Scripture and apology as the constitution of the Jews' government, the patriarchate of the second-century Land of Israel. The nature of Israelite life, lacking all capacity to distinguish as secular any detail of the common culture, made it natural to wonder about a deeper issue. How so? Scripture treats all aspects of Israel's life as subject to God's will. We realize what this means when we recall that God would punish Israel for sins against the poor and the weak as much as against the cult or ritual. Rites and rights form an undifferentiated realm. There is no claim that the one is religious, the other secular. All things are subject to God's will and may be made holy or profaned by human beings. So the choice of declaring the Mishnah to be essentially secular law, resting on authority other than God's revelation to Moses at Sinai, really did not present itself.

Israel understood its collective life and the fate of each individual under the aspect of God's loving concern, as expressed in the Torah. Accordingly, laws issued to define what people were supposed to do could not stand by themselves. They had to receive the imprimatur of Heaven, that is, they had to be given the status of revelation. To make its way in Israelite life, the Mishnah as a constitution and code demanded for itself a theory of beginnings at (or in relationship to) Sinai, with Moses, from God. Other new writings for a long time had proved able to win credence as part of the Torah, hence as revealed by God and so endowed with legitimacy. But they did so in ways not taken by the Mishnah's framers. How did the Mishnah differ? It was sent forth not in writing, but as a document to be memorized and handed on orally.

It was in the medium of writing that, in the view of all Israel until about 200 C.E., God had been understood to reveal the divine

Word and Will. The Torah was a written book. People who claimed to receive further messages from God usually wrote them down. They had three choices in securing acceptance of their account. All three involved linking the new to the old. In claiming to hand on revelation, they would first sign their books with the names of biblical heroes. Second, they would imitate the style of biblical Hebrew. Or third, they would present an exegesis of existing written verses, validating their ideas by supplying proof-texts for them. From the closure of the Torah literature in the time of Ezra, ca. 450 B.C.E. to the time of the Mishnah, nearly seven hundred years later, we do not have a single book alleged to be holy and at the same time standing wholly out of relationship, in one of these three ways, to the Holy Scriptures of ancient Israel. The pseudepigraphic writings fall into the first category, the Essene writings at Qumran into the second and third. I may point also to the Gospels, which take as a principal problem the demonstration of how Jesus had fulfilled the prophetic promises of the Old Testament and in other ways carried forward and even embodied Israel's Scripture.

Insofar as a piece of Jewish writing did not find a place in relationship to Scripture, its author laid no claim to present a holy book. The contrast between Jubilees and the Testaments of the Patriarchs, with their constant and close harping on biblical matters, and the several books of Maccabees, shows the difference. The former claim to present revealed truth, the latter, history. So a book was holy because in style, in authorship, or in (alleged) origin, it contained Scripture. Therefore it found a place (at least in the author's mind) within the canon, or because it provided an exposition on Scripture's meaning.

But the Mishnah made no such claim. As we have seen in Chapter 2, it entirely ignored the style of biblical Hebrew, speaking in a quite different kind of Hebrew altogether. It is silent on its authorship through sixty-two of the sixty-three tractates. Nowhere but at M. Avot 1:1 does the Mishnah contain the claim that God had inspired the authors of the document. These authors are not given biblical names. They certainly are not alleged to have been biblical saints. Most of the book's named authorities flourished within the same century as its anonymous arrangers and redactors, not in remote antiquity. Above all, the Mishnah contains scarcely a handful of exegeses of Scripture. These, where they occur, play a trivial and tangential role, as at M. Taanit 1. So here is the problem of the Mishnah: different from Scripture in language and style, indifferent to the claim of authorship by a biblical hero or divine inspiration, stunningly aloof from allusion to verses of Scripture for nearly the whole of its discourse—yet authoritative for Israel.

The crux of the matter, therefore, is that the Mishnah was not a statement of theory alone, telling us only how things will be in the **eschaton.** Nor was it a wholly sectarian document, reporting the view of a group without standing or influences in the larger life of Israel. True, in some measure it bears both of these traits of eschatology and sectarian provenance. But the Mishnah was (and is) law for Israel. It entered the government and courts of the Jewish people, both in the motherland and also overseas, as the authoritative constitution of the courts of Judaism. The advent of the Mishnah therefore marked a turning in the life of the nation-religion. The document demanded explanation and apology.

The one thing one could not do, as a Jew in third-century Tiberias, Sepphoris, Caesarea, or Beth Shearim, in Galilee, was ignore the thing. True, one might refer solely to ancient Scripture and tradition and live life out within the inherited patterns of the familiar Israelite religion-culture. But as soon as a Jew dealt with the Jewish government in charge of everyday life—went to court over the damages done to a crop by a neighbor's ox, for instance—such a one came up against a law in addition to the law of Scripture, a document the principles of which governed and settled all matters. So the Mishnah rapidly came to confront the life of Israel. The people who knew the Mishnah, the rabbis or sages, came to dominate that life. And their claim, in accord with the Mishnah, to exercise authority and the right to impose heavenly sanction, came to perplex. Now the crisis is fully exposed.

So, to conclude, on the surface Scripture plays little role in the Mishnaic system. How could the Mishnah be part of the Torah? The Mishnah rarely cites a verse of Scripture, refers to Scripture as an entity, links its own ideas to those of Scripture or, even by indirect or remote allusion to a scriptural verse or teaching, lays claims to originate in what Scripture has said. Superficially, the Mishnah is totally indifferent to Scripture. It is not related to the Torah at all. That impression, moreover, is reinforced by the traits of the language of the Mishnah. The framers of Mishnaic discourse never attempt to imitate the language of Scripture, as do those of the Essene writings at Qumran. The very redactional structure of Scripture, found so serviceable by the writer of the Temple scroll, is of no interest whatever to the organizers of the Mishnah and its tracates, except in a few cases (Yoma, Pesahim).

Formally, redactionally, and linguistically, the Mishnah stands in splendid isolation from Scripture. This is something that had to be confronted as soon as the Mishnah came to closure and was presented as authoritative to the Jewish community of the holy land and of Babylonia. It is not possible to point in Israelite writings to many parallels—that is, cases of anonymous books, received as holy, in which the forms and formulations (specific verses) of Scripture play so slight a role. Jews who wrote holy books commonly imitated the Scripture's language; they cited concrete verses, or they claimed (at the very least) that direct revelation has come to them, as in the angelic discourses of Ezra and Baruch, so that what they say stands on an equal plane with Scripture. The internal evidence of the Mishnah's sixty-two tractates, by contrast, in no way suggests that anyone pretended to talk like Moses and write like Moses, claimed to cite and correctly interpret things that Moses had said, or even alleged himself to have had a revelation like that of Moses and so to stand on the mountain with Moses. There is none of this. So the claim of scriptural authority for the Mishnah's authors and the claim of scriptural foundations for the Mishnah's doctrines and institutions are difficult to locate within the internal evidence of the Mishnah itself.

THE PLACE OF SCRIPTURE IN THE MISHNAIC TRADITION

We cannot be surprised that, in consequence of this amazing position of autonomous authority implicit in the character of Mishnaic discourse, the Mishnah should have demanded in its own behalf some sort of apologetic. Nor should we be surprised that the Mishnah attracted its share of hostile criticism. The issue, in the third century, would be precisely the issue phrased when we ask in general about the authority of tradition in Judaism: Why should we listen to this mostly anonymous document, which makes statements on the nature of institutions and social conduct, statements we obviously are expected to keep? Who are Meir, Yose, Judah, Simeon, and Eleazar—people who, from the perspective of the recipients of the document, lived fifty or a hundred years ago—that we should listen to what they have to say? God revealed the Torah. Is this Mishnah too part of the Torah? If so, how? What, in other words, is the relationship of the Mishnah to Scripture, and how does the Mishnah claim authority over us such as we accord to the revelation to Moses by God at Mount Sinai? There are two important responses to the question of the place of Scripture in the Mishnah tradition.

First and most radical then, is the apology of Avot: The Mishnah constitutes *torah*. It too is a statement of revelation, "Torah revealed to Moses at Sinai." But this part of revelation has come down in a form different from the well-known, written part, the Scripture. This tradition truly deserves the name "tradition," because for a long time it was handed down orally, not in writing, until given the written formulation now before us in the Mishnah. This sort of apologetic for the Mishnah emerges in Avot's stunning Chapter 1, linking Moses on Sinai through the ages to the earliest-named authorities of the Mishnah itself, the five pairs, on down to Shammai and Hillel. Since, as I said, some of the named authorities in the chain of tradition appear throughout the materials of the Mishnah, the claim is that what these people say comes to them from Sinai through the processes of *qabbalah* and *massoret* —handing down, traditioning.

So the reason from the perspective of the Torah theory of the Mishnah supplied in Avot is that the Mishnah did not cite Scripture because it did not have to. The Mishnah stood on the same plane as Scripture. It enjoyed the same authority as Scripture. This radical position is still more extreme than that taken by pseudepigraphic writers, who imitate the style of Scripture, or who claim to speak within that same gift of revelation as Moses. It is one thing to say one's holy book is Scripture because it is like Scripture, or to claim that the author of the holy book has a revelation independent of that of Moses. These two positions concede to the Torah of Moses priority over their own holy books. The Mishnah's apologists in Avot made no such concession, when they alleged that the Mishnah is part of the Torah of Moses. They appealed to the highest possible authority in the Israelite framework, claiming the most one can claim in behalf of the book which, in fact, bears the names of men who lived fifty years before the apologists themselves. That seems to me remarkable courage.

So that takes care of this matter of the Mishnah's not citing Scripture. When we consider the rich corpus of allusions to Scripture in other holy books, both those bearing the names of authors and those presented anonymously, we realize that the Mishnah claims its authority to be coequal with that of Scripture, while so many other holy books are made to lay claim to authority only because they depend upon the authority of Scripture and state the true meaning of Scripture. That fact brings us to the second answer to the question of the place of Scripture in the Mishnaic tradition, which we shall take up in the next chapter.

But let me prepare you, in advance, for a surprise. The claim made in behalf of the Mishnah that that document was equal to, and autonomous of, the written Torah proved too radical for some. They sought a different and more conservative answer altogether to the question of the standing and authority of the Mishnah. Perhaps because they could not concede the fundamental claim in behalf of sages laid down by the authors of tractate Avot, these other thinkers, also in good standing in the movement of sages or rabbis, took up exactly the opposite position.

How so? They held that the Mishnah not only did not stand on the same plane with Scripture, but it also was not autonomous of the written Torah. Rather, the Mishnah depended for each of its statements upon statements already made in Scripture. So what the Mishnah said was true found its validation in the written Torah. Only when we can provide a verse of the written Scriptures to prove a point—hence a "proof-text"—may we claim certainty about a position we find in the oral Torah or Mishnah. This other position stands at the opposite corner from the one of the framers of tractate Avot. In Chapter 4 we shall examine the alternative to the view we now have examined.

Should we be surprised that sages—intellectuals—should differ among themselves upon fundamental questions? Only if we know no intellectuals in our own day, only if we do not read magazines or books, and do not listen to conversations and discussions among literate and concerned men and women. But no one who has read this far is unaware that thinking people disagree. It is what thought is all about.

So, two positions take shape.

First, as in Avot, tradition, in the form of the Mishnah, is deemed autonomous of Scripture and enjoys the same authority as that of Scripture. The reason is that Scripture and oral tradition are merely two media for conveying a single corpus of revealed law and doctrine.

Or, in the Talmuds and other writings, tradition in the form of the Mishnah is true because it is not autonomous of Scripture. Tradition is secondary and dependent upon Scripture.

Second, as in Avot, the authority of the sages of the Mishnah is the authority of Moses. That authority comes to the Mishnah directly and in an unmediated way, because the Mishnah's words were said by God to Moses at Mount Sinai and faithfully transmitted through a process of oral formulation and oral transmission from that time until those words were written down by Judah the Patriarch at the end of the second century.

Or, that authority comes to the Mishnah indirectly, in a way mediated through the written Scriptures, solely by learned sages.

Third, as in Avot, what the Mishnah says is what the Scripture says, rightly interpreted. The authority of tradition lies in its correct interpretation of the Scripture. Tradition bears no autonomous authority, is not an independent entity, correlative with Scripture. A technology of exegesis of grammar and syntax is needed to build the bridge between tradition as contained in the Mishnah and Scripture, the original utensil shaped by God and revealed to Moses to convey the truth of revelation to the community of Israel.

Or matters are otherwise. I hardly need to make them explicit. Instead of spelling things out further, let us turn directly to the documents that present the approach different from that of tractate Avot.

4. Explaining the Oral Torah The Sifra and the Yerushalmi (The Talmud of the Land of Israel)

The Sifra, a commentary to Leviticus, and the Yerushalmi, the Talmud of the Land of Israel, present a second theory of the Mishnah's place in the Torah, or of the Mishnah as the oral Torah. As I said in Chapter 3, their theory turned out to be more conventional, therefore more enduring, than that of Avot. What was it? In accord with this other view, the Mishnah says in its way exactly what the Scriptures say in theirs. In fact, everything important in the Mishnah can be shown to rest upon Scripture. To frame matters in terms of the Torah, the oral Torah takes a subordinated and contingent position to the written Torah. What is in the oral Torah is true only because a proof-text deriving from the written Torah proves it. It follows that the oral Torah builds upon the foundations of the written Torah.

The task of explanation of, or commentary upon, Mishnaic statements to begin with is to show where in the written Torah to find, for the oral Torah, proof for all propositions. So the two Talmuds commonly approach the exposition of a paragraph of the Mishnah by beginning with the question, "What is the source of this statement?" They invariably answer the question with the words, "As it is written . . . ," or "as it is said . . . ," followed by a citation of a verse of Scripture as a proof-text. That fixed feature of the Talmuds' exegesis of the Mishnah constitutes the definitive theory of the Mishnah's place in the Torah and of the Mishnah as the oral Torah *par excellence.*

How then, within this other, exegetical theory, does the Mishnah relate to Scripture? The two Talmuds and other legal-exegetical writings produced in the two hundred years after the closure of the Mishnah take the position that the Mishnah can be shown to derive directly from Scripture. So the Mishnah is deemed distinct from, and subordinate to, Scripture. This position is expressed in an obvious way. "As it is said in Scripture," endlessly repeated in the Talmud's Mishnah—exegesis, constitutes a powerful defense for the revealed truth of the Mishnah.

THE SIFRA

That the search for the scriptural basis for the Mishnah's laws constitutes both an apologetic for, and a critique of, the Mishnah is shown in the character of a correlative response to the Mishnah, namely, the Sifra and its exegesis of Leviticus. The Sifra presents a verse-by-verse explanation of the book of Leviticus. One of the important themes in that explanation concerns propositions of law covered in the book of Leviticus and also treated in a passage of the Mishnah. The author of the Sifra will present, sometimes verbatim, the law of the Mishnah. He will then ask whether this law is (merely) a matter of logic, or whether we must refer to Scripture (the verse of Leviticus before us) to provide the basis for the law. He will always demonstrate that logic by itself is insufficient and that proof in Scripture, the written Torah, is required.

This rhetorical exegesis follows a standard syntactical-redactional form. A verse of Scripture will be cited. Then a statement will be made about its meaning, or a statement of law correlative to that Scripture will be given. Finally, the author of the Sifra may state, "Now is that not (merely) logical?" And the point of that statement will be, Can this position not be gained through the working of mere logic, based upon facts supplied (to be sure) by Scripture? The polemical power of the Sifra lies in its repetitive demonstration that the stated position (commonly, though not always, a verbatim or near-verbatim citation of a Mishnah pericope) is not only *not* the product of logic unaided by Scripture, but it is, and can only be, the product of exegesis of Scripture.

The point, then, is that logic is not enough. Why not? Because it is uncertain and leads to results one can overturn through argument. Certainty lies in a clear statement of Scripture, and that fact bears a deep implication for the character of the authority and propositions of the Mishnah. The Mishnah, according to this view, depends for authority and the truth of its propositions upon the proof supplied by the written Torah, Scripture alone. So the Mishnah is not autonomous and correlative to Scripture. It is contingent and dependent upon Scripture. The oral Torah, represented by the Mishnah, does not stand for tradition handed on separate from Scripture, but as exegesis of Scripture. In this way the teachings of the Mishnah are shown to be based upon exegesis of the formal traits of scriptural grammar and syntax.

So the polemic of the Sifra and the Talmuds later on is against the positions that (1) what the Mishnah says (in the Mishnah's own words) is merely logical; and (2) that the position taken by the Mishnah can have been reached in any way other than through grammatical-syntactical exegesis of Scripture. That other way, the way of reading the Scripture through philosophical logic or practical reason, is explicitly rejected time and again. Philosophical logic is inadequate. Formal exegesis is shown to be not only adequate, but necessary and indeed inexorable. It follows that the Sifra undertakes to demonstrate precisely what the framers of the opening pericopes of the Talmuds' treatment of the Mishnah's successive units of thought also wish to show. The Mishnah is *not* autonomous. It is *not* independent. It is *not* correlative, that is, separate but equal. It is contingent, secondary, derivative, resting wholly on the foundations of the (written) revelation of God to Moses at Mount Sinai. Therein, too, lies the authority of the Mishnah as tradition.

Let us proceed to texts that express the Sifra's and the Talmuds' theory of the oral Torah. Of the two Talmuds, we take up the

Yerushalmi first, because that document came to closure at ca. 400 C.E., at least a century, and possibly two centuries, before the Bavli. The date for the Sifra is less certain. All named authorities lived in the time of the Mishnah, and so the document is regarded as Mishnaic in provenance, that is, earlier than ca. 200. But the Sifra cites as independent and completed materials passages of both the Mishnah and the Tosefta. The Sifra therefore comes after the closure of the Mishnah in ca. 200. In any event the polemic is at issue, and to that we turn forthwith.

The Sifra presents a systematic, running, line-by-line commentary to the book of Leviticus. The mode of commentary is episodic. The Sifra's authors will cite a clause on possibly a whole verse of Leviticus and then comment on it, sometimes simply spelling out its obvious sense, at other times imputing to the verse issues important only to the exegetes themselves. Of interest here is the relationship to the Mishnah of this exegesis of the book of Leviticus. There are, in point of fact, two distinct exegetical exercises that express that relationship.

The first, and simpler, is a treatment of the cited verse, simply joined to a citation of the Mishnah's relevant materials. The Mishnah-paragraph will be parachuted down, with such language as "on this basis" (referring to the cited verse) "they" (meaning, the Mishnah's authorities) "said." Then the Mishnah-paragraph will be cited verbatim. A simple example of this running exegesis of the book of Leviticus, interrupted by the intrusion of a Mishnah-citation, is as follows:

A. [And the priest shall examine him] on the seventh [day] (Lev. 13:-5)—

B. Might one say, Whether by day or by night?

C. Scriptures says, On [the seventh] day (Lev. 13:5), and not by night.

(Sifra Parashat Negaim Pereq N2*:1)

D. Might one say, In any light of the day they should be suitable [for examination]?

E. Scripture says, *In accord with whatever the priest shall see* (Lev. 13:12).

F. And just as [we speak of] a priest, excluding the one the light of whose eyes has darkened, so [we speak of] the day, excluding [a day] which has grown dark [lit.: the light of whose eyes has darkened].

(Sifra *Parashat* Negaim Pereq N2*:2)

G. On this basis have they said:

H. *They do not examine the plagues at dawn or at sunset, and not inside the house, and not on a cloudy day, because the dim appears bright, and not at noon, because the bright appears dim.*

I. *When do they examine [plagues]? At three, four, five, seven, eight, and nine, the words of R. Meir. R. Judah says, At four, five, six, eight, and nine* [= M. Negaim 2:2]

J. R. Yose says, "At four, five, nine, ten."

K. But he said, "I see the words of Rabbi."

(Sifra *Parashat* Negaim Pereq N2*:3)

A–E form a complete unit, in the established exegetical pattern. F forms the link to G–K, and it is a good one, for it clearly wishes to refer to the dispute materials of I and explain that under dispute are specific times of day. Yet the point of F is that we do not examine the skin ailments referred to in Leviticus 13–14 toward sunset (or at sunrise), but the dispute of I–K is about the middle of the day; all parties agree about the earlier and later hours. The time of noon is not too dim, but too bright. A–C pose no problems. The examination must be in the daytime, proved by a simple exegesis. D–F follow the same form. The conclusion of F excludes a cloudy day. H is directly pertinent to F. The important point for us comes at G–K. The underlined words come verbatim from the Mishnah-tractate that deals with the same topic as Leviticus 13–14, namely, tractate Negaim. H, I, of Sifra's passage, given in italics, correspond to Mishnah-tractate Negaim 2:2. The upshot of this exercise, for our inquiry, is self-evident. We see the effort to point up those passages of the Mishnah that express what in fact Scripture makes explicit. In this way the Mishnah is linked to Scripture, paragraph by paragraph and verse by verse.

The polemic to which I referred, in which the Sifra's authors give to the Mishnah-paragraph what the Mishnah's authors did not see fit to provide, is a commonplace in the Sifra, and in the Yerushalmi (and, later, the Bavli) as well. In the passage that follows, a statement of the Mishnah is not only linked to a verse of Leviticus but also interpreted within the limits of that verse. Specifically, what we have is the familiar citation of a statement of the Mishnah. In the passage that follows, C cites M. Negaim 12:6H–I. Then comes the important point. At D we ask whether one may extend the rule, given in the Mishnah, to cover yet another case. The answer is that we may not apply the rule to yet another case. Why not? Because *Scripture* indicates that one may not do so. The polemic, then, is that the Mishnah must be read in line with Scripture, and a position based on mere reason—for the proposal of D is surely a reasonable one—is to be rejected on account of the rule of Scripture.

> B. *And they shall take down* (Lev. 14:40)—this teaches that both of them take down the stones.
>
> C. On this basis have they said: *Woe to an evil person, woe to his neighbor. Both of them take down the stones, both of them bring the stones.*
>
> D. Might one say that both of them should take down the wall which is near the open air?
>
> E. Scripture says, *And after he has taken down the stones* (Lev. 14:43).
>
> F. How so?
>
> G. A wall which is between his house and that of his fellow do they both take down, but a wall which is facing the open air he alone takes down.

> **(Parashat Mesora' Pereq 4 M4:2)**

The use of the plural is understood to mean the neighbor participates. Since E refers to dismantling by one party alone, it is assumed to be the outer wall. Thus a further polemic in the Sifra carries forward the point at hand. A verse of Scripture is cited and spelled out. The rule is given as the verse specifies it. Then it is asked, "But is that not a matter of logic?" The sense of the question is why a verse of Scripture is required to prove what we could on our own discover. Not uncommonly, the proposition based on reason unaided by revelation will turn out to be a viewpoint contained in the Mishnah, and at some points the Mishnah-paragraph will be cited verbatim. Then the polemical exercise will proceed to show that logic alone cannot provide a firm foundation for the rule at hand. It will follow that only Scripture, that is, the written Torah, constitutes the reliable source for the rule. Where the rule is that of the Mishnah, and where the Mishnah's authorities fail to cite a proof-text (and, as we know, they rarely cite proof-texts), the point is clear. It is to apply rigorous logic to the exegesis of Scripture and to demonstrate that revelation, not logic alone, is necessary for the discovery of the law.

THE YERUSHALMI

The Yerushalmi, or the Talmud of the Land of Israel, is one of the two systematic expansions of the Mishnah accomplished in late antiquity, the Bavli being the other. Independently, the two Talmuds provided a commentary upon a single text, namely, the Mishnah. They took up a common task. But each group of sages carried on the work in its own way. Hence we define "the Talmud" as a set of two systematic commentaries to the Mishnah, the one now under discussion produced in the Land of Israel (mainly in Tiberias, Sepphoris, and Caesarea) in the third and fourth centuries C.E. The Yerushalmi is important because it carries forward the explanation and application of the oral portion of "the one whole Torah of Moses, our rabbi."

A remarkably limited repertoire of approaches to the explanation of the Mishnah was available to the framers of the Yerushalmi's discussions of that document. They usually chose and carried out one of a handful of procedures. Essentially, these may be reduced to two: first, to explain the simple meaning of a passage; and second, to expand and theorize about one passage in the light of other passages (or of a problem common to several passages). Exegesis, therefore, may take the form of exposition of the meaning, or expansion upon the meaning, of a given paragraph of the

Mishnah. It follows that if we understand what the Talmud does with a single item, we may confidently claim to describe and make sense of what the Talmud is apt to do with a great many such items.

THE YERUSHALMI AND THE MISHNAH

Let us turn to the Yerushalmi's theory of the Mishnah. Since the Mishnah stands forth as the principal authority for the law and theology of Judaism, so far as the Yerushalmi portrayed both, one conclusion must follow. The Mishnah constituted the stable foundation for certainty, the basis for authority, legitimating whatever the talmudic sages did in their work of governance of Israel in its land. The character of the Yerushalmi makes it clear that the Mishnah constituted the foundation and set goal of the Yerushalmi's sages' quest for authority. By this I mean a simple thing. The character of talmudic discourse tells us sages believed that if they knew precisely what the Mishnah said and meant, they then knew what they were supposed to do, how things were supposed to be. So the proper interpretation of the Mishnah, in relationship to Scripture to be sure, served as the ultimate guarantee of certainty.

We therefore should anticipate a splendid myth of the origin and authority of the Mishnah, on which, for sages, all else rested. Yet the Yerushalmi presents no explicit theory of the Mishnah. Implicitly, however, the Yerushalmi judgment of the Mishnah is self-evident, hardly demanding specification. Why so? Because the Yerushalmi presents its ideas about bits and pieces of the Mishnah, so the authors of the Yerushalmi treat the work of explanation of the Mishnah as the critical and important enterprise of their day. What follows is a simple fact. In their view, after Scripture, the Mishnah is the authoritative law code of Israelite life, the center, the focus, the source. From it all else flows. Beyond the Mishnah is only Scripture.

The Yerushalmi knows full well the theory that there is a tradition separate from, and in addition to, the written Torah. But there is ample evidence, implicit in what happens to the Mishnah in the Yerushalmi, to allow a reliable description of how the Talmud's founders viewed the Mishnah. That view may be stated very simply. The Mishnah rarely cites verses of Scripture in support of its propositions. The Yerushalmi routinely adduces scriptural bases for the Mishnah's laws. The Mishnah seldom undertakes the exergesis of verses of Scripture for any purpose. The Yerushalmi consistently investigates the meaning of verses of Scripture, and does so for a variety of purposes. Accordingly, the Yerushalmi, subordinate as it is to the Mishnah, regards the Mishnah as subordinate to, and contingent upon, Scripture. That is why, in the Yerushalmi's view, the Mishnah requires the support of proof-texts of Scripture. That fact can mean only that, by itself, the Mishnah exercises no autonomous authority and enjoys no independent standing or norm-setting status. The task of the framers of the Yerushalmi is not only to explain Mishnah-law, but to prove *from Scripture* the facticity of rules of the Mishnah. Accordingly, so far as the Yerushalmi has a theory about the Mishnah as such, as distinct from a theory about the exposition, amplification, and application to the court system of various laws in the Mishnah, it is quite clear.

To state matters negatively (and the absence of articulate statements makes this the wiser choice), the Mishnah does not enjoy autonomous and uncontingent authority as part of the one whole Torah of Moses revealed by God at Sinai. The simple fact that one principal task facing the sages is to adduce proof-texts for the Mishnah's laws, makes this conclusion ineluctable. It follows that, without such texts, those laws lack foundation. We now turn to the ways in which the Yerushalmi does this work of founding upon the secure basis of the written Torah the fundamental propositions of the Mishnah's laws.

Most units of discourse in the Yerushalmi take up the exegesis and amplification of the Mishnah. Exegesis for the talmudic sages means many things, from the close reading of a line and explanation of its word choices to large-scale, wide-ranging, and encompassing speculation on legal principles expressed, among other places, in the passage at hand.

The Yerushalmi's sages rarely, if ever, set out to twist the meaning of a Mishnah passage out of its original shape. Whatever problems they wish to solve in the statement of the Mishnah's rule, they do not resort to deliberately fanciful or capricious readings of what is at hand. At the same time the Yerushalmi's sages constantly cite verses of Scripture when reading statements of the Mishnah. These they read in their own way. References to specific verses of Scripture are as uncommon in the Mishnah as they are routine in the Talmuds.

For the framers of the Talmuds, certainty for the Mishnah's rules depended upon adducing scriptural proof-texts. The entire system—the laws, courts, the power of lawyer-philosophers themselves—thus is seen to rest upon the written revelation of God to Moses at Sinai, and on that alone. What this means for the sages' view of the Mishnah is that the details of the document depended for validity upon details contained within Mosaic revelation, in the written Torah.

HOW THE YERUSHALMI'S AUTHORS READ THE MISHNAH

Let us now proceed to review the ways in which the Yerushalmi presents proof-texts for allegations of statements of the Mishnah. We begin with the simplest examples, in which a passage of the Mishnah is cited, then linked to a verse of Scripture, deemed to constitute self-evident proof for what has been said. The Mishnah's rule is given in italics.

Y. Avodah Zarah 4:4.III

A. [Citing M.A.Z. 4:4] *An idol belonging to a gentile is prohibited forthwith,* in line with the following verse of Scripture: "You shall surely destroy [all places where the nations whom you shall dispossess served their gods]" (Deut. 12:2)—forthwith.

B. *And one belonging to an Israelite is prohibited only after it has been worshipped,* in line with the following verse of Scripture: "Cursed be the man who makes a graven or molten image."

C. There are those who reverse the matter.

D. An idol belonging to an Israelite is prohibited forthwith, as it is written, "Cursed be the man who makes a graven or molten image."

E. And one belonging to a gentile is prohibited only after it has been worshipped, as it is written, "You shall surely destroy all the places where the nations whom you shall dispossess served their gods."

F. R. Isaac bar Nahman in the name of Samuel derived that same view [that an idol belonging to a gentile is prohibited only after it has been worshiped] from the following: If one has inherited [the idol] when it [already] is deemed a god, "in fire shall you burn it, and if not: "where the nations whom you shall dispossess . . . their gods," ["You shall tear down their altars and dash in pieces their pillars and burn their Asherim with fire . . . "] (Deut. 12:2–3).

Y. Avodah Zarah 4:4.IV

A. [With reference to the following passage of the Mishnah: *A gentile has the power to nullify an idol belonging either to himself or his fellow, but an Israelite has not got the power to nullify an idol belonging to a gentile (Y.A.Z. 4:4)].* R. Yohanan in the name of R. Yannai derived that view from the following verse of Scripture: "You shall not covet the silver or the gold that is on them or take it for yourselves" (Deut. 7:25). "*You* may not covet and take [that gold], but *others* may covet [the gold], and then you may take it."

Y. Niddah 2:6

A. *Five [colors of] blood are unclean in a woman.*

II. A. Whence do we derive evidence that there are five varieties of unclean blood specified by the Torah?

B. Said R. Joshua b. Levi: " 'And she has uncovered the fountain of her bloods' (Lev. 20:18) [= two], 'And she will be clean from the source of her bloods' [= two], a discharge of blood from her body (Lev. 15:19) [= one, thus five]."

C. And lo: "And if a woman has a discharge of blood" (Lev. 15:25) —this blood [too] should be part of that number.

III. A. And how do we know that there is unclean blood, and there is clean blood[, so not all blood is unclean, but only the five which are listed]?

B. R. Hama bar Joseph in the name of R. Hoshaiah: "It is written, If any case arises requiring a decision . . . (Deut. 17:8). Now 'between blood and (W) blood' is not written, *but of one kind of blood from (L) another.*

C. "On this basis there is proof that there is blood that is unclean and blood that is clean."

Y. Horayot 1:6

A. *"[If] the court made an [erroneous] decision, and the entire community [of Israel], or the greater part of the community carried out their decision, they bring a bullock.*

B. *"In the case of idolatry (Num. 14:24), they bring a bullock and a goat," the words of R. Meir.*

C. *R. Judah says, "Twelve tribes [individually] bring twelve bullocks.*

D. *"And in the case of idolatry, they bring twelve bullocks and twelve goats."*

E. *R. Simeon says, "Thirteen bullocks, and in the case of idolatry, thirteen bullocks and thirteen goats:*

F. *"a bullock and a goat for each and every tribe, and [in addition] a bullock and a goat for the court."*

III. A. R. Abun in the name of R. Benjamin bar Levi: "There is a verse of Scripture that supports the position of the one [Judah, Simeon] who says, 'Each tribe is called a congregation.'

B. "For it is written, 'A nation and a congregation of nations will come from you' (Gen. 35:11).

C. "And yet [at the time that that statement was made], Benjamin had not yet been born. [So the reference to a coming *congregation* applied to a single tribe.]"

Y. Shebuot 1:4

A. *And for that [uncleanness] for which there is no awareness [of uncleanness] either at the beginning or at the end,*

B. *"the goats offered on festivals and the goats offered on new months effect atonement," the words of R. Judah.*

I. A. R. Eleazar in the name of R. Hoshaiah: "The Scriptural basis for the position of R. Judah is as follows: 'Also one male goat for a sin offering to the Lord' (Num. 28:15, in context of the offerings of the beginnings of the months)—for a sin about which only the Lord knows this goat effects atonement."

B. I thus have information concerning the goat offered on the beginning of the new month. How do I know that that same rule applies to the goats offered on the occasion of festivals?

C. Said R. Zira, " 'Also a goat . . . '—the use of the word also adds
to the first matter under discussion [this other one, namely, the
goats offered on the festivals]."

The preceding instances all follow a single pattern. A statement of
the Mishnah is given, followed by a verse of Scripture regarded as
proof of the antecedent conception. The first instance, Y.A.Z. 4:4,
is the most obvious, since all we have are sentences from the one
document, the Mishnah, juxtaposed to sentences from the other,
the Scripture. In the next, out of the same passage, Yohanan-Yan-
nai first cite a verse, then restate its meaning. In the third, at Y.
Niddah 2:6, the words of a verse of Scripture are treated one by
one, each yielding a number of types of blood. So the sense of the
verse is less important than its formal character.

By contrast, at the next example, Y. Hor. 1:6, the substance and
sense of the verse, not some minor detail, govern the matter. The
same is the case for Hoshaiah's view at Y. Sheb. 1:4, in contrast to
Zira's. In this last instance we see that a mixture of approaches to
the reading of a verse will be accepted, so that the positions of
both parties to a disagreement enjoy the support of a single passage of Scripture. But all of these instances of the use of Scripture
to sustain allegations of a rule of the Mishnah have in common
their simplicity.

Y. Sanhedrin 1:1.1.

A. And whence shall we produce evidence from Scripture [for the
factual statement of M. San. 1:1A]?

B. " 'And these things shall be for a statute and ordinance' (Num.
35:29).

C "On the basis of this verse I draw the conclusion that [the reference to both statute and ordinance bears this meaning:] careful
cross-examination of witnesses is required not only for capital
cases but also for property ones.

D. "And then how do we know that property cases require three
[and not twenty-three judges, as in the case of capital cases]?

E. " 'The owner of the house shall come near to the judges' (Ex.
22:8)—thus encompassing one judge.

F. " 'The case of both parties shall come before the judges' (Ex. 22:9)—thus encompassing a second judge.

G. " ' . . . he whom the judges shall condemn shall pay . . . ' (Ex. 22:9)—lo, here is yet a third," the words of R. Josiah.

I. But: " . . . to the judge . . . . '—lo, one judge is required.

J. " . . . whom the judge shall condemn . . . "—lo, two judges.

K. "Now a court cannot be made up of an even number of judges, so they add yet a third judge, so that there are three in all on the court."

Y. Baba Mesia 2:1

Mishnah text:

A. *What lost items are [the finder's], and which ones is he liable to proclaim [in the lost-and-found]?*

B. *These lost items are his [the finder's]:*

C. *"[If] he found pieces of fruit scattered about, coins scattered about, small sheaves in the public domain, cakes of figs, baker's loaves, strings of fish, pieces of meat, wool shearings [as they come] from the country [of origin], stalks of flax, or tongues of purple—lo, these are his," [the words of R. Meir].*

I.   A. [Since the operative criterion in M.B.M. 2:1 is that, with undistinguished items such as these, the owner takes for granted he will not recover them and so despairs of them, thus giving up his rights of ownership to them, we now ask:] Whence do we know from the Torah the law of the owner's despair [of recovering his property constitutes relinquishing rights of ownership and declaring the property to be ownerless, hence available to whoever finds it]?

B   R. Yohanan in the name of R. Simeon b. Yehosedeq: " 'And so you shall do with his ass; so you shall do with his garment; so you shall do with any lost thing of your brother's, which he loses and you find; you may not withhold your help' (Deut. 22:23)—

C. "That which is [perceived as] lost by him and found by you, are you liable to proclaim [as having been found], and that which is not [perceived as] lost by him [because he has given up hope of recovering it anyhow] and found by you, you are not liable to proclaim.

D. "This then excludes that for which the owner has despaired, which is lost to him and to any one."

Y. Baba Mesia 3:1

A. *He who deposits with his fellow a beast or utensils,*

B. *and they were stolen or lost,*

C. *[if the bailee] made restitution and was unwilling to take an oath—*

D. *(For they have said, "An unpaid bailee takes an oath and thereby carries out his obligation [without paying compensation for the loss of the bailment]".)—*

E. *[if] then the thief was found,*

F. *[the thief] pays twofold restitution.*

G. *[If] he had slaughtered or sold the beast, he pays fourfold or fivefold restitution.*

H. *To whom does he pay restitution?*

I. *To him with whom the bailment was left.*

I.   A. Whence do you bring evidence [for the proposition of M.B.M. 3:1H–I that in a case in which the bailee pays compensation, he is given the double indemnity which is collected from the thief]?

    B. "[If a man steals an ox or a sheep and kills it or sells it, he shall pay five oxen for an ox, and four sheep for a sheep. He shall make restitution; if he has nothing, then he shall be sold for his theft.] If the stolen beast is found alive in his possession [whether it is an ox or an ass or a sheep, he shall pay double]" (Ex. 22:1–4).

    C. Now do we not already know [from Ex. 22:7] that if the thief is found, he will pay a double-indemnity?

    D. So why does Scripture state, "He shall pay double"?

    E. If it does not apply to the matter at hand, then treat it as referring to a further matter, [that is, if it does not mean the thief pays a double-indemnity to the one from whom he stole, which we know from other references,] then treat the point of application as that before us. [For the rules governing bailments state, "If a man delivers to his neighbor money or goods to keep, and it is stolen out of the man's house, then, if the thief is found, he shall pay double" (Ex. 22:7).]

What is striking in the preceding instances is the presence of a secondary layer of reasoning about the implications of a verse of Scripture. The process of reasoning then derives from the verse a principle not made explicit therein, and that principle turns out to be precisely what the Mishnah's rule maintains. Accordingly, the Mishnah's law is shown to be merely a corollary of the Scripture's, that is, the obverse side of the coin. Or the Scripture's rule is shown to deal only with the case pertinent to the Mishnah's law, rather than to what, on the surface, that biblical law seems to contain.

We proceed to instances in which a disputed point of the Mishnah is linked to a dispute on the interpretation of the pertinent verses of Scripture. What is important is that the dispute in the Mishnah is made to depend not upon principles of law, but upon readings of the same pertinent verses of Scripture. Once again the net effect is to turn the Mishnah into a set of generalizations of what already is explicit in Scripture, a kind of restatement in other language of what is quite familiar, therefore well-founded.

Y. Makkot 2:2

Mishnah text:

A. *[If] the iron flew from the helf and killed someone,*

B. *Rabbi says, "He does not go into exile."*

C. *And sages say, "He goes into exile."*

D. *[If] it flew from the wood which is being split,*

E. *Rabbi says, "He goes into exile.*

F. *And sages say, "He does not go into exile."*

I. A. What is the Scriptural basis for the position of Rabbi [at M. 2:2D–E]?

B. Here it is stated, " . . . [and the head] slips [from the handle and strikes his neighbor so that he dies . . .]" (Deut. 19:5).

C. And later on, the same verb root is used: "[. . . for your olives] shall drop off . . . " (Deut. 28:40).

D. Just as the verb root used later means, "dropping off," so here it means, "dropping off."

E. What is the Scriptural basis for the position of the rabbis [at M. 2:2]F?

F. Here the verb root "slipping" is used.

G. And later on elsewhere we have the following" . . . and clears away many nations before you . . . " (Deut. 7:1).

H. Just as the verb root, clearing away, refers to an [active] blow there, so here too it speaks of an [active] blow [by an object which strikes something, e.g., the ax, not chips of wood].

Y. Baba Mesia 3:9.11

A. What is the Scriptural basis for the opinion of the House of Shammai [that one who expresses the intention of making use of a bailment is liable for any damage done to it, as if he had made use of it (M. B.M. 3:9E–F)]?

B. "For *every* breach of trust . . . " (Ex. 22:9)—[even one merely in intention].

C. And how does the House of Hillel deal with the cited verse, "For *every* breach of trust"?

D. One might suppose that the law applies only to the [bailee] himself. [If his slave or his agent does the deed, how do we know that he is liable?]

E. Scripture states, "For every breach of trust"—even if it is by a man bailee's agent, he is liable. [Even though the law of agency does not apply to a sin, in this case Scripture has expanded the range of culpability by its statement, "For every breach of trust."]

Y. Sanhedrin 9:3

A. *He who hits his fellow, whether with a stone or with his fist,*

B. *and they diagnosed him as likely to die,*

C. *[but] he got better than he was,*

D. *and afterward he got worse, and died—*

E. *he is liable.*

F. *R. Nehemiah says, "He is exempt,*

G. *"for there is a basis to the matter [of thinking that he did not die from the original injury.]"*

II. A. What is the Scriptural basis for R. Nehemiah's opinion?

B. "[When men quarrel and one strikes the other with a stone or with his fist and the man does not die but keeps his bed,] then if the man rises again and walks abroad with his staff, he that struck him shall be clear" (Ex. 21:18–19).

C. Now would it have entered your mind that this one should be walking about in the marketplace, while the other is put to death on his account? [Obviously not, and so the purpose of

Scripture's statement is as follows:] Even though the victim should die after he was originally examined and diagnosed as dying, the other party is exempt [should the man's condition improve in the meantime].

D. What is the Scriptural basis for rabbis' opinion?

E. "And the man does not die but keeps his bed."

F. Now do we not know that if he "does not die but keeps his bed"? [Why does Scripture specify both his not dying and also his going to bed]?

G. It is to speak of a case in which they did not make prognosis that he would die. [That is, Scripture is to be interpreted to mean, "if he does not die," that is, they did not reach a prognosis that he would die, but that he would not die.]

H. In this case it is written, "Then if the man rises again and walks abroad with his staff, he that struck him shall be clear" (Ex. 21:19).

I. [This then means that] lo, if he does not get up, the one who struck him is liable.

J. If then they reached the prognosis that he would die, in such a case it is written, "Only he shall pay for the loss of his time, and shall have him thoroughly healed" (Ex. 21:19). [That is, if he was not expected to die, the one who hit him nonetheless must pay the costs of his recovery.]

We see that in the first case both parties to the Mishnah's dispute read the same verse. The difference then depends upon their prior disagreement about the meaning of the verse. The same is so in the second dispute, but now at issue is the force of a particular word in the biblical verse. In the third, each party claims that implicit in what the Scripture says is an excluded, self-evident case. Once more, therefore, the same verse is read in opposed ways, resulting in the dispute in the Mishnah. The underlying supposition is that the Mishnah simply restates in general language the results of the exegesis of biblical law.

We consider, finally, instances in which the Yerushalmi's discussion consists wholly in the analysis of the verses of Scripture deemed to prove the Mishnah's point. The outcome is that we deal not with a mere formality, but with a protracted, sustained inquiry. That is to say, the discussion of the Talmud transcends the limits of the Mishnah and becomes a well-developed discourse upon *not* the Mishnah's rule, but Scripture's sense.

What is important in the next item is the fact that the search for proof texts in Scripture sustains not only propositions of the Mishnah, but also those of the Tosefta as well as those of the Yerushalmi's own sages. This is a stunning fact. It indicates that the search of Scriptures is primary; the source of propositions or texts to be supported by those Scriptures is secondary. There is no limit, indeed, to the purposes for which scriptural texts will be found relevant.

Y. Sanhedrin 3:8.11

Tosefta:

A. *How do they carry out a judgment?*

B. *The judges seat themselves, and the litigants remain standing before them.*

C. *Whoever brings claim against his fellow is the one who opens the proceedings [T. San. 6:3],*

D. as it said, " . . . Who ever has a complaint, let him go to them [Aaron and Hur, as judges]" (Ex. 24:14).

E. And how do we know that the one who lays claim against his fellow bears the burden of proof?

F. R. Qerispa [Crispus] in the name of R. Hananiah b. Gamaliel: " ' . . . let him go to them . . . , " [meaning,] Let him bring his evidence to them."

G. R. Yohanan raised the question, "In the case of a childless sister-in-law, who brings claim against whom?"

H. R. Eleazar replied, "And is it not written, ' . . . then the brother's wife shall go up to the gate to the elders' (Deut. 25:7)?"

I. R. Yohanan said, "Well did R. Eleazar teach me."

Y. Sanhedrin 10:4.11

A. *The party of Korah has no portion in the world to come and will not live in the world to come [M. San. 10:4].*

B. What is the Scriptural basis for this view?

C. "[So they and all that belonged to them went down alive into Sheol;] and the earth, closed over them, and they perished from the midst of the assembly" (Num. 16:33).

D. The earth closed over them"—in this world.

E. "And they perished from the midst of the assembly" in the world to come [M. San. 10:4D–F].

F. It was taught: R. Judah b. Batera says, "[The contrary view] is to be derived from the implication of the following verse:

G. "I have gone astray like a lost sheep: seek thy servant [and do not forget thy commandments]' (Ps. 119:176).

H. "Just as the lost object which is mentioned later on is the end in going to be searched for, so the lost object which is stated herein is destined to be searched for" [T. San. 13:9].

I. Who will pray for them?

J. R. Samuel bar Naham said, "Moses will pray for them:

K. " 'Let Reuben live, and not die, [nor let his men be few]' (Deut. 33:6)."

L. R. Joshua b. Levi said, "Hannah will pray for them."

M. This is the view of R. Joshua b. Levi, for R. Joshua b. Levi said, "Thus did the party of Korah sink ever downward, until Hannah went and prayed for them and said, 'The Lord kills and brings to life; he brings down to Sheol and raises up' (1 Sam. 2:6)."

At Y. San. 3:8, we see, the search for proof-texts is provoked equally by citation of a passage of the Tosefta and by an opinion of a rabbi; D, E–F, give an instance of the former, and G–I, the latter. There is no differentiation between the two processes. At Y. San. 10:4 we have a striking sequence of proof-texts, serving, one by one, the cited statement of the Mishnah, A–C, then an opinion of a rabbi in the Tosefta, F–H, then the position of a rabbi, J–K, L–M. The process of providing proof-texts treats as a matter of indifference, the source of the proposition to be proved.

We began with the interest in showing how the Scripture is made to supply proof-texts for propositions of the Mishnah. But we see at the end that the search for appropriate verses of Scripture vastly transcends the purpose of study of the Mishnah, exegesis of its rules, and provision of adequate authority for the document and its laws. In fact, any proposition to be taken seriously, whether in the Mishnah, in the Tosefta, or in the mouth of a Yerushalmi's sage himself, will elicit interest in scriptural support.

So the main thing is that the Scripture is at the center and focus. A verse of Scripture settles all pertinent questions, wherever located, whatever their source. That is the Yerushalmi's position. The quest for certainty lay through the Torah of Moses—the written Torah, there alone.

If the sages of the second century, who made the Mishnah as we know it, spoke in their own name and in the name of the logic of their own minds, those who followed, certainly the ones who flourished in the later fourth century, took a quite different view. Reverting to ancient authority, like others of the age they turned back to Scripture, deeming it the sole reliable source of certainty about truth. Unlike their masters in the Mishnah, theirs was a quest for a higher authority than the logic of their own minds. The shift from age to age then is clear. The second-century masters took commonplaces of Scripture, well-known facts, and stated them wholly in their *own* language and context. Fourth-century masters of the Yerushalmi phrased commonplaces of the Mishnah or banalities of worldly wisdom, so far as they could, in the language of *Scripture* and in its context.

But, as we saw at the end, this quest in Scripture for certainty far transcended the interest in supplying the Mishnah's rules with proof-texts. On the contrary, the real issue turns out to have been not the Mishnah at all, not even the indication of its diverse sayings one by one. Once the words of a sage, not merely a rule of the Mishnah, are made to refer to Scripture for proof, it must follow that, in the natural course of things, a rule of the Mishnah and of the Tosefta will likewise be asked to refer also to Scripture.

In phrasing this as I have, I have turned matters upside down. The fact that the living sage validates his own words through Scripture explains why the sage *also* validates the words of the ancient sages of the Mishnah and Tosefta through verses of Scripture. It is one undivided phenomenon. The reception of the Mishnah constitutes merely one—though massive—testimony to a prevalent attitude of mind, important for the age, not solely for the Mishnah. The final passage we reviewed turns out, upon reflection, to be the most suggestive. In the quest for certainty, proof-texts for the Mishnah are beside the point. The main point is this: Certainty is in Scripture, which validates teachings of sages present and past, including sages of the Mishnah. The importance of this fact will become clear in the concluding chapter.

5. Recasting the Written Torah as the Oral Torah: Leviticus Rabbah

Leviticus Rabbah presents a deeply *religious* view of Israel's historical and salvific life, in much the same way that the Mishnah provides a profoundly *philosophical* view of Israel's everyday and sanctified existence. Just as the main themes of the Mishnah evoke the consideration of issues of being and becoming, the potential and the actual, mixtures and blends and other problems of physics, all in the interest of philosophical analysis, so Leviticus Rabbah presents its cogent and coherent agendum as well. That program of inquiry concerns the way in which, in the book of Leviticus, God set forth to Moses the entire scope and meaning of Israel's history among the nations and salvation at the end of days.

In a few words we may restate the conviction of the framers of the document: "We now know what will be then, just as Jacob had told his sons, just as Moses had told the tribes, because everything exists under the aspect of a timeless will, God's will, and all things express one thing, God's program and plan. Our task as Israel is to accept, endure, submit, and celebrate." So, as I said, in the Mishnah, we take up the philosophy of what we now call Judaism, and, in the polemical and pointed statements of the exegete-compositors of Leviticus Rabbah, we confront the theology of history of that same Judaism.

Leviticus Rabbah came to closure, all scholars generally concur, at the end of the fourth century and the beginning of the fifth. The document in its final form therefore emerges from that momentous century in which the Roman empire passed from pagan to Christian rule, and, in which, in the aftermath of Julian's abortive reversion to paganism, Christianity adopted that politics of repression of paganism that rapidly engulfed Judaism as well. The issue confronting Israel in the Land of Israel therefore proved immediate: the meaning of the new and ominous turn of history, the implications of Christ's worldly triumph for the other-worldly and supernatural people, Israel, whom God chooses and loves. The message of the exegete-compositors addressed the circumstance of historical crisis and generated remarkable renewal, a rebirth of intellect in the encounter with Scripture, now in quest of the rules not of sanctification—these had already been found—but of salvation. So the book of Leviticus, which portrays how all things had begun, would testify to the message and the method of the end: the coming salvation of patient, hopeful, enduring Israel.

Let me now place into the context of the unfolding of the Oral Torah the document at hand. We deal, in particular, with a systematic commentary on a biblical book. That is to say, the book of Leviticus is dealt with here much as elsewhere the various tractates of the Mishnah are subjected to systematic explanation. So, to revert to the argument up to this point, we have seen the Oral Torah take shape in a straight line from the Mishnah. We now ask what has become of the Written Torah.

Specifically, the great masters of the Oral Torah took the Mishnah and systematically worked out the Mishnah's standing and relationship to the Written Torah.

Seen in its own terms and context, the written Torah demanded explanation alongside the Mishnah. The same authorities who stood behind the Yerushalmi and made a systematic interpretation of the Mishnah also produced compositions of interpretations of Scripture. These compositions, made up of explanations of verses of Scripture, follow the sequence of biblical verses of certain books of the written Torah, just as the tractates of the Yerushalmi follow the sequence of sentences and paragraphs of certain tractates of the oral Torah, the Mishnah. Stating a **midrash** or explanation of a verse of Scripture, the sages expanded upon Scripture by bringing to it those same beliefs and values that they brought to the Mishnah.

LEVITICUS RABBAH AND LEVITICUS

Leviticus Rabbah deals with a biblical book, not a Mishnah-tractate. But it approaches that book with a fresh plan, one in which exegesis does not dictate rhetoric, and in which amplification of an established text (whether Scripture or the Mishnah) does not supply the underlying logic by which sentences are made to compose paragraphs, and paragraphs completed thoughts. The framers of Leviticus Rabbah treat topics, not particular verses. They make generalizations that are free-standing. They express cogent propositions through extended compositions, not episodic ideas. Earlier, things people wished to say were attached to predefined statements based on an existing text, constructed in accord with an organizing logic independent of the systematic expression of a single, well-framed idea. Now the authors so collect and arrange their materials that an abstract proposition emerges. That proposition is not expressed only or mainly through episodic restatements, assigned to an order established by a base-text. Rather, it emerges through a logic of its own. What is new is the shift from discourse framed around an established text to syllogistic argument organized around a proposed proposition. What changes, therefore, is the way in which cogent thought takes place, as people move from discourse contingent on some prior principle of organization, to discourse autonomous of a ready-made program inherited from an earlier paradigm.

Leviticus Rabbah is topical, not exegetical. Each of its thirty-seven parashiyyot (equivalent to the Mishnah's tractates) pursues its given topic and develops points relevant to that topic. It is logical, in that (to repeat) discourse appeals to an underlying principle of composition and intelligibility, and that logic inheres in what is said. Logic is what joins one sentence to the next and forms the whole into paragraphs of meaning, intelligible propositions, each with its place and sense in a still larger, accessible system. Because of logic one mind connects to another, public discourse becomes possible, debate on issues of general intelligibility takes place, and an anthology of statements about a single subject becomes a composition of theorems about that subject. In this sense, after the Mishnah, Leviticus Rabbah constitutes the next major logical composition in the rabbinic canon. Accordingly, with Leviticus Rabbah rabbis take up the problem of saying what they wish to say not in an exegetical, but in a syllogistic and freely discursive logic and rhetoric. They do not present a line-by-line explanation of a verse. They present an exposition of a topic and make a point about that topic, or answer a question concerning a given theme. This is how the sages of the Mishnah work out their ideas. They take a subject and they answer an important question concerning that subject. So the book of Leviticus in Leviticus Rabbah is treated in much the same way that a subject important to the authors of the Mishnah is treated in the Mishnah. The sages in both cases express significant propositions about a given subject by means of their comments, observations, and collections of facts. They present topical compositions, not merely anthologies of information.

LEVITICUS RABBAH AS ORAL TORAH

How does Leviticus Rabbah find a place in the oral Torah? Let me state with appropriate emphasis: *Sages here treat the written Torah exactly as they do the oral Torah.* In the pages of Leviticus Rabbah the sages at hand read the Scriptures exactly as, when they approach the oral Torah, they read the Mishnah. So they accomplish a labor of naturalizing the written Torah (in this case, the book of Leviticus) into the frame of reference of, and also into the mode of discourse established for, the oral Torah. It is an amazing transformation of the ancient Israelite Scriptures into something quite other than what they had been.

Let me spell out exactly how I think the work at hand—the oral Torah represented by Leviticus Rabbah—treats Scripture, specifi-

cally, the book of Leviticus, in the ways in which the authors of
the Mishnah have taught them to think and speak and as the authors of the Talmud treat a Mishnah-tractate.

The Mishnah makes its principal points by collecting three or
five examples of a given rule. The basic rule is rarely stated, but it
is always exemplified through the several statements of its application. The reader then may infer the generalization from its specific exemplifications. Sometimes, but not often, the generalization will be made explicit. The whole then constitutes an exercise
in rhetoric and logic carried out through list-making. The same is
true in Leviticus Rabbah, but it makes lists of different things from
those of the Mishnah. The authors of the Mishnah make a point
by collecting a list of facts, all pointed toward a single conclusion.
The authors of Leviticus Rabbah do the same. But the authors of
the Mishnah take up everyday things, rules governing the workaday world and its affairs. The sages of Leviticus Rabbah, on the
other hand, address not commonplace situations, but historical
events and moral issues. That is to say, the framers of Leviticus
Rabbah revert to sequences of events, all of which exhibit the same
definitive traits and the same ultimate results (e.g., arrogance, and
its downfall), not one time but many; humility and salvation, over
and over again; and so throughout. So the authors of Leviticus
Rabbah are looking for rules, just as much as the writers of the
Mishnah teach rules and laws. But the rules in Leviticus Rabbah
are historical laws, meaning, if you do this, that will happen. If
you are arrogant, you will sin and be punished. Then we shall
have a long list of relevant facts, meaning, cases of arrogance followed by downfall. So Leviticus Rabbah presents laws of society
and rules of historical morality, and the Mishnah presents laws of
the household and the hearth. The mode of thought and argument
remains, in both compositions, one and the same: one whole
Torah of Moses, our rabbi. If I had to select a single paramount
trait of argument in Leviticus Rabbah, it would be the theorem
stated by the making of a list of similar examples. The search for
the rules lies through numerous instances that, all together, yield
the besought rule.

In context, therefore, we have in the *parashiyyot* of Leviticus Rabbah the counterpart to the list-making that the philosophers of the Mishnah used to make their points. Through composing lists of common items, the framers produce underlying rules that are always applicable. Here the authors make lists of facts of history. Then show the laws that lay the foundations of social life. All of this is framed in very definite terms (e.g., Nebuchadnezzar, Senacherib, David, Josiah did so-and-so with such-and-such result). So the mode of argument at hand is to assemble instances of a common law of history or morality. The argument derives from the proper construction of a statement of that law in something close to a syllogism. The syllogistic statement often, though not invariably, occurs at the outset, all instances of so-and-so produce such-and-such a result, followed by the required catalogue.

In short, Leviticus Rabbah takes up the modes of thought and argumentation characteristic of the Mishnah and accomplishes the logically necessary task of applying them to society. Speaking of society, the authors turn to, among other records, the history book, Scripture, which provides examples of the special laws governing Israel, the physics of Israel's fate. In Scripture, but not only there, the authors find rules and apply them to their own day.

Just as Greek science focused upon physics, the laws of Israel's salvation serve as the physics of the sages as scientists. But Greek science derived facts and built theorems on the basis of other sources besides physics; the philosophers also studied ethnography, ethics, politics, and history. For the sages of the Mishnah, along these same lines, parables, exemplary tales, and completed paragraphs of thought deriving from other sources, not to exclude the Mishnah, Tosefta, Sifra, Genesis Rabbah, and such literary compositions that had been made ready for the Yerushalmi—these too make their contribution of data subject to analysis. All of these sources of truth together were directed toward the discovery of philosophical laws for the understanding of Israel's life, now and in the age to come.

The written Torah, Scripture, is naturalized into the oral Torah because its facts are taken over and turned into those same sorts of laws as the Mishnah, the oral Torah, for its part, contributes as well. So both the written and the oral Torahs in Leviticus Rabbah served a new, deeply philosophical inquiry. In our own day, we should call that work a labor of science in the deepest sense: systematic and rigorous learning through reasoning into the principles of order and proportion of social history and natural life.

PARASHAH 1 OF LEVITICUS RABBAH

Before we proceed, let us consider a complete *parashah* of Leviticus Rabbah, taking account of the traits of its individual units and noting how it develops its large ideas. The translation is my own, based on the critical text and commentary of M. Margulies. My individual comments on each unit of thought of the *parashah* should not obscure our main interest, which is to see how the plan of the framer of the document pursues a theme, rather than verse-by-verse exegesis of individual verses. The theme, moreover, does not impose an order based on the sequence of specific verses of scripture. So the mode of organizing and laying out comments on Mishnah-tractates—familiar in the Talmud of the Land of Israel and of Babylonia, and biblical books, well known in such exercises as Sifra on Leviticus, Sifre on Numbers, Sifre on Deuteronomy, and Genesis Rabbah—is abandoned. A quite different mode is at hand.

1:1

1.   A. "The Lord called Moses [and spoke to him from the tent of meeting, saying, 'Speak to the children of Israel and say to them, "When any man of you brings an offering to the Lord, you shall bring your offering of cattle from the herd or from the flock" ']."

     B. R. Tanhum bar Hinilai opened [discourse by citing the following verse]: " 'Bless the Lord, you his messengers, you mighty in strength, carrying out his word, obeying his word' (Ps. 103:20).

     C. "Concerning whom does Scripture speak?

     D. "If [you maintain that] Scripture speaks about the upper world's creatures, [that position is unlikely, for] has not [Scripture in the very same passage already referred to them, in stating], 'Bless the Lord, all his hosts [his ministers, who do his word]' (Ps. 103:21)?

E. "If [you maintain that] Scripture speaks about the lower world's creatures, [that position too is unlikely,] for has not [Scripture in the very same passage already referred to them, in stating], 'Bless the Lord, [you] his messengers' (Ps. 103:20)? [Accordingly, concerning whom does Scripture speak?]

F. "[We shall now see that the passage indeed speaks of the lower ones.] But, since the upper world's creatures are perfectly able to fulfill the tasks assigned to them by the Holy One, blessed be he, therefore it is said, 'Bless the Lord, *all* of his hosts.' But as to the creatures of the lower world [here on earth], who cannot fulfill the tasks assigned to them by the Holy One, blessed be he, [the word *all* is omitted, when the verse of Scripture states,] 'Bless the Lord, [you] his messengers'—but not *all* of his messengers."

2.   A. Another matter: Prophets are called messengers [creatures of the lower world], in line with the following passage, "And he sent a messenger and he took us forth from Egypt" (Num. 20:16).

B. Now was this a [heavenly] messenger, [an angel]? Was it not [merely] Moses [a creature of the lower world]?

C. Why then does [the verse of Scripture, referring to what Moses did,] call him a "messenger?"

D. But: It is on the basis of that usage that [we may conclude] prophets are called "messengers" [in the sense of creatures of the lower world].

E. Along these same lines, "And the messenger of the Lord came up from Gilgal to Bochim" (Judges 2:1). Now was this a [heavenly] messenger, [an angel]? Was it not [merely] Phineas?

F. Why then does [the verse of the Scripture, referring to Phineas], call him a "messenger"?

G. Said R. Simon, "When the holy spirit rested upon Phineas, his face burned like a torch."

H. [There is better proof of the allegation concerning Phineas, deriving from an explicit reference, namely:] rabbis said, "What did Manoah's wife say to him [concerning] Phineas]? 'Lo, a man of God came to me, and his face was like the face of a messenger of God' (Judges 13:6).

I. [Rabbis continue,] "She was thinking that he was a prophet, but he was in fact a [heavenly] messenger [so the two looked alike to her]."

3. A. Said R. Yohanan, "From the passage that defines their very character, we derive evidence that the prophets are called 'messengers,' in line with the following passage: 'Then said Haggai, the messenger of the Lord, in the Lord's agency, to the people, "I am with you, says the Lord"' (Hag. 1:13).

B. "Accordingly, you must reach the conclusion that on the basis of the passage that defines their very character, we prove that the prophets are called 'messengers.'"

4. A. [Reverting to the passage cited at the very outset,] "You mighty in strength, carrying out his word [obeying his word]" (Ps. 103:20).

B. Concerning what [sort of mighty man or hero] does Scripture speak?

C. Said R. Isaac, "Concerning those who observe the restrictions of the Seventh Year [not planting, and sowing their crops in the Sabbatical Year] does Scripture speak.

D. "Under ordinary conditions a person does a religious duty for a day, a week, a month. But does one really do so for all of the days of an entire year?

E. "Now [in Aramaic] this man sees his field lying fallow, his vineyard lying fallow, yet he pays his *anona*-tax [a share of the crop] and does not complain.

F. "[In Hebrew] Do you know of a greater hero than that!"

G. "Now if you maintain that Scripture does not speak about those who observe the Seventh Year, [I shall bring evidence that it does].

H. "Here it is stated, 'Carrying out his word' (Ps. 103:20) and with reference to the Seventh Year, it is stated, 'This is the word concerning the year of release' (Deut. 15:2).

I. "Just as the reference to 'word' stated at that passage applies to those who observe the Seventh Year, so reference to 'word' in the present passage applies to those who observe the Seventh Year."

5. A. [Continuing discussing of the passage cited at the outset:] "Carrying out his word" (Ps. 103:20):

B. R. Huna in the name of R. Aha: "It is concerning the Israelites who stood before Mount Sinai that Scripture speaks, for they first referred to doing [what God would tell them to do], and only afterward referred to hearing [what it might be], accordingly stating, 'Whatever the Lord has said we shall carry out and we shall hear' (Ex. 24:7)."

6.   A. [Continuing the same exercise:] "Obeying his word" (Ps. 103:-20):

B. Said R. Tanhum bar Hinilai, "Under ordinary circumstances a burden which is too heavy for one person is light for two, or too heavy for two is light for four.

C. "But is it possible to suppose that a burden that is too weighty for six hundred thousand can be light for a single individual?

D. "Now the entire people of Israel were standing before Mount Sinai and saying, 'If we hear the voice of the Lord our God any more, then we shall die' (Deut. 5:22). But, [for his part], Moses heard the voice of God himself and lived.

E. "You may find evidence that that is the case, for, among all [the Israelites], the [act of] speech [of the Lord] called only to Moses, on which account it is stated, 'The Lord called Moses' (Lev. 1:1)."

Leviticus 1:1 intersects with Psalms 103:20 to make the point that Moses was God's messenger *par excellence,* the one who blesses the Lord, is mighty in strength, carries out and obeys God's word. This point is made first at No. 1 by proving that the verse speaks of earthly, not heavenly, creatures. Then it is made explicit at No. 6. No. 1 presents two sets of proofs, 1.A–F and G–M. The second may stand by itself. It is only the larger context that suggests otherwise. No. 2–3 is continuous with 1.G–M, No. 3 is equally continuous with 1.G–M, to which explicit reference is made. No. 4 and No. 5 refer back to the cited verse, Ps. 103:20, but not to the context of Leviticus 1. So we have these units:

1.A–F   Psalms 103:20 refers to earthly creatures.
1.G–M, 2, 3   Prophets are called messengers.
4.   Psalms 103:20 refers to a mighty man who observes the Sabbatical Year.

5.   Psalms 103:20 refers to the Israelites before Mount Sinai.

6.   Psalms 103:20 refers to Moses.

1:2

1.   A. R. Abbahu opened [discourse by citing the following verse]: "They shall return and dwell beneath his shadow, they shall grow grain, they shall blossom as a vine, their fragrance shall be like the wine of Lebanon' (Hos. 14:7).

      B. " 'They shall return and dwell beneath his shadow'—these are proselytes who come and take refuge in the shadow of the Holy One, blessed be he.

      C. " 'They shall grow grain'—they are turned into [part of] the root, just as [any other] Israelite.

      D. "That is in line with the following verse: 'Grain will make the young men flourish, and wine the women' (Zech. 9:17).

      E. " 'They shall blossom as a vine'—like [any other] Israelite.

      F. "That is in line with the following verse: 'A vine did you pluck up out of Egypt, you did drive out the nations and plant it' (Ps. 80:9)."

2.   A. Another item [= Genesis Rabbah 66:3]: "They shall grow grain"—in Talmud.

      B. "They shall blossom as a vine"—in lore.

3.   A. "Their fragrance shall be like the wine of Lebanon [and Lebanon signifies the altar]"—

      B. Said the Holy One, blessed be he, "The names of proselytes are as dear to me as the wine-offering that is poured out on the altar before me."

4.   A. And why [is that mountain called] "Lebanon"?

      B. In line with [the following verse]: "That goodly mountain and the Lebanon" (Deut. 3:25).

      C. R. Simeon b. Yohai taught, "Why is it called Lebanon? Because it whitens the sins of Israel like snow.

      D. "That is in line with the following verse: 'If your sins are red as scarlet, they shall be made white as snow' (Is. 1:18)."

      E. R. Tabyomi said, "It is [called Lebanon] because all hearts (LBB) rejoice in it.

      F. "That is in line with the following verse of Scripture: 'Fair in situation, the joy of the whole world, even Mount Zion, at the far north' (Ps. 48:3).''

G. And rabbis say, "It is [called Lebanon] because of the following verse: 'And my eyes and heart shall be there all the days' (1 Kings 9:3).''

So far as we have a sustained discourse, we find it as Nos. 1, 3. No. 2 is inserted whole because of its interest in the key verse, Hoshaiah 14:7. Reference at that verse to "Lebanon" explains the set-piece treatment of the word at No. 4. These units may travel together. Someone clearly drew together this anthology of materials on, first, Hos. 14:7, and, by the way, second, the word Lebanon.

1:3

1. A. R. Simon in the name of R. Joshua b. Levi, and R. Hama, father of R. Hoshaiah, in the name of Rab: "The Book of Chronicles was revealed only for the purposes of exegetical exposition."

2. A. "And his wife Jahehudijah bore Jered, the father of Gedor, and Heber, the father of Soco, and Jekuthiel the father of Zanoah—and these are the sons of Bithiah, the daughter of Pharaoh, whom Mered took" (1 Chr. 4:17).

    B. "And his wife, Hajehudijáh [= the Judah-ite]"—that is Jochebed.

    C. Now was she from the tribe of Judah, and not from the tribe of Levi? Why then was she called Hajehudijah [the Judah-ite]?

    D. Because she kept Jews (Jehudim) alive in the world [as one of the midwives who kept the Jews alive when Pharaoh said to drown them].

3. A. "She bore Jered"—that is Moses.

    B. R. Hanana bar Papa and R. Simon:

    C. R. Hanana said: "He was called Jered because he brought the Torah down from on high to earth."

    D. "Another possibility: 'Jered'—for he brought down the Presence of God from above to Earth."

    E. Said R. Simon, "The name Jered connotes only royalty, in line with the following verse: 'May he have dominion from sea to sea, and from the river to the end of the earth' (Ps. 72:8).

F. "And it is written, 'For he rules over the entire region on this side of the River' (1 Kings. 5:4)."

4. A. "Father of Gedor"—

B. R. Huna in the name of R. Aha said, "Many fence-makers stood up for Israel, but this one [Moses] was the father of all of them."

5. A. "And Heber"—

B. For he joined Israel to their father in heaven.

C. Another possibility: "Heber"—for he turned away punishment from coming upon the world.

6. A. "The father of Soco"—

B. This one was the father of all the prophets, who perceive by means of the holy spirit.

C. R. Levi said, "It is an Arabic word. In Arabic they call a prophet 'sakya.' "

7. A. "Jekuthiel"—

B. R. Levi and R. Simon:

C. R. Levi said, "For he made the children hope in their Father in heaven."

D. Said R. Simon, "When the children sinned against God in the incident of the Golden Calf . . . "

E. 'The father of Zanoah'—

F. "Moses came along and forced them to give up that transgression.

G. "That is in line with the following verse of Scripture: '[And he took the calf which they had made and burned it with fire and ground it to powder] and strewed it upon the water' (Ex. 32:-20)."

8. A. "And these are the sons of Bithiah, the daughter of Pharaoh"—

B. R. Joshua of Sikhnin in the name of R. levi: "The Holy One, blessed be he, said to Bithiah, the daughter of Pharaoh, 'Moses was not your child, but you called him your child. So you are not my daughter, but I shall call you my daughter' [thus daughter of the Lord]."

9. A. "These are the sons of Bithiah . . . whom Mered took"—

B. [Mered] is Caleb.

C. R. Abba bar Kahana and R. Judah bar Simon:

D. R. Abba bar Kahana said, "This one [Caleb] rebelled against the counsel of the spies, and that one rebelled against the counsel of the father [Pharaoh, as to murdering the babies]. Let a rebel come and take as wife another rebellious spirit."

E. [Explaining the link of Caleb to Pharaoh's daughter in a different way], R. Judah b. R. Simon said, "This one [Caleb] saved the flock, while that one [Pharaoh's daughter] saved the shepherd [Moses]. Let the one who saved the flock come and take as wife the one who saved the shepherd."

10. A. Moses [thus] had ten names [at 1 Chr. 4:17]: Jered, Father of Gedor, Heber, Father of Soco, Jekuthiel, and Father of Zanoah [with the other four enumerated in what follows].

B. R. Judah bar Ilai said, "He also was called [7] Tobiah, in line with the following verse: 'And she saw him, that he was good' (Ex. 2:2). He is Tobiah."

C. R. Ishmael bar Ami said, "He also was called [8] Shemaiah."

11. A. R. Joshua bar Nehemiah came and explained the following verse: " 'And Shemaiah, the son of Nethanel the scribe, who was of the Levites, wrote them in the presence of the king and the princes and Zadok the priest and Ahimelech the son of Abiathar' (1 Chr. 24:6).

B. "[Moses was called] Shemaiah because God heard his prayer.

C. "[Moses was called] the son of Nethanel because he was the son to whom the Torah was given from Hand to hand.

D. " 'The scribe,' because he was the scribe of Israel.

E. " 'Who was of the Levites,' because he was of the tribe of Levi.

F. " 'Before the king and the princes'—this refers to the King of kings of kings, the Holy One blessed be he, and his court.

G. " 'And Sadoq the priest'—this refers to Aaron the priest.

H. " 'Ahimeleh'—because [Aaron] was brother ('H) of the king.

I. " 'The son of Abiathar'—the son through whom the Holy One, blessed be he, forgave the deed of the Golden Calif."

12. A. R. Tanhuma in the name of R. Joshua b. Qorhah, and R. Menehemah in the name of R. Joshua b. Levi: "He also was called [9] Levi after his eponymous ancestor: 'And is not Aaron, your brother, the Levite' (Ex. 4:14)."

B. And [he of course was called] [10] Moses—hence [you have] ten names.

C. Said the Holy One, blessed be he, to Moses, "By your life! Among all the names by which you are called, the only one by which I shall ever refer to you is the one which Bithiah, the daugher of Pharaoh, gave to you: 'And she called his name Moses' (Ex. 2:10), so God called Moses."

D. So: "He called Moses" (Lev. 1:1).

The passage at hand stands fully by itself, leading to the climax at the very end, at which the opening words of the opening verse of the book of Leviticus are cited. The point of the entire, vast construction is the inquiry into the various names of Moses. From that standpoint we have a strikingly tight composition. But still, the passage *is* a composite, since it draws together autonomous and diverse materials. The first passage, No. 1, is surely independent, yet it makes for a fine superscription to the whole. Then the pertinent verse, at No. 2A, 1 Chronicles 4:17, is cited and systematically spelled out, Nos. 2, 3, 4, 5, 6, 7, 8, 9. Not only so, but at No. 10, we review the matter and amplify it with an additional, but completely appropriate, set of further names of Moses, Nos. 10 plus 13, to be viewed, in line with No. 12, as a unified construction. No. 11 is inserted and breaks the thought. Then 12C tells us the point of it all, and that brings us back to Leviticus 1:1, on the one side, and to No. 8. But, as we have seen, we cannot refer to No. 8 without drawing along the whole set, Nos. 2–9. So the entire passage forms a single sustained discussion, in which diverse materials are determinedly drawn together into a cogent statement.

1:4

1. A. R. Abin in the name of R. Berekhiah the Elder opened [discourse by citing the following verse]: " 'Of old you spoke in a vision to your faithful one, saying, "I have set the crown upon one who is mighty, I have exalted one chosen from the people" ' (Ps. 89:20).

   B. "[The Psalmist] speaks of Abraham, with whom [God] spoke both in word and in vision.

   C. "That is in line with the following verse of Scripture: 'After these words the word of God came to Abram in a vision saying . . . ' (Gen. 15:1).

   D. " '. . . to your faithful one'—'You will show truth to Jacob, faithfulness to Abraham' (Mic. 7:20).

   E. " ' . . . saying, "I have set the crown upon one who is mighty" ' —for [Abraham] slew four kings in a single night.

F. "That is in line with the following verse of Scripture: 'And he divided himself against them by night . . . and smote them' (Gen. 14:15)."

2. A. Said R. Phineas, "And is there a case of someone who pursues people already slain?

   B. "For it is written, 'He smote them and he [then] pursued them' (Gen. 14:15).

   C. "But [the usage at hand] teaches that the Holy One, blessed be he, did the pursuing, and Abraham did the slaying.

3. A. [Abin continues,] " 'I have exalted one chosen from the people' (Ps. 89:20).

   B. " 'It is you, Lord, God, who chose Abram and took him out of Ur in Chaldea' (Neh. 9:7)."

4. A. ["I have exalted one chosen from the people" (Ps. 89:20] speaks of David, with whom God spoke both in speech and in vision.

   B. That is in line with the following verse of Scripture: "In accord with all these words and in accord with this entire vision, so did Nathan speak to David" (2 Sam. 7:17).

   C. "To your faithful one" (Ps. 89:20) [refers] to David, [in line with the following verse:] "Keep my soul, for I am faithful" (Ps. 86:2).

   D. " . . . saying, 'I have set the crown upon one who is mighty' " (Ps. 89:20)—

   E. R. Abba bar Kahana and rabbis:

   F. R. Abba bar Kahana said, "David made thirteen wars."

   G. And rabbis say, "Eighteen."

   H. But they do not really differ. The party who said thirteen wars [refers only to those that were fought] in behalf of the need of Israel [overall], while the one who held that [he fought] eighteen includes five [more, that David fought] for his own need, along with the thirteen [that he fought] for the need of Israel [at large].

   I. "I have exalted one chosen from the people" (Ps. 89:20)—"And he chose David, his servant, and he took him . . . " (Ps.78:70).

5. A. ["Of old you spoke in a vision to your faithful one . . . "] speaks of Moses, with whom [God] spoke in both speech and vision, in line with the following verse of Scripture: "With him do I speak mouth to mouth [in a vision and not in dark speeches]" (Num. 12:8).

B. "To your faithful one"—for [Moses] came from the tribe of Levi, the one concerning which it is written, "Let your Thummim and Urim be with your faithful one" (Deut. 33:8).

C. " . . . saying, 'I have set the crown upon one who is mighty' "—

D. the cited passage is to be read in accord with that which R. Tanhum b. Hanilai said, "Under ordinary circumstances a burden which is too heavy for one person is light for two, or too heavy for two is light for four. But is it possible to suppose that a burden that is too weighty for six hundred thousand can be light for a single individual? Now the entire people of Israel were standing before Mount Sinai and saying, 'If we hear the voice of the Lord our God any more, then we shall die' (Deut. 5:27). But, for his part, Moses heard the voice of God himself and lived" [= 1:1.6.B–D].

E. You may know that that is indeed the case, for among them all, the act of speech [of the Lord] called only to Moses, in line with that verse which states, "And [God] called to Moses" (Lev. 1:1).

F. "I have exalted one chosen from the people" (Ps. 89:20)—"Had not Moses, whom he chose, stood in the breach before him to turn his wrath from destroying them" [he would have destroyed them] (Ps. 106:23).

The whole constitutes a single, beautifully worked-out composition, applying Psalms 89:20 to Abraham, David, then Moses, at Nos. 1, 3 (Abraham), 4 (David), and 5 (Moses). No. 2 is a minor interpolation, hardly spoiling the total effect. No. 5D is jarring and obviously inserted needlessly. That the purpose of the entire construction was to lead to the climactic citation of Lev. 1:1 hardly can be doubted, since the natural chronological (and eschatological) order would have dictated Abraham, Moses, David. That the basic construction, moreover, forms a unity is shown by the careful matching of the stichs of the cited verse in the expositions of how the verse applies to the three heroes. If we had to postulate an "ideal form," it would be simply the juxtaposition of verses, A illustrated by X, B by Y, and so forth, with little or no extraneous language. But where, in the basic constituents of the construction, we do find explanatory language or secondary development, in the main it is necessary for sense. Accordingly, we see as perfect a construction as we are likely to find: whole, nearly entirely essential, with a minimum of intruded material. To be sure, what really looks to be essential is the notion of God's communicating by two media to the three great heroes. That is the clear point of the most closely corresponding passages of the whole. In that case, the reorganization and vast amplification comes as an after thought, provoked by the construction of a passage serving Leviticus 1:1.

1:5

1.   A. R. Joshua of Sikhnin in the name of R. Levi opened [discourse by citing the following verse]: " 'For it is better to be told, "Come up here," than to be put lower in the presence of the prince' (Prov. 25:7)."

     B. R. Aqiba repeated [the following tradition] in the name of R. Simeon b. Azzai, "Take a place two or three lower and sit down, so that people may tell you, 'Come up,' but do not go up [beyond your station] lest people say to you, 'Go down,' It is better for people to say to you, 'Come up, come up,' than that they say to you, 'Go down, go down.' "

     C. And so did Hillel say, "When I am degraded, I am exalted, but when I am exalted, I am degraded."

     D. What is the pertinent biblical verse? "He who raises himself is to be made to sit down, he who lowers himself is to be [raised so that he is] seen" (Ps. 113:5).

     E. So too you find that, when the Holy One, blessed be he, revealed himself to Moses from the midst of the bush, Moses hid his face from him.

     F. That is in line with the following verse of Scripture: "Moses hid his face" (Ex. 3:6).

2.   A. Said to him the Holy One, blessed be he, "And now, go, (LKH), I am sending you to Pharaoh" (Ex. 3:10).

     B. Said R. Eleazar, "[Taking the word 'Go,' LK, not as the imperative, but to mean, 'to you,' and spelled LKH, with an H at the end, I may observe that] it would have been sufficient to write, 'You (LK),' [without adding] an H at the end of the word. [Why then did Scripture add the H?] To indicate to you, 'If you are not the one who will redeem them, no one else is going to redeem them.'

C. "At the Red Sea, Moses stood aside. Said to him the Holy One, blessed be he, 'Now you, raise your rod and stretch out your hand [over the sea and divide it]' (Ex. 14:16).

D. "This is to say, 'If you do not split the sea, no one else is going to split it.'

E. "At Sinai Moses stood aside. Said to him the Holy One, blessed be he, 'Come up to the Lord, you and Aaron' (Ex. 24:1).

F. "This is to say, 'If you do not come up, no one else is going to come up.'

G. "At the [revelation of the instructions governing sacrifices at] the tent of meeting, [Moses] stood to the side. Said to him the Holy One, blessed be he, 'How long are you going to humble yourself? For the times demand only you.'

H. "You must recognize that that is the case, for among them all, the speech of God called only to Moses, as it is written, 'And [God] called to Moses' (Lev. 1:1)."

We have once more to work backward from the end to find out what, at the outset, is necessary to make the point of the unit as a whole. It obviously is the emphasis upon how the humble man is called to take exalted position and leadership, that is, No. 2.

1:6

1. A. R. Tanhuma opened [discourse by citing the following verse:] " 'There are gold and a multitude of rubies, but lips [that speak] knowledge are the [most] valuable ornament' (Prov. 20:15).

   B. "Under ordinary circumstances [if] a person has gold, silver, precious stones, pearls, and all sorts of luxuries, but has no knowledge—what profit does he have?

   C. "In a proverb it says, 'If you have gotten knowledge, what do you lack? But if you lack knowledge, what have you gotten?' "

2. A. "There is gold"—all brought their freewill offering of gold to the tabernacle.

   B. That is in line with the following verse of Scripture: "And this is the offering [which you shall take from them, gold] . . . " (Ex. 25:3).

   C. "And a multitude of rubies"—this refers to the freewill offering of the princes.

D. That is in line with the following verse of Scripture: "And the rulers brought [onyx stones and the stones to be set]" (Ex. 35:-27).

E. "But lips [that speak] knowledge are the [most] valuable ornament" (Prov. 20:15).

F. Now Moses was sad, for he said, "Everyone has brought his freewill offering for the tabernacle, but I have not brought a thing.' "

G. Said to him the Holy One, blessed be he, "By your life! Your words [of address to the workers in teaching them how to build the tabernacle] are more precious to me than all of these other things."

H. You may find proof for that proposition, for among all of them, the Word [of God] called only to Moses, as it is written, "And [God] called to Moses" (Lev. 1:1).

Once more we see a complete construction, with a seemingly irrelevant introduction, No. 1, serving to cite a verse in no way evoked by the passage at hand. The exposition of the verse, further, does not appear to bring us closer to the present matter. But at No. 2, both the cited verse and the exposition of the verse are joined to the verse before us. If we may venture a guess at the aesthetic *jeu d'esprit* involved, it is this: How do we move from what appears to be utterly irrelevant to what is in fact the very heart of the matter? The aesthetic accomplishment is then to keep the hearer or reader in suspense until the climax, at which the issue is worked out, the tension resolved. It must follow, of course, that we deal with unitary composition.

1:7

1. A. What subject matter is discussed just prior to the passage at hand? It is the passage that deals with the building of the tabernacle [in which each pericope concludes with the words,] "As the Lord commanded Moses" (cf. Ex. 38:22; 39:1, 5, 7, 21, 26, 29, 31, 42, 43; 40:16, 19, 21, 23, 25, 27, 29, 32).

    B. To what may this matter be compared? To a king who commanded his servant, saying to him, "Build a palace for me."

C. On everything that [the employee] built, he wrote the name of the king. When he built the walls, he inscribed the name of the king; when he set up the buttresses, he wrote the name of the king on them; when he roofed it over, he wrote the name of the king on [the roof]. After some days, the king came into the palace, and everywhere he looked, he saw his name inscribed. He said, "Now my employee has paid me so much respect, and yet I am inside [the building he built], while he is outside.' " He called him to enter.

D. So when the Holy One, blessed be he, called to Moses, "Make a tabernacle for me," on [every] thing that Moses made, he inscribed, " . . . as the Lord commanded Moses."

E. Said the Holy One, blessed be he, "Now Moses has paid me so much respect, and yet I am inside, while he is outside."

F. He called him to come in, on which account it is said, "And [God] called Moses" (Lev. 1:1).

The passage begins with the imputation to the verb QR' of the sense of invitation. The focus of exegesis shifts from Moses to God's calling him. The exegetical resource is the repeated reference, as indicated, to Moses' doing as God had commanded him. But this is now read as Moses' inscribing God's name everywhere on the tabernacle as he built it, and the rest follows.

1:8

1. A. R. Samuel bar Nahman said in the name of R. Nathan, "Eighteen times are statements of [God's] commanding written in the passage on the building of the tabernacle, corresponding to the eighteen vertebrae in the backbone.

   B. "Correspondingly, sages instituted eighteen statements of blessing in the Blessings of the Prayer, eighteen mentions of the divine name in the recitation of the *Shema,* eighteen mentions of the divine name in the Psalm, 'Ascribe to the Lord, you sons of might' (Ps. 29)."

   C. Said R. Hiyya bar Ada, "[The counting of the eighteen statements of God's commandment to Moses] excludes [from the count the entry prior to the one in the verse], 'And with him was Oholiab, son of Ahisamach of the tribe of Dan' (Ex. 38:23), [thus omitting reference to Ex. 38:22, 'And Bezalel, son of Uri son of Hur of the tribe of Judah, made all that the Lord commanded Moses']. [But the counting then includes all further such references to the end of the book [of Exodus]."

2.   A. To what is the matter comparable? To a king who made a tour of a province, bringing with him generals, governors, and lesser officers, and [in watching the procession], we do not know which one among them is most favored. But [when we see] to whom the king turns and speaks, we know that he is the favorite.

   B. So everyone surrounded the tabernacle, Moses, Aaron, Nadab and Abihu, and the seventy elders, so we do not know which one of them is the favorite. But now, since the Holy One, blessed be he, called to Moses and spoke to him, we know that he was the favorite of them all.

   C. On that account it is said, "And [God] called Moses" (Lev. 1:1).

3.   A. To what may the matter be compared? To a king who made a tour of a province. With whom will he speak first? Is it not with the market-inspector, who oversees the province? Why? Because he bears responsibility for the very life of the province.

   B. So Moses bears responsibility for Israel's every burden,

   C. saying to them, "This you may eat" (Lev. 11:2), "and this you may not eat" (Lev. 11:4), "This you may eat of whatever is in the water" (Lev. 11:9), and this you may not eat, "This you shall treat as an abomination among fowl" (Lev. 11:13), and so these you shall treat as an abomination, and others you need *not* abominate, "And these are the things that are unclean for you." (Lev. 11:29), so these are unclean, and those are *not* unclean.

   D. Therefore it is said, "And [God] called Moses" (Lev. 1:1).

No. 1 bears no relationship to what follows. It continues 1:7, with its interest in the repetitions of the statement about Moses' having done as God had commanded him. 1A–B however stand completely outside the present frame of reference, Lev. 1:1. 1C harmonizes the number of times the cited phrase actually occurs with the number of vertebrae in the backbone.

1:9

1.   A. "And [the Lord] called to Moses" (Lev. 1:1) [bearing the implication, to Moses in particular].

B. Now did he not call Adam? [But surely he did:] "And the Lord God called Adam" (Gen. 3:9).

C. [He may have called him, but he did not speak with him, while at Lev. 1:1, the Lord "called Moses and spoke to him"], for is it not undignified for a king to speak with his tenant-farmer [which Adam, in the Garden of Eden, was]?

D. " . . . and the Lord spoke to him" (Lev. 1:1) [to him in particular].

E. Did he not speak also with Noah? [But surely he did:] "And God spoke to Noah" (Gen. 8:15).

F. [He may have spoken to him, but he did not call him,] for is it not undignified for a king to speak with [better: *call*] his ship's captain [herding the beasts into the ark]?

G. "And [the Lord] called to Moses" (Lev. 1:1) [in particular].

H. Now did he not call Abraham? [But surely he did:] "And the angel of the Lord called Abraham a second time from heaven" (Gen. 22:15).

I. [He may have called him, but he did not speak with him,] for is it not undignified for a king to speak with his host [Gen. 18:1]?

J. "And the Lord spoke with him" (Lev. 1:1) [in particular].

K. And did he not speak with Abraham? [Surely he did:] "And Abram fell on his face, and [God] spoke with him" (Gen. 17:3).

M. But is it not undignified for a king to speak with his host?

2. A. "And the Lord called Moses" (Lev. 1:1), but not as in the case of Abraham.

B. [How so?] In the case of Abraham, it is written, "And an angel of the Lord called Abraham a second time from heaven" (Gen. 22:15). The angel did the calling, then the Word [of God] did the speaking.

C. "Here, [by contrast,] said R. Abin, "the Holy One, blessed be he, said, 'I am the one who does the calling, and I am the one who does the speaking.'

D. " 'I, even I, have spoken, yes, I have called him, I have brought him and he shall prosper in his way' " (Is. 48:15).

The point of No. 1 is clear, but the text is not. What is demanded is three instances in which God called someone but did not speak with him, or spoke with him but did not call him; in contrast with the use of both verbs, "call" and "speak," in regard to

Moses at Leviticus 1:1. If that is what is intended, then the pattern does not work perfectly for all three: Adam, Noah, and Abraham. 1A–D and E–G are smooth. With Abraham, however, the exposition breaks down, since the point should be that he called Abraham but did not actually speak with him, and it is only No. 2 that makes *that* point. The repetition of 3 at M therefore is only part of the problem of the version. We can readily reconstruct what is needed, of course, in the model of the passages for Adam and Noah.

No. 2 of course is independent of No. 1, and handsomely worked out. But No. 2 cannot have served the form selected by the framer of the triplet at No. 1.

1:10

1.   A. "[And the Lord called Moses and spoke to him] from the tent of meeting" (Lev. 1:1).

      B. Said R. Eleazar, "Even though the Torah [earlier] had been given to Israel at Sinai as a fence [restricting their actions], they were liable to punishment on account of [violating] it only after it has been repeated for [taught to] them in the tent of meeting.

      C. "This may be compared to a royal decree, that had been written and sealed and brought to the province. The inhabitants of the province became liable to be punished on account of violating the decree only after it had been spelled out for them in a public meeting in the province.

      D. "Along these same lines, even though the Torah had been given to Israel at Sinai, they bore liability for punishment on account of violating it[s commandments] only after it had been repeated for them in the tent of meeting.

      E. "That is in line with the following verse of Scripture: 'Until I had brought him into my mother's house and into the chamber of my teaching [lit.: parent]' (Song 3:4).

      F. " ' . . . into my mother's house' refers to Sinai.

      G. " ' . . . and into the chamber of my teaching' refers to the tent of meeting, from which the Israelites were commanded through instruction [in the Torah]."

The passage is formally perfect, running from the beginning, a general proposition, 1B, through a parable, C, explicitly linked to the original proposition, D, and then joined to the exposition of a seemingly unrelated verse of Scripture, which turns out to say exactly what the general proposition has said. So the original statement, B, is worked out in two separate and complementary ways, first, parabolic, second, exegetical.

1:11

1. A. Said R. Joshua b. Levi, "If the nations of the world had known how valuable the tent of meeting was to them, they would have sheltered it with tents and ballustrades.

    B. "[How so?] You note that before the tabernacle was erected, the nations of the world could hear the noise of [God's] speech and [fearing an earthquake(?)] they would rush out of their dwellings.

    C. "That is in line with the following verse of Scripture: 'For who is there of all flesh, who has heard the voice of the living God [speaking out of the midst of the first as we have, and lived]?' " (Deut. 5:23).

2. A. Said R. Simon, "The word [of God] went forth in two modes, for Israel as life, for the nations of the world as poison.

    B. "That is in line with the following verse of Scripture: ' . . . as you have, and lived'" (Deut. 4:33).

    C. "You hear [the voice of God] and live, while the nations of the world hear and die."

    D. That is in line with what R. Hiyya taught, " ' . . . from the tent of meeting' (Lev. 1:1) teaches that the sound was cut off and did not go beyond the tent of meeting."

1:12

1. A. Said R. Isaac, "Before the tent of meeting was set up, prophecy was common among the nations of the world. Once the tent of meeting was set up, prophecy disappeared from among them. That is in line with the following verse of Scripture: 'I held it' [the holy spirit, producing], 'and would not let it go [until I had brought it . . . into the chamber of her that conceived me]' (Song 3:4)."

B. They said to him, "Lo, Balaam [later on] practiced prophecy."

C. He said to them, "He did so for the good of Israel: 'Who has counted the dust of Jacob' (Num. 23:10). 'No one has seen iniquity in Jacob' (Num. 23:21). 'For there is no enchantment with Jacob' (Num. 23:23). 'How goodly are your tents, O Jacob' (Num. 24:5). 'There shall go forth a star out of Jacob' (Num. 24:17). 'And out of Jacob shall one have dominion' (Num. 24:19)."

"The chamber" of 1A is the tent of meeting, as before. In fact the passage at hand is continuous with the foregoing. As we shall see, the established theme then moves forward in what follows. The construction is of course unitary. "They said to him" of B simply sets up discourse; it is not meant to signify an actual conversation, rather serves as a convention of rhetoric. B then allows C to string out the relevant verses. We now continue the same matter of Balaam, prophet of the gentiles, and Israel.

1:13

1.   A. What is the difference between the prophets of Israel and those of the nations?

B. R. Hama b. R. Hanina and R. Issacher of Kepar Mandi:

C. R. Hama b. R. Hanina said, "The Holy One, blessed be he, is revealed to the prophets of the nations of the world only in partial speech, in line with the following verse of Scripture: 'and God called Balaam' (Num. 23:16). On the other hand, [he reveals himself] to the prophets of Israel in full and complete speech, as it is said, 'And [the Lord] called to Moses' (Lev. 1:-1)."

D. Said R. Issachar of Kepar Mandi, "Should that [prophecy, even in partial form] be [paid to them as their] wage? [Surely not, in fact there is no form of speech to gentile prophets, who are frauds]. [The connotation of] the language, 'And [God] called to Balaam' (Num. 23:16) is solely uncleanness. That is in line with the usage in the following verse of Scripture: 'That is not clean, by that which happens by night' (Deut. 23:11). [So the root is the same, with the result that YQR at Num. 23:16 does not bear the meaning of God's calling to Balaam. God rather declares Balaam unclean.]

E. "But the prophets of Israel [are addressed] in language of holiness, purity, charity, in language used by the ministering angels to praise God. That is in line with the following verse of Scripture: 'And they called (QR') one to another and said' (Is. 6:3)."

2. A. Said R. Eleazar b. Menahem, "It is written, 'The Lord is far from the evil, but the prayer of the righteous does he hear' (Prov. 5:29).

B. " 'The Lord is far from the wicked' refers to the prophets of the nations of the world.

C. " 'But the prayer of the righteous does he hear' refers to the prophets of Israel.

D. "You [furthermore] find that the Holy One, blessed be he, appears to the prophets of the nations of the world only like a man who comes from some distant place.

E. "That is in line with the following verse of Scripture: 'From a distant land they have come to me, from Babylonia' (Is. 39:3).

F. "But in the case of the prophets of Israel [he is always] near at hand: 'And he [forthwith] appeared [not having come from a great distance]' (Gen. 18:1), 'and [the Lord] called' (Lev. 1:1)."

3. A. Said R. Yose b. Biba, "The Holy One, blessed be he, is revealed to the prophets of the nations of the world only by night, when people leave one another: 'When men branch off, from the visions of the night, when deep sleep falls on men' (Job 4:13), 'Then a word came secretly to me' (Job 4:12). [Job is counted among the prophets of the gentiles.]"

4. A. R. Hanana b. R. Pappa and rabbis:

B. R. Hanina b. R. Pappa said, "The matter may be compared to a king who, with his friend, was in a hall, with a curtain hanging down between them. When [the king] speaks to his friend, he turns back the curtain and speaks with his friend."

C. And rabbis say, "[The matter may be compared] to a king who had a wife and a concubine. When he walks about with his wife, he does so in full public view. When he walks about with his concubine, he does so discreetly. So, too, the Holy One, blessed be he, is revealed to the prophets of the nations of the world only at night, in line with that which is written: 'And God came to Abimelech in a dream by night' (Gen. 22:24). 'And God came to Balaam at night' (Num. 22:20).

D. "To the prophets of Israel, however, [he comes] by day: '[And the Lord appeared to Abraham . . .] as he sat at the door of his tent in the heat of the day' (Gen. 18:1). 'And it came to pass by day that the Lord spoke to Moses in the land of Egypt' (Ex. 6:28). 'On the day on which he commanded the children of Israel' (Lev. 6:38). 'These are the generations of Aaron and Moses. God spoke to Moses by day on Mount Sinai' (Num. 3:1)."

Once the topic of comparing Israel's receiving of revelation to that of the nations of the world has arisen, at 1:12, we pursue it further, and, as we shall see, 1:14 adds still more pertinent material. We have a fine superscription, 1A, with three independent items strung together, 1B–D, 2, 3, and 4. Nos. 1B–D, 4, follow an obvious, simple pattern, and Nos. 2, 3 simply assign a protracted saying to a given name. We have no reason to suppose the entire set has come from a single hand. Since the same points are made by two or more authorities, it is likely that a redactor has chosen pertinent materials out of what he had available.

1:14

1. A. What is the difference between Moses and all the other [Israelite] prophets?
   B. R. Judah b. R. Ilai and rabbis:
   C. R. Judah said, "All the other prophets saw [their visions] through nine mirrors [darkly], in line with the following verse of Scripture: 'And the appearance of the vision which I saw was like the vision that I saw when I came to destroy the city; and the visions were like the vision that I saw by the River Chebar, and I fell on my face' (Ex. 43:3) [with the root R'H occurring once in the plural, hence two, and seven other times in the singular, nine in all].
   D. "But Moses saw [his vision] through a single mirror: 'in [one vision] and not in dark speeches' (Num. 12:8)."
   E. Rabbis said, "All other [Israelite] prophets saw [their visions] through a dirty mirror. This is in line with the following verse of scripture: 'And I have multiplied visions, and by the ministry of the angels I have used similitudes' (Hos. 12:11).

    F. "But Moses saw [his vision] through a polished mirror: 'And the image of God does he behold' (Num. 12:8)."

2.   A. R. Phineas in the name of R. Hoshaia: "[The matter may be compared] to a king who makes his appearance to his courtier in his informal garb [as an intimate].*

    B. "For in this world the Indwelling Presence makes its appearance only to individuals [one by one], while concerning the age to come, what does Scripture say? 'The glory of the Lord shall be revealed, and all flesh shall see [it together, for the mouth of the Lord has spoken]' (Is. 40:5)."

The continuous discourse continues its way, ignoring not only the passage at hand—Leviticus 1:1—but the several topics provoked by exposition of the theme under discussion in connection with the tent of meeting. Having compared Balaam to Israelite prophets, we proceed to compare Israelite prophets to Moses, with the predictable result, No. 1 preserves the matter. But No. 2 on the surface is wildly out of place, since Moses now is forgotten, and the contrast is between prophecy in this age and in the time to come—a subject no one has hitherto brought up. But the messianic *finis* is a redactional convention.

Having surveyed the first *parashah* of Leviticus Rabbah, we have now to ask what is new in this document.

To seek, through biblical exegesis, to link the Mishnah to Scripture, detail by detail, represented a well-trodden and firmly packed path. The Sifra has shown us what could be done. Scripture-exegesis by rabbis also was a commonplace, as the Yerushalmi indicates. One document opened a new road to Scripture, and that is Leviticus Rabbah. Not merely a phrase-by-phrase or verse-by-verse exegesis of a document, whether the Mishnah or Scripture itself, Leviticus Rabbah takes a new path. The framers of that composition undertook to offer propositions, declarative sentences. It was not through the exegesis of verses of Scripture in the order of Scripture, but through an order dictated by their own sense of the logic of syllogistic composition. That is how they would say what they had in mind. To begin with, they laid down

*Lieberman in Margulies, p. 870 commenting on Margulies, p. 32.

their own topical program, related to, but essentially autonomous of, that of the book of Leviticus. Second, in expressing their ideas on these topics, they never undertook simply to cite a verse of Scripture and then to claim that that verse states precisely what they had in mind to begin with. Accordingly, through rather distinctive modes of expression, the framers said what they wished to say in their own way—just as had the authors of the Mishnah itself. True, in so doing, the composers of Leviticus Rabbah treated Scripture as had their predecessors. That is to say, to them as to those who had gone before, Scripture provided a rich treasury of facts.

THE AS-IF WAY

The paramount and dominant exegetical construction in Leviticus Rabbah is the base-verse/intersecting verse exegesis. *Parashah* 1:1 provides an ample instance. In this construction, a verse of Leviticus is cited (hence: base-verse), and another verse, from such books as Job, Proverbs, Qohelet, or Psalms, is then cited. The latter, not the former, is subjected to detailed and systematic exegesis. But the exegetical exercise ends up by leading the intersecting verse back to the base-verse and reading the latter in terms of the former. In such an exercise, what in fact do we do? We read one thing in terms of something *else*. To begin with, it is the base-verse in terms of the intersecting verse. But it also is the intersecting verse in other terms as well—a multi-layered construction of analogy and parable. The intersecting verse's elements always turn out to stand for, to signify, or to speak of, something other than that to which they openly refer. If water stands for Torah, the skin disease for evil speech, the reference to something for some other thing entirely, then the mode of thought at hand is simple. One thing symbolizes another, speaks not of itself but of some other thing entirely.

How shall we describe this mode of thought? It seems to me we may call it an *as-if* way of seeing things. That is to say, it is *as if* a common object or symbol really represented an uncommon one.

Nothing says what it means. Everything important speaks metonymically, elliptically, parabolically, symbolically. All statements carry deeper meaning. The profound sense, then, of the base-verse emerges only through restatement within and through the intersecting verse—*as if* the base-verse spoke of things that, on the surface, we do not see in it at all.

Accordingly, if we ask the single prevalent literary construction to testify to the prevailing frame of mind, its message is that things are never what they seem. All things demand interpretation. Interpretation begins in the search for analogy, for that to which the thing is likened. All exegesis at hand is a quest for that for which the thing in its deepest structure stands.

Exegesis as we know it in Leviticus Rabbah (and not only there) consists in an exercise in analogical thinking—something is like something else, stands for, evokes, or symbolizes that which is quite outside itself. It may be the opposite of something else, in which case it conforms to the exact opposite of the rules that govern that something else.

These observations bring us back to the question with which we began: exactly how do the authors of Leviticus Rabbah treat the written Torah? What relationship does this document posit between the written Torah and the oral Torah? We seek to know exactly what we can say for the position of Scripture in this composition in particular, and what Scripture contributed.

We ask first about the use of Scripture in the mode of thought at hand: Where, why, and how did Scripture find its central place in the minds of people who thought in the way in which the framers of our document did? The answer is that Scripture contributed that other world that underlay this one. From Scripture came that other set of realities to be discovered in the ordinary affairs of the day. Scripture defined the inner being, the mythic life, that sustained Israel. The world is to be confronted *as if* things are not as they seem, because it is Scripture that tells us how things always are—not one time, in the past only; not one-time, in the future only; but now and always. So the key to the system is what happens to, and through, Scripture. The lock that is opened is the deciphering of the code by which people were guided in their denial of one thing and recognition and affirmation of the presence of some other. It was not general, therefore mere lunacy; but specific, therefore culture.

The mode of thought pertained to a particular set of ideas. People did not engage ubiquitously and individually in an ongoing pretense that things always had to be other than how they seemed. Had they done so, the Jewish nation would have disintegrated into a collectivity of pure insanity. The insistence on the *as-if* character of reality collectively focused upon one, and only one, alternative existence. All parties (so far as we know) entered into and shared that same and single interior universe. It was the one framed by Scripture.

What happens in Leviticus Rabbah and in other documents of the same sort? Reading one thing in terms of something else, the builders of the document systematically adopted for themselves the *reality* of the Scripture, its history and doctrines. They transformed that history from a sequence of one-time events, leading from one place to some other, into an ever-present mythic world. No longer was there one Moses, one David, one set of happenings of a distinctive and never-to-be-repeated character. Now whatever happens, of which the thinkers propose to take account, must enter and be absorbed into that established and ubiquitous pattern and structure founded in Scripture. It is not that biblical history repeats itself. Rather, biblical history no longer constitutes history as a story of things that happened once, long ago, and pointed to some moment in the future. Now, biblical history becomes an account of things that happen every day, hence, an ever-present mythic world.

A rapid glance at Leviticus Rabbah and its fellows tells us that Scripture supplies the document with its structure, its content, its facts, its everything. But a deeper analysis also demonstrates that Scripture never provides the document with the structure, contents, and facts, that it now exhibits. Everything is reshaped and reframed. Whence the paradox?

Scripture as a whole does not dictate the order of discourse, let alone its character. Just as the talmudic authors destroyed the wholeness of the Mishnah and chose to take up its bits and pieces, so the exegetical writers did the same to Scripture. They chose in Leviticus itself a verse here, a phrase there (e.g., Leviticus 1:1 in our sample). These then presented the pretext for propositional discourse commonly quite out of phase with the cited passage. Verses that are quoted ordinarily shift from the meanings they convey to the implications they contain, speaking—as I have made clear—about something, anything, other than what they seem to be saying. So the *as-if* frame of mind brought to Scripture brings renewal to Scripture, seeing everything with fresh eyes.

The result of the new vision was a re-imagining of the social world envisioned by the document at hand, that is the everyday world of Israel in its land in that difficult time. For what the sages now proposed was a reconstruction of existence along the lines of the ancient design of Scripture as they read it. This meant that, from a sequence of one-time and linear events, everything that happened was turned into a repetition of known and already experienced paradigms, hence, once more, a mythic being. The source and core of the myth, of course, derive from Scripture— Scripture reread, renewed, constructed along with the society that revered Scripture.

So, to summarize, the mode of thought that dictated the issues and the logic of the document, that told the thinkers to see one thing in terms of something else, addressed Scripture in particular and collectively. And thinking as they did, the framers of the document saw Scripture in a new way, just as they saw their own circumstance afresh, rejecting their world in favor of Scripture's, reliving Scripture's world in their own terms.

That, incidentally, is why they did not write history, an account of what was happening and what it meant. It was not that they did not recognize or appreciate important changes and trends reshaping their nation's life. They could not deny that reality. In their apocalyptic reading of the dietary and leprosy laws, they made explicit their close encounter with the history of the world as they knew it. But they had another mode of responding to history. It was to treat history *as if* it were already known and readily understood. Whatever happened had already happened. That is why the oral Torah contains not one history tractate or book. Scripture dictated the contents of history, laying forth the structures of time, the rules that prevailed and were made known in events. Self-evidently, these same thinkers projected into Scripture's day the realities of their own, turning Moses and David into rabbis, for example. But that is how people think in that mythic, enchanted world in which, to begin with, reality blends with dream, and hope projects onto future and past alike how people want things to be.

Everything in Scripture is relevant everywhere else in Scripture. It must follow, the Torah defines reality under all specific circumstances. Obviously we did not have to come to the specific literary traits of the document at hand to discover those prevailing characteristics of contemporary and later documents of the rabbinic canon. True, every exercise in referring one biblical passage to another expands the range of discourse to encompass much beyond the original referent. But that is a commonplace in the exegesis of Scripture, familiar wherever *midrash*-exegesis was undertaken, in no way particular to rabbinic writings.

THE MAJOR PROPOSITIONS OF LEVITICUS RABBAH

The message of Leviticus Rabbah comes to us from the ultimate framers. It is delivered through their selection of materials already available as well as through their composition of new ones. What we now require is a clear statement of the major propositions expressed in Leviticus Rabbah. That will emerge through classification of the statements, with the notion that the principal themes, and the messages on those themes, should coalesce into a few clear statements.

The recurrent message may be stated in a single paragraph: God loves Israel, so gave them the Torah, which defines their life and governs their welfare. Israel is alone in its category *(sui generis)*, as in *Parashah* 1, so what is a virtue to Israel is a vice to the nations, life-giving to Israel, poison to the gentiles. True, Israel sins, but God forgives that sin, having punished the nation on account of it. Such a process has yet to come to an end, but it will culminate in Israel's complete regeneration. Meanwhile, Israel's assurance of God's love lies in the many expressions of special concern, for even the humblest and most ordinary aspects of the national life: the food the nation eats, the sexual practices by which it procreates. These life-sustaining, life-transmitting activities draw God's special interest, as a mark of his general love for Israel. Israel then is supposed to achieve its life in conformity with the marks of God's love.

These indications moreover signify also the character of Israel's difficulty, namely, subordination to the nations in general, but to the fourth kingdom, Rome, in particular. Both food laws and skin diseases stand for the nations. There is yet another category of sin, also collective and generative of collective punishment, and that is social. The moral character of Israel's life, the treatment of people by one another, the practice of gossip and small-scale thuggery— these too draw down divine penalty. The nation's fate therefore corresponds to its moral condition. The moral condition, however, emerges not only from the current generation. Israel's richest hope lies in the merit of the ancestors, thus in the scriptural record of the merits attained by the founders of the nation, those who originally brought it into being and gave it life.

The world to come upon the nation is so portrayed as to restate these same propositions. Merit overcomes sin, and doing religious duties or supererogatory acts of kindness will win merit for the nation that does them. Israel will be saved at the end of time, and the age, or world, to follow will be exactly the opposite of this one. Much that we find in the account of Israel's national life, worked out through the definition of the liminal relationships, recurs in slightly altered form in the picture of the world to come.

If we now ask about further recurring themes or topics, there is one so commonplace that we should have to list the majority of paragraphs of discourse in order to provide a complete list. It is the list of events in Israel's history, meaning, in this context, Israel's history solely in scriptural times, down through the return to Zion. The one-time events of the generation of the flood, Sodom and Gomorrah, the patriarchs and the sojourn in Egypt, the Exodus, the revelation of the Torah at Sinai, the golden calf, the Davidic monarchy and the building of the Temple, Sennacherib, Hezekiah, and the destruction of northern Israel, Nebuchadnezzar and the destruction of the Temple in 586, the life of Israel in Babylonian captivity, Daniel and his associates, Mordecai and Haman —these events occur over and over again. They turn to to serve as paradigms of sin and atonement, steadfastness and divine intervention, and equivalent lessons. We find, in fact, a fairly standard repertoire of scriptural heroes or villains, on the one side, and conventional lists of Israel's enemies and their actions and downfall, on the other. The boastful, for instance, include the generation of the flood, Sodom and Gomorrah, Pharaoh, Sisera, Sennacherib, Nebuchadnezzar, the wicked empire (Rome)— contrasted to Israel, "despised and humble in this world." The four kingdoms recur again and again, always ending, of course, with Rome, with the repeated message that after Rome will come Israel. But Israel has to make this happen through its faith and submission to God's will. Lists of enemies ring the changes on Cain, the Sodomites, Pharaoh, Sennacherib, Nebuchadnezzar, and Haman.

Accordingly, the mode of thought brought to bear upon the theme of history remains exactly the same as before: list-making, with data exhibiting similar taxonomic traits drawn together into lists based on common monothetic traits of definitions. These lists then through the power of repetition make a single enormous point or prove a social law of history. The catalogues of exemplary heroes and historical events serve a further purpose. They provide a model of how contemporary events are to be absorbed into the biblical paradigm. Since biblical events exemplify recurrent happenings—sin and redemption, forgiveness and atonement —they lost their one-time character. At the same time and in the same way, current events find a place within the ancient, but eternally present, paradigmatic scheme. So no new historical events, other than exemplary episodes in lives of heroes, demand narration because, through what is said about the past, what was happening in the times of the framers of Leviticus Rabbah would also come under consideration. This mode of dealing with biblical history and contemporary events produces two reciprocal effects. The first is the mythicization of biblical stories, their removal from the framework of ongoing, unique patterns of history and sequences of one-time events, and their transformation into accounts of things that happen all the time. The second is that contemporary events—what happens in the present—also lose their specificity and enter the paradigmatic framework of established mythic existence. So (1) the Scripture's myth happens every day, and (2) every day produces reenactment of the Scripture's myth.

In seeking the substance of the mythic being invoked by the exegetes at hand, who read the text as if it spoke about something else and viewed this world as if it lived out the next world, we uncover a simple fact. At the center of the pretense, that is, the *as-if* mentality of Leviticus Rabbah and its framers, we find a simple proposition: Israel is God's special love. That love is shown in a simple way. Israel's present condition of subordination derives from its own deeds. It follows that God cares, so Israel may look forward to redemption on God's part in response to Israel's own regeneration through repentance.

The message of Leviticus Rabbah attaches itself to the book of Leviticus, as if that book had come from prophecy, with its interest in history, and addressed the issue of salvation at the end of time. But it came from the priesthood and spoke of sanctification. The paradoxical syllogism—the *as-if* reading, the opposite of how things seem—of the composers of Leviticus Rabbah therefore reaches simple formulation. In the very setting of cultic rules of sanctification we find the promise of salvation. In the topics of the cult and the priesthood we uncover the national and social issues of the moral life and redemptive hope of Israel. The repeated comparison and contrast of priesthood and prophecy, sanctification and salvation, turn out to produce a complement, which comes to most perfect union in the text at hand.

The basic mode of thought—denial of what is at hand in favor of a deeper reality—proves remarkably apt. The substance of thought confronts the crisis too. Let me state the message.

"Are we lost for good to the fourth empire, now-Christian Rome?" "No, we may yet be saved."

"Has God rejected us forever?" "No, aided by the merit of the patriarchs and matriarchs and of the Torah and religious duties, we gain God's love."

"What must we do to be saved?" "We must *do* nothing, we must *be* something: sanctified."

That status is gained through keeping the rules that make Israel holy. So salvation is through sanctification, all embodied in Leviticus read as rules for the holy people.

The Messiah will come not because of what a pagan emperor does, nor, indeed, because of Jewish action either, but because of Israel's own moral condition. When Israel enters the right relationship with God, then God will respond to Israel's condition by restoring things to their proper balance. Israel cannot, but need not, so act as to force the coming of the Messiah. Israel can so attain the condition of sanctification, by forming a moral and holy community, that God's response will follow the established prophecy of Moses and the prophets.

So the basic doctrine of Leviticus Rabbah is the metamorphosis of Leviticus. Instead of holy caste, we deal with holy people. Instead of holy place, we deal with holy community, in its holy land. The deepest exchange between reality and inner vision, therefore, comes at the very surface: the rereading of Leviticus in terms of a different set of realities from those to which the book, on the surface, relates. No other biblical book would have served so well; it had to be Leviticus. Only through what the framers did on that particular book could they deliver their astonishing message and vision.

So to state the main conclusion, which stands paramount and dominant, Scripture contributed everything but the main point. That point comes to us from the framers of Leviticus Rabbah, from them alone. So far as Leviticus Rabbah transcends the book of Leviticus, and that means in the whole of its being, the document speaks for the framers, conveys their message, pursues their discourse, makes the points they wished to make. For they are the ones who made of Leviticus the book, Leviticus Rabbah, that *greater* Leviticus (the word *rabbah* means great); the document that spoke of sanctification but, in its augmented version at hand, meant salvation. As closely related to the book of Leviticus as the New Testament is to the Old, Leviticus Rabbah delivers the message of the philosophers of Israel's history.

I have emphasized that Leviticus Rabbah carries a message of its own, which finds a place within, and refers to, a larger system. The method of thought and mode of argument act out a denial of one reality in favor of the affirmation of another. That dual process of pretense at the exegetical level evokes the deeper pretense of the mode of thought of the larger system, and, at the deepest layer, the pretense that fed Israel's soul and sustained it. Just as one thing evokes some other, so does the rabbinic system overall turn into aspects of myth and actions of deep symbolic consequence what to the untutored eye were commonplace deeds and neutral transactions. So too the wretched nation really enjoyed God's special love. Thus, as I stated at the outset, what is important in the place and function accorded to Scripture derives significance from the host and recipient of Scripture, that is to say, the rabbinic system itself.

THE PLACE OF SCRIPTURE IN THE ORAL TORAH

But so far as Leviticus Rabbah stands for and points toward that larger system, what are the commonplace traits of Scripture in this other, new context altogether?

1. Scripture, for one thing, forms a timeless present, with the affairs of the present day read back into the past and the past into the present, with singular events absorbed into Scripture's paradigms.

2. Scripture is read whole and atomistically. Everything speaks to everything else, but only one thing speaks at a time.

3. Scripture is read as an account of a seamless world, encompassing present and past alike, and Scripture is read atemporally and ahistorically.

Scripture is read whole, because the framers pursue issues of thought that demand all data pertaining to all times and all contexts. The authors are philosophers, looking for rules and their verification. Scripture tells stories, to be sure. But these exemplify facts of social life and national destiny: The laws of Israel's life.

Scripture is read atomistically, because each of its components constitutes a social fact, ever relevant to the society of which it forms a part, with that society everywhere uniform.

Scripture is read as a source of facts pertinent to historical and contemporary issues alike, because the issues at hand when worked out will indicate the prevailing laws, the rules that apply everywhere all the time, to everyone of Israel.

Accordingly, there is no way for Scripture to be read except as a source of facts about that ongoing reality that forms the focus and the center of discourse, the life of the unique social entity, Israel. But, as we have seen, the simple logic conveyed by the parable also contributes its offering of facts. As we shall see in Chapter 7, the simple truth conveyed by the tale of the great man, the exemplary event of the rabbinic sage, the memorable miracle —these too serve as well as facts of Scripture. The several truths therefore stand alongside, and at the same level as, the truths of Scripture, which thus is not the sole source of rules or cases. The facts of Scripture stand no higher than those of the parable, on the one side, or of the tale of the sage, on the other. Why not? Because to philosophers and scientists, facts are facts, whatever their origin or point of application.

What we have in Leviticus Rabbah, therefore is the result of the mode of thought not of prophets or historians, but of philosophers and scientists. The framers propose not to lay down, but to discover, rules governing Israel's life. I state with necessary emphasis: *As we find the rules of nature by identifying and classifying facts of natural life, so we find rules of society by identifying and classifying the facts of Israel's social life.* In both modes of inquiry we make sense of things by bringing together like specimens and finding out whether they form a species, then bringing together like species and finding out whether they form a genus—in all, classifying data and identifying the rules that make possible the classification. That sort of thinking lies at the deepest level of list-making, which is, as I said a work of offering a proposition and facts (for social rules) as much as a genus and its species (for rules of nature). Once discovered, the social rules of Israel's national life of course yield explicit statement, such as that God hates the arrogant and loves the humble. The readily assembled syllogism follows: If one is arrogant, God will hate him, and if he is humble, God will love him. The logical status of these statements about physics, ethics, or politics, as these emerge in philosophical thought, is equivalent to those found in the text at hand. What differentiates the statements of Leviticus Rabbah is not their logical status—as sound, scientific philosophy—but only their subject matter on the one side, and distinctive rhetoric on the other. Both sorts of statements rest on acknowledged facts and shared premises of logical argument.

So Leviticus Rabbah is anything but an exegetical exercise. We err if we are taken in by the powerful rhetoric of our document, which resorts so ubiquitously to the citation of biblical verses and, more important, to the construction, out of diverse verses, of a point transcendent of the cited verses. At hand is not an exegetical composition at all, nor even verses of Scripture read as a corpus of proof-texts. We have, rather, a statement that stands by itself, separate from Scripture, and which makes its points only secondarily, along the way, by evoking verses of Scripture to express and exemplify those same points. We miss the main point if we posit that Scripture plays a definitive or even central role in providing the program and agenda for the framers of Leviticus Rabbah. Their program is wholly their own. but of course Scripture then serves their purposes very well indeed. So what we have in this component of the oral Torah is yet another Mishnah, a document that presents its own message, in its own way, and nonetheless demands a hearing as part of the Torah of Moses, received from God at Mount Sinai.

6. The Written Torah and the Oral Torah in Conclusion: The Bavli (The Talmud of Babylonia)

The path from the Mishnah leads through the Yerushalmi and then takes us to Leviticus Rabbah. The problem posed by that amazing document has now to come to the fore, since we shall not understand the Bavli's success until we realize the impasse that the authors of the Bavli confronted. The impasse was reached when people realized the full implications of the stunning approach to the written Torah taken by the authors of Leviticus Rabbah. What those writers accomplished, we now realize, was to treat the written Torah as if it were the oral Torah. That is to say, they turned Scripture into another Mishnah. What I mean by that simple sentence has taken the whole of Chapter 5 to work out, so let us move directly to state the problem at hand.

If the Scripture now turns out to be another Mishnah—or, to speak in the language of the Torah, if the written and the oral Torahs constitute "one whole Torah"—then how are we to demonstrate that fact? Specifically, can sages find a way to organize their ideas and received traditions so as to treat both Torahs in one and the same way, as "one whole Torah"? As we shall now discover, the authors of the Bavli found an answer to that question, an answer as astonishing in its way as the breakthrough in the philosophical reading of Scripture accomplished by the writers of

Leviticus Rabbah in their way. Let us turn back to the Yerushalmi as one route to the Bavli, and take up its approach to the issue of the oral Torah.

HOW THE BAVLI RELATES TO THE YERUSHALMI

Since everything characteristic of the Yerushalmi's sages' treatment of the Mishnah also defines the work of the Bavli's authorities, we turn directly to the important question about the Bavli and its theory of both the oral and the written Torahs.

The Bavli did not emerge alone and all by itself. It flowed from three or four centuries of continuous tradition, beginning with the Mishnah and passing through a sequence of documents devoted to the exegesis of the Mishnah. We cannot pretend that, wholly on its own, the Bavli came to expression and realization. Then we must find out in what ways the Bavli relates to what had gone before. So we ask how the Bavli relates to the Yerushalmi. Why the Yerushalmi in particular? The answer derives from two distinct facts. First, the authors of both the Yerushalmi and the Bavli organized their materials around the exegesis of the Mishnah. The materials they produced, moreover fall into essentially the same taxonomic framework. Accordingly, out of all of the documents of the canon of Judaism of late antiquity, the Yerushalmi and the Bavli stand closest both to the source on which both comment, and also to one another. Second, when I investigated the formation of critical ideas in the symbolic and mythic structure of the Judaism presented by the canon as a whole, I repeatedly reached a single conclusion. Whatever data we find in the many other components of the canon as a whole, one group of facts here, another sort of emphases there, nearly all of the data of a given symbol or myth find a place in the two Talmuds and nowhere else. So the Yerushalmi and the Bavli both stand together and also take up a position separate from the remainder of the canon. They therefore form a subdivision of the canon as a whole.

Since the distinctive approach of the authors of the Bavli to the relationship of the Mishnah to Scripture is at issue, let me state up front what is important. The exposition will then occupy the remainder of the present chapter. A somewhat complicated fact forms the centerpiece of the argument, but I will express it as simply as I can. As we shall see, the Yerushalmi and the Bavli do many things in one and the same way. But there is one thing that the Bavli's framers do in their own way.

When it comes to organizing their materials, the compositors of the Yerushalmi organize large-scale discourse only around the exposition of the Mishnah. They of course include units of thought of an episodic character on two other matters: first, lives and teachings of sages; second, exposition of verses or themes of Scripture. When, however, it comes to putting the whole together, no *protracted* discussions in the Yerushalmi take shape around lives of sages or passages of Scripture. The Mishnah and that alone defines the fundamental redactional framework for the Yerushalmi.

The compositors of the Bavli organize *protracted* discussion—many consecutive units of discourse—not only around the amplification of the Mishnah. They also present us with sizable sequences of units of discourse drawn together as exposition of Scripture, that is, of consecutive verses of Scripture (as much as consecutive passages of the Mishnah) or of cogent themes or topics of Scripture. *In resorting to Scripture, as much as to the Mishnah, for the framework for the organization and proportioning of large-scale discourse, the authors of the Bavli did what those of the Yerushalmi did not do.*

In so doing, they accomplished a feat that was all their own. They absorbed Scripture into the framework defined by their modes of Mishnah-exegesis and amplification. They made Scripture over into a kind of Mishnah, but joined the Mishnah and Scripture into a single construction. In literary terms, they took the written Torah and revised it into a component of close-to-equal structural standing with the Mishnah, the oral Torah.

What facts show this to be true? My probe of three tractates (Sukkah, Sotah, and Sanhedrin) in both Yerushalmi and Bavli shows that as much as 35 to 40 percent of the Bavli's large-scale sequences of units of discourse pursue Scriptural exegeses, along with 60 percent of such units on Mishnah-exegesis. In the Yerushalmi's corresponding tractates, *all* large-scale sequences of units of discourse seem to take shape around Mishnah-exegesis, none around protracted Scripture-exegesis. While these figures can only be rough estimates, they are sufficiently one-sided to sustain the conclusions stated here. that is, by the Bavli's authors, the oral Torah, focused upon the Mishnah, and the written Torah, focused upon Scripture, were reworked into that "one whole Torah of Moses, our rabbi," to which, as we see in Chapter 8, the Bavli gives the first unequivocal expression in the unfolding of the rabbinic writings of late antiquity, that is, of the oral Torah as we now have it.

Let me now go back and unpack the assertions of the preceding paragraphs, since my intent is to show exactly where and how the oral Torah came to that full and final expression that we find in the Bavli. Why, specifically, the Bavli became the paramount authority for Judaism, moreover, is the character of the Bavli itself. That character is defined, above all else, by the Bavli's treatment of the problem of the two Torahs, written and oral, and making them one. So what is at issue is no small matter.

THE ORGANIZATION OF THE BAVLI

When the final organizers of the Talmud of Babylonia (who, it is commonly alleged, flourished ca. 500 to 600 C.E.,) considered the redactional choices made by their predecessors, two will have appeared the most likely. They might take up and organize such materials as they had in their hands around the categories of Scripture, as had some of their precursers in bringing into being compositions made up of exegesis of Scripture *(midrashim)*. Or they might follow the order of the Mishnah and compose a systematic commentary and amplification of that document, as had their precursers who created the Talmud of the Land of Israel a century or so before. When they considered their task, however, they had to recognize that they in fact had in hand a tripartite corpus of inherited materials awaiting composition into a final, closed document.

First, they took up materials, in various states and stages of completion, pertinent to the Mishnah, or to the laws that the Mishnah had originally brought to articulation.

Second, they had in hand received materials, again in various conditions, pertinent to the Scripture, both as the Scripture related to the Mishnah and also as the Scripture laid forth its own narratives.

Finally, they had in hand materials focused on sages. These were framed around twin biographical principles, either as strings of stories about great sages of the past, or as collections of sayings and comments drawn together solely because the same name stands behind the sayings. The decision the framers of the Bavli reached was to adopt the two redactional principles inherited from the antecedent century or so, and to reject the one already rejected by their predecessors, even while honoring it.

First, they organized the Bavli around the Mishnah. Second, however, they adapted and included vast tracts of antecedent materials organized as scriptural commentary. And, finally, while making provision for compositions built upon biographical principles, preserving both strings of sayings from a given master (and often a given tradent of a given master), as well as tales about authorities of the preceding half-millennium, they did nothing new. That is to say, they never created redactional compositions of a sizable order, focused upon given authorities, even though sufficient materials lay at hand to allow doing so. In the three decisions, two of what to do and one of what not to do, the final compositors of the Bavli indicated what they proposed to accomplish: to give final form and fixed expression, through their categories of the organization of all knowledge, to what had been known, sifted, searched, approved, and handed down, even from the remote past to their own day. So the compositors of the Bavli were encyclopedists. Their creation turned out to be the encyclopedia of Judaism, its summa, its point of final reference, its court of last appeal, its definition, its conclusion, its closure—so they thought, and so thought those that followed, to this very day.

Shall we then draw so grand a conclusion from so modest a fact as how people sorted out available redactional categories? It sounds disproportionate. But in fact the modes by which thinkers organize knowledge leads us deep into the theses by which useful knowledge rises to the surface, while what is irrelevant or unimportant or trivial sinks to the bottom. If we want to know what people thought and how they thought it, we can do worse than to begin by asking about how they organized what they knew, and about the choices they made in laying out the main lines of the structure of knowledge. When we approach a document so vast and complex as the Bavli, resting as it does on a still larger and more complex antecedent corpus of writings, we do best to begin at the very beginning, at the surface of things.

The document as a whole lays itself out as a commentary to the Mishnah. So the framers wished us to think that whatever they wanted to tell us would take the form of Mishnah-commentary. Their place in the oral Torah was as explainers and completers. But a second glance indicates that the document is made up of enormous composites, themselves closed prior to inclusion in the Bavli. Some of these composites—around 35 to 40 percent of the Bavli's volume, if my sample is indicative—were selected and arranged along lines dictated by a logic other than that deriving from the requirements of Mishnah-commentary. In these the logic of redaction—what (self-evidently) comes first, what (obviously) goes below—emerges from a different sort of exegetical task from Mishnah-commentary. It was Scripture-commentary, for, as I said, people focused upon passages of Scripture in making up and putting together their compositions.

It goes without saying that people who copy what others had earlier done on the surface laid no claim upon originality. That would be so for the Bavli's editors except for one fact. Before their time the three principles of composition and redaction—Mishnah-exegesis, Scripture-exegesis, and biographical-collection—flourished more or less in isolation from one another. How do we know? The first is fully exposed in the Yerushalmi, the second, in earlier compilations of scriptural exegeses. The third accounts for the available biographical composites. To be sure, these never were gathered into "tractates" or other large and autonomous units of literary expression before the time of the nineteenth- and earlier twentieth-century biographers of talmudic rabbis. It is clear, therefore, that the antecedent redactors, before the age of the Bavli's own compositors, thought that the three things could be done pretty much separately.

The framers of the Bavli then drew together the results of these three types of editorial work, which people prior to their own labors already had created in abundance. They made of them one document, the Bavli—or, in the later tradition of Judaism, *the* Talmud. Whatever the place and role of the diverse types of compositions circulating before and in the time of the Bavli—compilations of scriptural exegeses, the Yerushalmi, not to mention the exegeses of pentateuchal laws in Sifra and the Sifres, the Tosefta, Pirqe Avot and Avot de R. Natan, and on and on, the Bavli superseded them all. It took pride of place. It laid the final seal upon the past and defined not only what would succeed for an unknown future, but the very form and topical order and program of all that would pass into the hands of the future.

TYPES OF CONSTRUCTIONS

Since the critical issue, for the Bavli, is the organization of large-scale discourse around the order of verses or the exposition of themes or topics of Scripture, let us begin by reviewing examples of the type of constructions I regard as so critical to the interpretation of the Bavli's theory of the relationship of the oral to the written Torah. These scriptural exegeses are of several types. My examples all derive from the Yerushalmi, but the critical importance of the Bavli will soon become clear.

First, a sequence of verses may be subjected to systematic discussion, or a single scriptural topic or event is amplified. The principle of conglomeration rests upon Scripture's own presentation of the verses as a group. The passage then is organized around Scripture's sequence of verses. Here is a simple example of a sequence of units of discourse devoted to the exposition of a set of verses, in rough order and sequence. The principle of conglomeration derives from Scripture.

Y. Sotah 1:8

II. A. It is written, "[Then Samson went down with his father and mother to Timnah,] and he came to the vineyards of Timnah" (Judges 14:5).

B. Said R. Samuel bar R. Isaac, "This teaches that his father and his mother showed him the vineyards of Timnah, sewn in mixed seeds, and they said to him, 'Child! Just as [17b] their vineyards are sewn with mixed seeds, so their daughters are sewn with mixed seeds.'

C. "His father and mother did not know that it was from the Lord; for he was seeking an occasion against the Philistines" (Judges 14:4).

D. Said R. Eleazar, "In seven places it is written, 'You should not intermarry with them.'"

E. Said R. Abin, "This is to prohibit intermarriage with the seven peoples [of the Land.]

F. "And here why does it say [that Samson was punished for marrying a Philistine woman, when there is no prohibition in the Torah against marrying Philistines]?"

G. Said R. Isaac, "'Toward the scorners he is scornful, [but to the humble he shows favor]' (Prov. 3:34). [Since Samson got involved with scornful people, he was punished.]"

III. A. It is written, "And the spirit of the Lord began to stir him in Mahaneh-dan, between Zorah and Eshtaol" (Judges 13:25).

B. There are two Amoraim who interpret this passage.

C. One of them said, "When the Holy Spirit rested upon him, his footsteps were as if from Zorah and Eshtaol."

D. The other one said, "When the Holy Spirit rested on him, his hair grew stiff like a bell, and the sound went as between Zorah and Eshtaol."

IV. A. "[And the woman bore a son, and called his name Samson; and the boy grew] and the Lord blessed him" (Judges 13:24).

B. R. Huna in the name of R. Yose: "For [despite his great strength,] his sexual capacities were like those of any other man [and so he could enjoy sexual relations with a normal woman]."

V.   A. It is written, "[Then Samson called out to the Lord and said, 'O Lord God, remember me, I pray thee, and strengthen me, I pray thee, only this once, O God,] that I may be avenged upon the Philistines for one of my two eyes'" (Judges 16:28).

B. Said R. Aha, "He said before Him, 'Lord of the world! Give me the reward of one of my eyes in this world, and let the reward for the other eye be readied for me in the world to come.'"

VI.   A. One verse of Scripture states, "He judged Israel forty years." [This verse is not in the present version.]

B. And yet another verse of Scripture says, "He had judged Israel twenty years" (Judges 16:31).

C. Said R. Aha, "It teaches that the Philistines feared him for twenty years after his death just as they feared him for twenty years when he was alive."

Second, a common theme, independent of a single scriptural passage, is illustrated by scriptural verses. In this type of Scripture-unit of discourse, the introduction of scriptural verses is central to the rhetoric of the passage. The principle of conglomeration therefore derives from the subject matter, that is to say, the point that the framer wishes to make about a given topic, or the exposition of that topic from a variety of perspectives. Materials are joined together because they are relevant to that common topic. Here is an example of the use of Scripture to deal with a problem distinct from the verses at hand, yet closely related to them.

Y. Sotah 5:6

I.   A. When did Job live?

B. R. Simeon b. Laquish in the name of Bar Qappara: "In the days of Abraham, our father, did he live.

C. "This is in line with that which is written, 'There was a man in the land of Uz, whose name was Job, [and that man was blameless and upright, one who feared God, and turned away from evil]' (Job. 1:1).

D. "And it is written, '[Now after these things it was told to Abraham, 'Behold, Milcah also has born children to your brother Nahor:] Uz the first-born, [Buz his brother, Kemuel the father of Amram, Chesed, Hazo, Pildash, Jidlaph, and Bethuel]'" (Gen. 22:20–21).

E. R. Abba said, "It was in the days of our father, Jacob, and his wife was Dinah.

F. "This is in line with that which is written, '[But he said to her,] You speak as one of the foolish women would speak' (Job 2:10).

G. "And it is written, '[The sons of Jacob came in from the field when they heard of it; and the men were indignant and very angry,] because he had wrought folly in Israel [by laying with Jacob's daughter, for such a thing ought not to be done]' " (Gen. 34:7).

H. R. Levi said, "It was in the time of the tribes that he lived.

I. "That is in line with that which is written, '[I will show you, hear me; and what I have seen I will declare,] what wise men have told, and their fathers have not hidden' " (Job. 15:17–18).

J. R. Yose b. Halafta said, "He was among those who went down to Egypt, and when they came up, he died.

K. "It may be compared to a shepherd, to whose flock a shepherd came along and joined up. What did he do? He set up the bellwether against him.

L. "That is in line with the following verse of Scripture, 'God gives me up to the ungodly, and casts me into the hands of the wicked' " (Job 16:11).

M. R. Ishmael taught, "Job was one of the servants of Pharaoh. He was one of the great members of his retinue.

N. "That is in line with the following verse of Scripture: 'Then he who feared the word of the Lord among the servants of Pharaoh made his slaves and his cattle flee into the houses' (Ex. 9:20).

O. "And concerning him it is written, 'And the Lord said to Satan, Have you considered my servant Job, [that there is none like him on the earth,] a blameless and upright man, who fears God and turns away from evil?' " (Job 1:8).

P. R. Yose bar Judah says, "He was in the time in which the judges ruled Israel.

Q. "That is indicated in the following verse of Scripture: 'Behold, all of you have seen it yourselves; why then have you become so vain?' (Job 27:12).

R. "You have seen the deeds of my generation.

S. "For they collected tithes at the threshing floors: '[Rejoice not, O Israel! Exult not like the peoples; for you have played the harlot, forsaking your God.] You have loved a harlot's hire upon all the threshing floors' " (Hos. 9:1).

T. R. Samuel bar Nahman in the name of R. Jonathan: "He lived in the time of the kingdom of the Sabeans, for it is said, 'And the Sabeans fell upon them and took them, [and slew the servants with the edge of the sword; and I alone escaped to tell you]' " (Job 1:15).

U. R. Nathan said, "He lived in the time of the Chaldeans, for it is said, '[While he was yet speaking, there came another, and said,] The Chaldeans formed three companies, [and made a raid upon the camels and took them, and slew the servants with the edge of the sword; and I alone have escaped to tell you]' " (Job 1:17).

V. R. Joshua b. Qorha said, "He lived in the days of Ahasueros, for it is said, '[Then the king's servants said,] Let beautiful young virgins be sought out for the king' (Esther 2:2).

W. "And it is written, 'And in all the land there were no women so fair as Job's daughters; [and their father gave them inheritance among their brothers]' " (Job 42:15).

X. R. Joshua b. Levi said, "He was among those who came up from the Exile."

Y. R. Yohanan said, "He was among those who came up from the Exile, but he was an Israelite."

Z. On that account R. Yohanan derived from his behavior rules governing conduct in the time of mourning.

AA. "Then Job arose, and rent his robe, [and shaved his head, and fell upon the ground, and worshipped]" (Job 1:20).

BB. R. Judah b. Pazzi in the name of R. Yohanan, "On the basis of the cited verse we learn that a mourner has to tear his garment while standing up."

CC. R. Hiyya taught, "In my realm [?] there was a righteous gentile [such as Job, who was not an Israelite], and I paid him his wage, and I dismissed him from my realm."

DD. R. Simeon b. Laqish said. "Job never existed and never will exist."

EE. The opinions attributed to R. Simeon b. Laqish are at variance with one another.

FF. There R. Simeon b. Laqish said in the name of Bar Qappara, "He lived in the time of Abraham, our father," and here [at B] has he said this?

GG. But he really did exist, while the sufferings ascribed to him never really took place.

HH. And why were these sufferings ascribed to him? It is to indicate that if such sufferings had come to him, he would have been able to endure them.

We return, now, to the second principle by which compositors of documents selected and organized materials, in addition to that dictated by Mishnah-exegesis. As is clear, this redactional framework was defined by Scripture-exegesis. What did this mean? Quite simply, redactors would gather materials of Scripture-exegesis and organize them in the order of appearance of verses of Scripture or of the unfolding of a story in Scripture. At the outset, in the earliest scriptural-exegetical documents (generally assumed to be, as we saw, Sifra, also the two Sifres, followed by Genesis Rabbah and Leviticus Rabbah), people adhered to the exegetical and redactional pattern already established for the Mishnah, of going from one sentence to the next. For Scripture too they followed the order of verses of a biblical book, just as the framers of the Yerushalmi followed the order of Mishnah-sentences of a given tractate. They undertook to explain words or phrases, imposing upon Scripture that set of values that they regarded as self-evident and factual, the values of sages' worldview and way of life.

Since, it is usually alleged, the Yerushalmi took shape ca. 400 C.E. and the earlier compilations of scriptural exegeses in that same time (Genesis Rabbah, then Leviticus Rabbah in the period of, and shortly after, the Yerushalmi, with less certain dates for Sifra and the two Sifres, probably prior to the Yerushalmi), we need hardly be surprised at a simple fact. The same modes of exegesis and organization—that is, the same logic and topical program—that determined the content of self-evident comment in self-evident order on the Mishnah also dictated what would be done on Scripture. So the original work of collecting and arranging the compilations of exegeses of Scripture followed the patterns set in collecting and arranging exegeses of the Mishnah. Just as the Talmud, which is Mishnah exegesis, treats the Mishnah, so the earliest collections of scriptural exegesis treat Scripture.

APPROACHES TO REDACTION

Now that I have spelled out the different approaches to building up large-scale and protracted discussions taken by the authors of the Yerushalmi and the Bavli, with the Bavli building extensive passages and the Yerushalmi not doing so, let me go on to spell out, in some modest detail, the definition of the distinction between the two approaches to redaction. At the end, I shall explain why I think the distinction between the documents has made all the difference. So the question is this: In what ways do the two groups do the same thing, and in what ways do the Bavli's authors do their own distinctive work, in dealing with the written Torah?

As is clear from the examples given just now, sizable units of discourse in both Talmuds take up the exegesis of verses or passages of Scripture. The purpose in composing such Scripture-units proves diverse. Some such compositions take shape around problems of law, either to link rules of the Mishnah to proof-texts of Scripture or to explore in a context autonomous of the Mishnah the legal implications of legal passages of Scripture (as we saw in Chapter 4). These units of discourse in general link up to the Mishnah, one way or the other, and prove common in both Talmuds. But in both Talmuds other Scripture-units exhibit no link to the Mishnah or to problems of legal theory. They prove propositions through statements of Scripture; they elaborate values or ideals by reference to scriptural cases; they focus upon the meaning of a verse or a sequence of verses of Scripture. While the intent of the authors of units of discourse such as these cannot be exhaustively described, we can point to at least one reason they did their work. It is clear that, in some cases, their purpose was systematically to expound, in terms of a quite separate set of issues from those explicit in the passage at hand, the sense of a verse or sequence of verses in Scripture. In other such constructions we find a manifest interest in a virtue or a vice, with verses of Scripture supplying ample proof-texts or examples to prove that said virtue brings reward, or vice, punishment. In further instances we have a single verse subjected to close reading and exposition. In others, there are groups of verses.

The main point is simply that Scripture, as much as the Mishnah, served some authors of units of discourse and editors of conglomerates of units of discourse as the frame or the structure around which to organize ideas. What we now ask is only how much of the work of those authors of Scripture-units of discourse found its way into one Talmud—the Bavli—as against the other—the Yerushalmi. Then we inquire about what sort of work each set of compositors, those for the Yerushalmi, those for the Bavli, appears to have preferred. The question at hand therefore remains simple: whether or not on the basis of proportions of Scripture-units of discourse in each of the two Talmuds, we are able to differentiate one Talmud from the other. As we shall now see, the evidence is quite decisive.

Our first point of differentiation between Yerushalmi and Bavli is to ask whether one Talmud devotes a larger proportion of its interest to Scripture-units of discourse than does the other. The matter proves fundamental. While we do not know what choices the framers of the Talmuds faced, the sorts of material they rejected not being available now, we do have in our hands precisely what has survived of what they preferred. The Talmuds tell us. So we ask to begin with about their policies of selection and composition: where and how units of discourse devoted to systematic exposition of a verse or verse of Scripture for other than legal-exegetical purposes made their appearance. In surveying three tractates—Sotah, Sukkah, and Sanhedrin—we simply review the particular items devoted to Scripture and indicate their proportion of the large composite in which they appear. Let me state the question simply. How many units of discourse serving a given Mishnah-paragraph focus not upon the Mishnah, but upon Scripture; and what proportion of the total units of discourse serving said paragraph is devoted to Scripture?

The result is consistent and one-sided. While the Yerushalmi contains a negligible proportion of Scripture-units of discourse—5.9 percent in Sotah, 0.7 percent in Sukkah, and 6.5 percent in Sanhedrin—in the Bavli editors made use of sizable numbers and vastly larger proportions of the same sort of units. In proportion to the whole, these are 32.1 percent in Sotah, 2.9 percent in Sukkah, and 35.3 percent in Sanhedrin, five times the percentage for Sotah, four times for Sukkah, and five times for Sanhedrin. We need not suppose that the work of composing Scripture-units of discourse took place mainly in Babylonia; nor can we imagine that the work got underway mainly after the Yerushalmi had come to closure. These hypotheses are not relevant here. The sole evidence at hand hardly permits us to entertain such propositions. All we know, after all, is what the framers of the two Talmuds have given us, not what they decided not to include. Thus far, therefore, all we have done is differentiate the two documents by showing that the compositors of the Bavli have made far more extensive use of Scripture-units of discourse than did those of the Yerushalmi. To point toward the meaning of the facts at hand, we have now to undertake a further exercise of differentiation.

At issue next is whether or not a single system of classification serves both Talmuds. If it does, then the difference in proportion proved just now bears one set of meanings. If it does not, then that same difference requires a different set of interpretations. So the heart of matters lies in the sort of taxonomic structure I am able to propose for sorting out the types of Scripture-units of discourse. How so? The trait in common among the units of discourse at hand—their focus upon Scripture—has now to yield to consideration of the traits that differentiate one type of such unit of discourse from the next. One fundamental and ubiquitous question is simple: On what basis did the author or composer of a given sustained unit of discourse gather and join the materials that he used? What struck the framer as a point in common among the diverse materials he assembled?

Once we define as our point of differentiation the principle of aggregation of materials, we see two completely distinct theories. In one, a sequence of verses of Scripture e.g., a chapter of Scripture) clearly formed the center of interest for the compositors. This sort we saw above with Samson. The authors of the passage proposed, therefore, to collect sayings relevant to the sequence of verses and to arrange them into a composite given unit, proportion, and sense by the verses that are cited. In a second theory, a fundamental ideal or value formed the focus of discourse. Verses of Scripture, drawn from diverse passages, find their way into such a unit of discourse because they serve in some way to exemplify or clarify the virtue of value at hand.

The differentiation for taxonomic purposes then is both formal and functional. In a formal sense, a unit of discourse finds structure in the framework of a chapter (or a large sequence of verses) of Scripture. Or a unit of discourse takes shape around the inner logic or sense of a given ideal or virtue. It is that ideal (for example, study of Torah) that will guide the author to verses of Scripture suitable for his larger Scripture-unit of discourse. In that case, in a formal sense, a unit of discourse will skip about biblical books, picking and choosing verses out of their own context and moving those verses into the context of the ideal or value under discussion (as in the case of Job). So the question at hand is why and how the framer of a given unit of discourse has chosen and joined the various items. In that case, we seek to differentiate among Scripture-units of discourse not in terms of the function these units serve in their larger, talmudic context. Then we look upon the larger setting, not only upon the inner architectonic. Once we clarify the principle that, within a given unit of discourse, holds things together and imparts to Scripture its role and purpose in the larger statement of the unit viewed whole and complete, we look also to the reason for including a Scripture-unit.

Let me now state the answers to those questions. Unlike the Yerushalmi, the Bavli makes substantial use of Scripture-units of discourse for a purpose *other* than Mishnah exegesis, on the one side, or the amplification of points established in the context of legal or theological exposition, on the other. Scripture-units of this sort in the Bavli occur out of context, thus are used "for their own sake." The Bavli's framers therefore were prepared to organize their larger composition around more than the single focus of that context of discourse dictated by the Mishnah or by points of law or theology deemed pertinent to the Mishnah. The main point is not what the Bavli's compositors found more useful. It is *that* they were prepared to build large-scale discourse around a framework of verses of Scripture and not only of sustained Mishnah–exegesis.

The upshot is that, for the Bavli's authors, two distinct principles guided selection and arrangement of Scripture-units of discourse. One, available, as we know from the Yerushalmi, instructed them to use Scripture-units of discourse, as these served the larger and established purposes of Mishnah-exegesis and amplification. The other, not generated by the needs of Mishnah-exegesis and amplification, told them to allow Scripture-units of discourse, especially rather substantial ones, to find a place within their composition out of all relationship with the frame of reference defined by the available program of inquiry. Let me state with emphasis: *In this simple, redactional framework, while the Yerushalmi builds its lines of structure around paragraphs of the Mishnah alone, the Bavli utilizes a second redactional focus. It is redactional construction upon passages of Scripture, which, linked one way or another, serve as suitably as do passages of the Mishnah.* So the Yerushalmi rests upon a simple, and the Bavli upon a complex, principle of what both defines redactional logic and also dictates inner cogency between units of discourse. The one speaks to the Mishnah, the other to the Mishnah but also Scripture. In this way the Bavli thus joins the two Torahs and makes them one.

So, to conclude, the Yerushalmi contains a negligible proportion of Scripture-units of discourse composed around sequences of verses. The Bavli contains units of discourse that find cogency in Scripture, not in the Mishnah, on the one side; or in some well-established value or virtue, on the other. Just as much as the Mishnah serves the Bavli, in units of discourse of this type Scripture too defines for the Bavli a principle of redactional cogency and rhetorical coherence. The Bavli finds itself entirely at home in the utilization of such units of discourse—which, we recognize, can as readily have served the purposes of the redactors of exegeses of Scripture *(midrashim),* such as Genesis Rabbah or Leviticus Rabbah or Lamentations Rabbah. Just as the Yerushalmi's redactors composed large-scale discourse on a principle of law, rather than on a particular Mishnah-paragraph, so they put together equivalently sizable units of discourse in which a single theme, topic, value or ideal formed the focus, which then is amplified, illustrated, or validated by scriptural verses. But we find in our probe no examples at all in the Yerushalmi of large composites of units of discourse built up around the exposition of verses of Scripture. The framers of the Yerushalmi in the tractates surveyed did not resort to Scripture in search of principles of cogency and coherence of sustained discourse. Those of the Bavli did. And that has made all the difference.

What did the Bavli's framers accomplish in organizing and composing units of discourse? They formed a synthesis of two of the available components of the Torah, the oral and the written, the Mishnah and Scripture. First, they made far more ample use than did the authors of the Yerushalmi of units of discourse focused upon exegesis of Scripture, rather than upon that of the Mishnah. Second, they drew upon the redactional structure supplied by Scripture, as much as upon that provided by the Mishnah, when they went about organizing their units of discourse into large-scale compositions. That is why the Bavli's more sizable stretches of exposition will be made up of two quite distinct types of materials: first, those focused upon the Mishnah-paragraph; second, others centered upon verses of Scripture.

In selecting as redactional principles the order of the Mishnah, the framers of the Bavli followed the example of the authors of the Yerushalmi. In asking Scripture to dictate the sequence of discourse, they followed the example of the authors of Sifra, as we saw, as well as of Leviticus Rabbah (and other compositions, not treated here). So, viewed from a literary angle, as compositors and redactors of large-scale compositions, the authors of the Bavli constructed a vast synthesis of the two principles of composition and redaction employed prior to their time in available and distinct types of literature. These, as is clear, were Mishnah-exegesis in the Yerushalmi, and Scripture-exegesis in the collection of scriptural exegeses *(midrashim)*.

To conclude, the Bavli differs from the Yerushalmi in the clear and self-evident program of its compositors and redactors. Specifically, these compositors and redactors synthesized the two formerly distinct principles of (1) redaction of completed units of discourse concerning Scripture, and (2) composition or conglomeration of cogent units of discourse using Scripture. Their Talmud is not like the one that had come before, specifically because it appealed to two components of the available canon, not only for law and theology, but also for the logic and rhetoric of cogent discourse. To state the result in one sentence: Scripture, as much as the Mishnah, told the Bavli's, but not the Yerushalmi's, authors and compositors how to organize completed thoughts, and how to hold together the components of completed thoughts and make of them a cogent statement of size and consequence. The Bavli, the Torah of two Torahs thus joined not formally alone, but in the basic structure of knowledge, the unchanging monument of intellect that, to begin with, God had revealed at Sinai: the one whole Torah of Moses, our rabbi.

THE BAVLI: THE TWO STREAMS BECOME ONE

The Bavli became the summa of Judaism, and the Yerushalmi did not. To state matters in the language of Judaism, the Bavli, above all, constituted *the* Torah. For generations of learned Jews, therefore, the route to the written Torah, Scripture, passed through the oral Torah, the Bavli above all. The Bavli thus defined that one whole Torah of Moses, our rabbi, which told, and still tells, faithful Israel what God wants of humanity.

One thing, then, distinguishes the Bavli from the Yerushalmi: the Bavli's complete union of the Mishnah and Scripture, the two Torahs into one. In presenting a summa of Judaism, the Bavli joined the two streams, which until its time had flowed separate and distinct within the same banks. The one stream, coursing from the source of the Mishnah, and the other stream, emanating from the source of Scripture, mingled only in eddies, at the edges. But the banks of the mighty river had been set from Sinai, and (in the mythic dimension) the two streams had been meant to flow together as one mighty river.

In the Yerushalmi, Scripture found a place along the sides. In the collection of scriptural exegeses *(midrashim)*, Scripture had flowed all by itself, apart from the Mishnah. In the Bavli, for the first time, the waters not only flowed together but mingled in common and sustained discourse. So the Bavli for the first time from Sinai (to speak within the Torah-myth) joined together in a whole and complete way, in both literary form and doctrinal substance, the one whole Torah of Moses, our rabbi.

That is why the Bavli became the Torah *par excellence,* the Torah through which Israel would read both Scripture and Mishnah, the Torah all together, the Torah all at once, as God at Sinai had revealed it to Moses, our rabbi. It was because the Bavli's writers accomplished the nearly perfect union of Scripture and Mishnah in a single document that the Bavli became Israel's fullest Torah. That is why for the next fifteen hundred years, when the people of the Torah—Israel, the Jewish people—wished to approach the Mishnah, it was through the reading of the Bavli. It is why when that same people wished to address and interpret Scripture, it was through the reading of the Bavli. All the other authentic and authoritative component of the canon stood in line behind the primary reading of the Bavli. It is no accident that authentic avatars of the classical literature of Judaism even today learn Scripture through the Bavli's citations of verses of Scripture, just as much as, commonly, they learn the Mishnah and assuredly interpret it exactly as the Bavli presents it.

For many good reasons the Bavli has formed the definitive statement of Judaism from the time of its closure to the present day. The excellence of its composition, the mastery and authority of those who everywhere studied it and advocated its law, the sharpness of its exegesis and discussion, the harmonious and proportionate presentation of all details—virtues of taste and intellect, these may well have secured for the document a paramount position. Far larger in sheer volume than the first Talmud, the Babylonian Talmud moreover incorporated a far broader selection of antecedent mateials than any other document that reaches us out of Judaism in late antiquity—far more, for instance, than the Yerushalmi. This vast selection, in addition, was so organized and put together that systematic accounts of numerous important problems of biblical exegesis, law and theology, alike emerged in the

Bavli's pages. Consequently, the Bavli would readily have served from its closure as both an encyclopedia of knowledge and a summa of the theology and law of Judaism. But what to begin with gained for the Bavli the priority it would enjoy was not its intellectual elegance, but the comprehensive character of its statement, based as it was on both the Scripture's and the Mishnah's redactional framework. No one had done that before, no one had to do it again.

7. Our Sages of Blessed Memory: Torah in the Flesh

Both Talmuds contain stories and sayings of three types. The first sort takes up the exegesis and amplification of the Mishnah, the oral Torah. The second does the same for Scripture, the written Torah. The third type of sayings and stories, which concerns the sages, presents the Torah in the flesh. Incidents in sages' lives and teachings deemed characteristic of individuals comprise the contents of this third component of "the one whole Torah of Moses, our rabbi." The authorship of the Yerushalmi organized its materials around only the first of the three types. The redactors of the Bavli developed large-scale conglomerations of materials of both Mishnah- and Scripture-exegesis.

The compositors of the two Talmuds did not treat the third type of received materials in the same way. Stories about sages and collections of sayings of individuals in the Bavli seldom define the boundaries of systematic and protracted analysis, and, in the Yerushalmi, they do so still more rarely. Yet, at the same time, sizable composites of sayings and stories—if not sustained and extended—did take shape around names of sages, and the literature of the oral Torah preserved these composites.

Then what about the sizable compositions that are organized not around Scripture or the Mishnah, but around lives and teachings of individual sages? How do these fit in to the "one whole Torah of Moses, our rabbi?" We shall discover that the teachings and actions of sages came under sustained analysis in accord with exactly the same canons of inquiry as did the teachings and actions of biblical heroes and of masters represented in the Mishnah and the Tosefta. What sages said and did thus was treated as part of the Torah. That fact, once established, will present the basis for the claim that the oral Torah, as much as the written Torah, at the end emerged in three forms: (1) the written Torah and (2) the oral Torah, on the one side; and (3) the sage, Torah complete and incarnate, on the other. The Bavli in particular, as the synthesis of the two Torahs into the "one whole Torah of Moses, our rabbi," found its counterpart in the figure of the sage. He was represented as the Torah in the flesh, the Torah incarnate. So the Bavli in literary form and the sage in living form stood for exactly the same thing: the image, the likeness of what God had revealed. Each took a substantial position within the Torah. To put matters in more secular language, along with Scripture, each formed a component of the canon of Judaism.

Let me now respond to this paradox, the curious fact that sizable quantities of stories and sayings came into the hands of the compositors of the Talmuds and were preserved by them, yet were not utilized as principal modes of organization and redaction. Why not organize discourse around sages' lives and teachings, as much as around exposition of the Mishnah (Yerushalmi) or the Mishnah and Scripture (Bavli)?

In my view, it was because the sages' share of the Torah would always remain in its entirely oral form. The sages' part of the Torah would be something to be remembered, to be renewed in the lives of age succeeding age. Lives of saints would not be written. The sages' part of the canon would not enter the main frame of the written-down version of the oral Torah because it did not have to. The sages' version of the Torah, alongside both the written Torah and oral Torah, which had long been memorized and finally written down, represented in the person of living men (and finally, in our day, women too), the Torah in the flesh, the Torah incarnate, the image, the ageless likeness.

The proposition at hand represents the sage as a supernatural figure. But the sage carried out political and this-worldly tasks. That is why, we remember, the Mishnah mattered to begin with:

It consitituted a political document, not merely a philosophical system of a rather curious order. Let us consider how the Talmuds, through particularly the Yerushalmi, represent the sage in his role as both holy man and also this-worldly authority.

HOLY MAN AND TEMPORAL AUTHORITY

The sage stood on the intersecting borders of several domains: political and private, communal and individual. He served as both legal and moral authority, decisor and exemplar, judge and clerk, administrator and governor, but also holy man and supernatural figure. It is this last aspect of the sage as public authority that we take up when we turn to stories about how the sage as a public official was expected to, and did, perform certain supernatural or magical deeds. These stories place the rabbi at the border between heaven and earth, as much as he stood at the frontier between Israel and the nations: wholly liminal, entirely exemplary, at one and the same time. What is important here is the representation of the sage as *public* authority deemed to exercise *supernatural* power. These tales are separate from views of the sage as a supernatural figure in general, which we shall review below. In the present setting, the wonder-working sage as a civic figure, in particular, comes to the fore. His task was to use his supernatural power in pretty much the same context and for the same purpose as he used his political-judicial and legal power and learning, on the one side, and his local influence and moral authority on the other.

In the following stories, the responsibility of rabbis to stop fire is taken for granted. What is striking is that, in the tales, they exercise that responsibility equally through this-worldly and other-worldly means: in the first story, by getting gentiles to do the work; in the second, by using Heaven through calling down rain; in the third, by some sort of merit (not made specific); and in the fourth, by a rabbi's spreading out a cloak, which drove the flames away.

Y. Nedarim 4:9.I.

> C. In R. Ami's time there was a fire in town [on the Sabbath]. R. Ami sent out a proclamation in the marketplace of the Aramaeans, saying, "Whoever does the work will not lose out by it." [Ami could not ask the people to do the work, because of the restrictions of the Sabbath on the employees of Israelites. Accordingly, he solved the problem in the way proposed in the present context.] . . .
>
> G. There was a case in which a fire broke out in the courtyard of Yose b. Simai in Shihin, and the soldiers of the camp of Sepphoris came down to put it out. But he did not let them do so.
>
> H. He said to them, "Let the tax collector come and collect what is owing to him."
>
> I. Forthwith clouds gathered, and rain came and put the fire out. After the Sabbath he sent a *sela* to every soldier, and to their commander he sent fifty *denars*.
>
> J. Said R. Haninah, "It was not necessary to do so."
>
> K. There was a Samaritan who was R. Jonah's neighbor. A fire broke out in the neighborhood of R. Jonah. The Samaritan came and wanted to put it out, but R. Jonah did not let him do so.
>
> L. [The Samaritan] said to him, "Will it be on your responsibility if it burns up my property?"
>
> M. [Jonah] said to him, "Yes." And the whole area was saved.
>
> N. R. Jonah of Kefar Ammi spread out his cloak over the grain, and the flames fled from it.

These several stories show that the sage was seen as bearing responsibility to put out fires, and a mixture of legal subterfuge, supernatural intervention, and sagacity is conveyed in the set of tales. When we call the rabbi a supernatural authority, we indicate that he was a communal official who, on occasion, was believed to invoke more than this-worldly power to carry out his civil duties.

In the following story the sage as public official protects the town from a siege and violence.

Y. Taanit 3:8.II

> A. As to Levi ben Sisi: troops came to his town. He took a scroll of the Torah and went up to the roof and said, "Lord of the ages!

If a single word of this scroll of the Light has been nullified [in our town], let them come up against us, and if not, let them go their way."

B. Forthwith people went looking for the troops but did not find them [because they had gone their way].

C. A disciple of his did the same thing, and his hand withered, but the troops went their way.

D. A disciple of his disciple did the same thing. His hand did not wither, but they also did not go their way.

E. This illustrates the following apothegm: "You can't insult an idiot, and the dead skin doesn't feel the scalpel."

The story is told to make its point, but, once more, it serves to convey a glimpse into the imagination, not merely the morality, of the storyteller and the Yerushalmi's framers. The power of the sage to ward off the siege was based upon his saintliness, which consisted in his obedience to the Torah and the people's obedience to him. So whatever public authority the rabbi exercised is credited, in the end, to his accurate knowledge and sincerity in living up to his own teachings, on the one side, and the people's willingness to accept his instructions, on the other.

Sages made rules on public fasting. For their part, they possessed sufficient merit so that, if they personally fasted, they were supposed to be able to bring rain. Yet another area in which supernatural, as distinct from this-worldly, authority came to the fore was in preventing epidemics. The first story provides a routine instance of rainmaking; the second, of bringing rain and stopping a pestilence, by two themes being joined together.

Y. Taanit 3:4.V

A. R. Aha carried out thirteen fasts, and it did not rain. When he went out, a Samaritan met him. [The Samaritan] said to him [to make fun of him], "Rabbi, take off your cloak, because it is going to rain."

B. He said to him, "By the life of that man [you]! Heaven will do a miracle, and this year will prosper, but that man will not live to see it."

C. Heaven did a miracle, and the year prospered, and that Samaritan died.

D. And everybody said, "Come and see the fruit [the man's corpse] [lying in the] sun."

Y. Taanit 3:4.I

A. There was a pestilence in Sepphoris, but it did not come into the neighborhood in which R. Haninah was living. And the Sepphoreans said, "How is it possible that that elder lives among you, he and his entire neighborhood, in peace, while the town goes to ruin?"

B. [Haninah] went in and said before them, "There was only a single Zimri in his generation, but on his account, twenty-four thousand people died. And in our time, how many Zimris are there in our generation? And yet you are raising clamor!"

C. One time they had to call a fast, but it did not rain. R. Joshua carried out a fast in the South, and it rained. The Sepphoreans said, "R. Joshua b. Levi brings down rain for the people in the South, but R. Haninah holds back rain for us in Sepphoris."

D. They found it necessary to declare a second time of fasting, and sent and summoned R. Joshua b. Levi. [Haninah] said to him, "Let my lord go forth with us to fast." The two of them went out to fast, but it did not rain.

E. He went in and preached to them as follows: "It was not R. Joshua b. Levi who brought down rain for the people of the South, nor was it R. Haninah who held back rain from the people of Sepphoris. But as to the Southerners, their hearts are open, and when they listen to a teaching of Torah, they submit [to accept it], while as to the Sepphoreans, their hearts are hard, and when they hear a teaching of Torah, they do not submit [or accept it]."

F. When he went in, he looked up and saw that the [cloudless] air was pure. He said, "Is this how it still is? [Is there no change in the weather?]" Forthwith, it rained. He took a vow for himself that he would never do the same thing again. He said, "How shall I say to the creditor [God] not to collect what is owing to him."

The tale about Joshua and Haninah is most striking, because it presents a thoroughly rationalistic picture of the supernatural framework at hand. True, God could do miracles. But if the people caused their own disasters by not listening to sages' Torah teachings, they could hardly expect God always to forego imposing the sanction for disobedience, which was holding back rain. Accordingly, there were reliable laws by which one could deal with the supernatural world, which also kept those laws. The particular power of the rabbi was in knowing the law. The storyteller took for granted, to be sure, that in the end the clerk could bring rain.

Stories in both Talmuds expressly link salvation to keeping the law. This means that the issues of the law were drawn upward into higher realm of Israelite consciousness. Keeping the law in the right way is represented as not merely right or expedient. It is the way to bring the Messiah, the son of David. This is stated by Levi, as follows:

Y. Taanit 1:1.IX

X. Said R. Levi, "If Israel would keep a single Sabbath in the proper way, forthwith the son of David would come.

Y. "What is the Scriptural basis for the view? 'Moses said, Eat it today, for today is a sabbath to the Lord; today you will not find it in the field' (Ex. 16:25)."

Z. And it says, "For thus said the Lord God, the Holy One of Israel, 'In returning and rest you shall be saved; in quietness and in trust shall be your strength. And you would not' (Is. 30:15)."

This story explicitly links the coming of the Messiah to the proper observance of the law as sages propound it.

Clearly, the framers of the Talmud regarded the Torah as the source and guarantor of salvation. But what they understood by the word "Torah" took on meanings particular to rabbis. They took to heart as salvific acts what others, standing outside of sages' social and mythic framework, will have regarded as merely routine or hocus-pocus. For to the rabbis the principal salvific deed was to "study Torah," by which they meant memorizing Torah sayings by constant repetition, and, as the Talmud itself amply testifies (for some sages), profound analytic inquiry into the meaning of those sayings. This act of "study of Torah" imparted supernatural power. For example, by repeating words of Torah, the sage could ward off the angel of death and accomplish other kinds of miracles as well. So Torah-formulas served as incantations. Mastery of Torah transformed the man who engaged in Torah learning into a supernatural figure, able to do things ordinary folk could not do.

In the nature of things, the category of "Torah" was vastly expanded so that the symbol of Torah, a Torah scroll, could be compared to a man of Torah, namely, a rabbi. Once it was established that salvation would come from keeping God's will in general, as Israelite holy men had insisted for so many years, it was a small step for rabbis to identify their particular corpus of learning, namely, the Mishnah and associated sayings, with God's will expressed in Scripture, the universally acknowledged revelation. In consequence "Torah" would include pretty much whatever rabbis knew (inclusive of Scripture) and did. It follows that the sage held in his hand the power to bring salvation to Israel. Torah as he taught it was the source of Israel's salvation. The supernatural power imputed to him even now was a foretaste of what would come when all Israel conformed to the Torah as the sage taught it. So tales of the supernatural or magical power of the rabbi have to be read in the larger setting of the salvific process posited by the Talmud's framers.

What was the theory behind the identification of rabbinical supernatural power or magical power with Israel's ultimate, historical redemption and not merely with immediate and personal salvation? It was an axiom of all forms of Judaism that, because Israel had sinned, it was punished by being given over into the hands of earthly empires; when it atoned, it was, and again would be, removed from their power. The means of atonement, reconciliation with God, were specified elsewhere as study of Torah, practice of commandments, and doing good deeds. Why so? The answer is distinctive to the matrix of the Talmuds: When Jews in general had mastered Torah, they would become rabbis, just as some now had become rabbis, saints, or holy men. When all Jews had become rabbis, they would no longer lie within the power of the nations, that is, of history. Then the Messiah would come. Redemption therefore depended upon all Israel's accepting the yoke of the Torah. Why so? Because at that point all Israel would attain a full and complete embodiment of Torah, revelation. Thus conforming to God's will and replicating Heaven, Israel on earth, as a righteous, holy community, would exercise the supernatural power of Torah. They would be able as a whole to do what some few saintly rabbis now could do. With access to supernatural power, redemption would naturally follow.

The theory of salvation focused upon Torah addressed the circumstance of the individual as much as of the nation. This was possible because the same factor had caused the condition of both, namely, sin. Not doing the will of God led to the fall of Israel, the destruction of the Temple. Disobedience to the will of God—sin— is what causes people to suffer and die. The angel of death has power, specifically, over those not engaged in the study of Torah and performing of commandments.

That view is expressed in stories such as the following, which express the belief that while a sage is repeating Torah sayings, the angel of death cannot approach him.

Y. Moed Qatan 3:5.XXI

F. [Proving that while one is studying Torah, the angel of death cannot touch a person, the following is told:] A disciple of R. Hisda fell sick. He called two disciples with him, so that they would repeat Mishnah-traditions with him. [The angel of death] turned himself before them into a figure of a snake, and they stopped repeating traditions, and [the sick man] died.

G. A disciple of Bar Pedaiah fell ill. He sent to him two disciples to repeat Mishnah-traditions with him. [The angel of death] turned himself before him into a kind of star, and they stopped repeating Mishnah-traditions, and he died.

Repeating Mishnah-traditions thus warded off death. It is hardly surprising that stories were told about wonders associated with the deaths of various rabbis. These validated the claim of supernatural power imputed to the rabbis. A repertoire of such stories includes two sorts. First, there is a list of supernatural occurrences accompanying sages' deaths, as in the following.

Y. Abodah Zarah 3:1.II

A. When R. Aha died, a star appeared at noon.

B. When R. Hanah died, the statues bowed down.

C. When R. Yohanan died, the icons bowed down.

D. They said that [this was to indicate] there were no icons like him [so beautiful as Yohanan himself].

E. When R. Haninah of Bet Hauran died, the Sea of Tiberias split open.

F. They said that [this was to commemorate the miracle that took place] when he went up to intercalate the year, and the sea split open before him.

G. When R. Hoshaiah died, the palm of Tiberias fell down.

H. When R. Isaac b. Elisheb died, seventy [infirm] thresholds of houses in Galilee were shaken down.

I. They said that [this was to commemorate the fact that] they [were shaky and] had depended on his merit [for the miracle that permitted them to continue to stand].

J. When R. Samuel bar R. Isaac died, cedars of the land of Israel were uprooted.

K. They said that [this was to take note of the fact that] he would take branch [of a cedar] and [dance, so] praising a bride [at her wedding, and thereby giving her happiness].

L. The rabbis would ridicule him [for lowering himself by doing so]. Said to them R. Zeira, "Leave him be. Does the old man not know what he is doing?"

M. When he died, a flame came forth from heaven and intervened between his bier and the congregation. For three hours there were voices and thunderings in the world: "Come and see what a sprig of cedar has done for this old man!"

N. [Further] an echo came forth and said, "Woe that Samuel b. R. Isaac has died, the doer of merciful deeds."

O. When R. Yosa bar Halputa died, the gutters ran with blood in Laodicea.

P. They said [that the reason was] that he had given his life for the rite of circumcision.

Q. When R. Abbahu died, the pillars of Caesarea wept.

R. The [gentiles] said [that the reason was] that [the pillars] were celebrating. The Israelites said to them, "And do those who are distant [such as yourselves] know why those who are near [we ourselves] are raising a cry?"

What is important in the foregoing anthology is the linkage between the holy deeds of the sage and the miracles done at their demise. The sages' merit, attained through study of Torah or through acts of saintliness and humility and mastery of Torah, was demonstrated for all to see. So the sage was not merely a master of Torah. But his mastery of Torah laid the foundations for all the other things he was.

It is not only in the context of death scenes that miracles were imputed to rabbis. Their power was compared to that of other wonder-workers. Sages were shown to be more effective than other magicians—specifically in those very same settings in which, all parties conceded, other wonder-workers, as much as rabbis, were able to perform magical deeds. What is important in the following is the fact that in a direct contest between a rabbi and another sort of magician, an Israelite heretic, the sages were shown to enjoy superior magical power.

Y. Sanhedrin 7:12.III

A. When R. Eleazar, R. Joshua, and R. Aqiba went in to bathe in the baths of Tiberias, a *min* saw them. He said what he said, and the arched chamber in the bath [where idolatrous statues were put up] held them fast, [so that they could not move].

B. Said R. Eleazar to R. Joshua, "Now Joshua b. Haninah, see what you can do."

C. When that *min* tried to leave, R. Joshua said what he said, and the doorway of the bath seized and held the *min* firm, so that whoever went in had to give him a knock [to push by], and whoever went out had to give him a knock [to push by].

D. He said to them, "Undo whatever you have done [to let me go]."

E. They said to him, "Release us, and we shall release you."

F. They released one another.

G. Once they got outside, said R. Joshua to that *min*, "Lo, you have learned [from us whatever you are going to learn]."

H. He said, "Let's go down to the sea."

I. When they got down to the sea, that *min* said whatever it was that he said, and the sea split open.

J. He said to them, "Now is this not what Moses, your rabbi, did at the sea?"

K. They said to him, "Do you not concede to us that Moses, our rabbi, walked through it?"

L. He said to them, "Yes."

M. They said to him, "Then walk through it."

N. He walked through it.

O. Joshua instructed the ruler of the sea, who swallowed him up.

IV. A. When R. Eliezer, R. Joshua, and Rabban Gamaliel went up to Rome, they came to a certain place and found children making little piles [of dirt]. They said, "Children of the Land of Israel make this sort of thing, and they say, 'This is heave offering,' and 'That is tithe.' It's likely that there are Jews here."

B. They came into one place and were received there.

C. When they sat down to eat, [they noticed] that each dish which they brought into them would first be brought into a small room, and then would be brought to them, and they wondered whether they might be eating sacrifices offered to the dead. [That is, before the food was brought to them, it was brought into a small chamber, in which they suspected, sacrifices were taken from each dish and offered to an idol.]

D. They said to [the host], "What is your purpose, in the fact that, as to every dish which you bring before us, if you do not bring it first into a small room, you do not bring it to us?"

E. He said to them, "I have a very old father, and he has made a decree for himself that he will never go out of that small room until he will see the sages of Israel."

F. They said to him, "Go and tell him, 'Come out here to them, for they are here.' "

G. He came out to them.

H. They said to him, "Why do you do this?"

I. He said to them, "Pray for my son, for he has not produced a child."

J. Said R. Eliezer to R. Joshua, "Now, Joshua b. Hananiah, let us see what you will do."

K. He said to them, "Bring me flax seeds," and they brought him flax seeds.

L. He appeared to sow the seed on the table; he appeared to scatter the seed; he appeared to bring the seed up; he appeared to take hold of it, until he drew up a woman, holding on to her tresses.

M. He said to her, "Release whatever [magic] you have done [to this man]."

N. She said to him, "I am not going to release [my spell]."

O. He said to her, "If you don't do it, I shall publicize your [magical secrets]."

P. She said to him, "I cannot do it, for [the magical materials] have been cast into the sea."

Q. R. Joshua made a decree that the sea release [the magical materials] and they came up.

R. They prayed for [the host], and he had the merit of begetting a son, R. Judah b. Bathera.

S. They said, "If we came up her only for the purpose of begetting that righteous man, it would have been enough for us."

T. Said R. Joshua b. Hananiah, "I can take cucumbers and pumpkins and turn them into rams and hosts of rams, and they will produce still more."

These long extracts leave no doubt that the authors of the Yerushalmi imputed to Israel's sages precisely the powers generally assigned to magicians. There was no important distinction between the one and the other. We see no claim that the superior merit of the rabbi, based on his knowledge of Torah, accounted for his remarkable magical power. On the contrary, the sage did precisely what the magician did, only he did it better. When the magician then pretended to do what Moses had done, it was his end. The story about Joshua's magic in Rome is similar, in its explicit reference to sympathetic magic, K–L. The result was the discovery that the childless man had been subject to a spell. There can be no doubt that distinctions between magic and supernatural power meant nothing to the Talmud's storytellers. The clerks were not merely holy men; they were a particular kind of holy men.

THE SAGE AS THE MODEL OF THE LAW

Thus far we have seen that the Yerushalmi's authors held that the sage exercised magical-supernatural powers and could reward his friends and punish his enemies. We have now to show that the supernatural status accorded to the person of the sage endowed his deeds with normative, therefore revelatory power. What is the main point? It is that what the sage did had the status of law. That is why I claim that the sage was the model of the law, thus the human embodiment of the Torah: Torah incarnate. That mundane view has to be joined to the otherworldly notion, just now illustrated, that the sage was a holy man. For what made the sage distinctive was his combination of this-worldly authority and power and other-worldly influence. The clerk in the court and the holy man on the rooftop in the Talmuds' view were one and the same. Given the fundamental point of insistence of the Yerushalmi's and Bavli's writers, that the salvation of Israel will derive from keeping the law, there was no choice but to preserve the tight union between salvation and law, the supernatural power of the sage and his lawgiving authority. We turn now to spell out this definitive trait of the system as a whole, again as it is exemplified in the Yerushalmi. To state matters simply: If the sage exercised supernatural power as a kind of living Torah, his very deeds served to reveal law, as much as his word expressed revelation.

The capacity of the sage himself to participate in the process of revelation is illustrated in two types of materials. First of all, tales told about rabbis' behavior on specific occasions immediately are translated into rules for the entire community to keep. Accordingly, he was a source not merely of good example but of prescriptive law.

Y. Abodah Zarah 5:4:III

X. R. Aha went to Emmaus, and he ate dumpling [prepared by Samaritans].

Y. R. Jeremiah ate leavened bread prepared by them.

Z. R. Hezekiah ate their locusts prepared by them.

AA. R. Abbahu prohibited Israelite use of wine prepared by them.

These reports of what rabbis had done enjoyed the same authority, as statements of the law on eating what Samaritans cooked and as did citations of traditions in the names of the great authorities of old or of the day. What someone did served as a norm, if the person was a sage of sufficient standing.

Far more common in the literature of the oral Torah from the Mishnah through the Bavli are instances in which the deed of a rabbi is adduced as an authoritative precedent for the law under discussion. It was everywhere taken for granted that what a rabbi did, he did because of his mastery of the law. Even though a formulation of the law was not in hand, a tale about what a rabbi actually did constituted adequate evidence on how to formulate the law itself. So from the deed or concrete practice of an authority, a law might be framed quite independent of the person of the sage. The sage then functioned as a model and lawgiver, like Moses. Among many instances of that mode of generating law are the following.

Y. Abodah Zarah 3:11.II

A. Gamaliel Zuga was walking along, leaning on the shoulder of R. Simeon b. Laqish. They came across an image.

B. He said to him, "What is the law as to passing before it?"

C. He said to him, "Pass before it, but close [your] eyes."

D. R. Isaac was walking along, leaning on the shoulder of R. Yohanan. They came across an idol before the council building.

E. He said to him, "What is the law as to passing before it?"

F. He said to him, "Pass before it, but close [your] eyes."

G. R. Jacob bar Idi was walking along, leaning upon R. Joshua b. Levi. They came across a procession in which an idol was carried. He said to him, "Nahum, the most holy man, passed before this idol, and you will not pass by it? Pass before it but close your eyes."

Y. Abodah Zarah 2:2.III

FF. R. Aha had chills and fever. [They brought him] a medicinal drink prepared from the phalluses of Dionysian revelers. But he would not drink it. They brought it to R. Jonah, and he did drink it. Said R. Mana, "Now if R. Jonah, the patriarch, had known what it was, he would never have drunk it."

GG. Said R. Huna, "That is to say, 'They do not accept healing from something that derives from an act of fornication.' "

What is important is GG, the restatement of the story now as fixed and formalized verbal version of the law. The example of a rabbi served to teach how one should live a truly holy life. The requirements went far beyond the measure of the law, extending to refraining from deeds of a most commonplace sort.

Once we see that rabbis' deeds serve to define the law of Torah, we have to ask whether rabbis' statements enjoy exactly the same status accorded to the Torah in its written and oral forms. For it is one thing to supply precedents merely to illustrate the meaning of the written and oral Torahs. It is quite another to add through what one does to the teachings of the Torah. So we wish to see just how sages treated deeds and opinions of their predecessors and colleagues when they analyzed the law. Specifically, were these dealt with as equivalent to sayings of the written and oral Torah, or in some other way? What we shall now discover, through a few concrete and representative examples, is this: Precisely the modes of inquiry applicable to the analysis of teachings of the written Torah and of the oral Torah as written down in the Mishnah and the Tosefta came to bear upon statements and deeds of sages themselves.

I can think of no more probative evidence that the sage himself took his place within "the one whole Torah of Moses, our rabbi." He formed the third component of the tripartite canon of Judaism, along with the written Torah and the oral Torah. Why do I say so? Because what he did was not merely exemplary, but revelatory. How? Because what he did was analyzed in precisely the same way that revelation coming through other media—writing, memorization—was treated. Since revelation in those other two media, besides the medium of the living authority, constituted parts of the Torah and fell into the classification of the Torah, what the sage said and did as a living person also found a way into that same classification, defined by the same criteria of authority.

What is probative is that sages' statements in the Talmuds about the Mishnah are treated precisely as are statements found both *in* the Mishnah and *in* Scripture itself. Thus talmudic statements either form part of the *Torah,* or are wholly derivative from the Torah and hence of the same status and standing as the Torah. Let me unpack this argument.

We began our inquiry by pointing out that the Talmuds' principal mode of the exegesis of the Mishnah was to supply proof-texts for the Mishnah's various statements. This served to link what the Mishnah said to principles and rules of Scripture. We shall now again observe, through a single interesting instance, that exactly the same inquiry pertaining to the Mishnah applies without variation to statements made by sages of the contemporary period themselves. Indeed, precisely the same theological and exegetical considerations came to bear upon both the Mishnah's statements and opinions expressed by talmudic rabbis. Since these were not to be distinguished from one another in the requirement that opinion be suitably grounded in Scripture, they also should be understood to have formed part of precisely the same corpus of (scriptural) truths. What the Mishnah and the later sages said further expressed precisely the same kind of truth: revelation, through the medium of Scripture, whether contained in the Mishnah or in the opinion of the sage himself. While this matter is familiar from our interest in the role of Scripture in the exegesis of the Mishnah, we review it to establish the main point of the present chapter.

The way in which this search for proof-texts applies equally to the Mishnah, the Tosefta, and to the rabbi's opinion is illustrated in the following passage:

Y. Sanhedrin 10:4

    A. *The party of Korah has no portion in the world to come, and will not live in the world to come [M. Sanhedrin 10:4].*

    B. What is the Scriptural basis for this view?

    C. "So they and all that belonged to them went down alive into Sheol; and the earth closed over them, and they perished from the midst of the assembly" (Num. 16:33).

D. *"The earth closed over them"—in this world.*

E. *"And they perished from the midst of the assembly"—in the world to come [M. Sanhedrin 10:4D–F].*

F. It was taught: *R. Judah b. Batera says, "The contrary view is to be derived from the implication of the following verse:*

G. *" 'I have gone astray like a lost sheep; seek thy servant and do not forget thy commandments' (Ps. 119:176).*

H. *"Just as the lost object which is mentioned later on in the end is going to be searched for, so the lost object which is stated herein is destined to be searched for" [Tosefta Sanhedrin 13:9].*

I. Who will pray for them?

J. R. Samuel bar Nahman said, "Moses will pray for them.

K. [This is proved from the following verse:] " 'Let Reuben live, and not die, [nor lest his men be few]' (Deut. 33:6)."

L. R. Joshua b. Levi said, "Hannah will pray for them."

M. This is the view of R. Joshua b. Levi, for R. Joshua b. Levi said, "Thus did the party of Korah sink ever downward, until Hannah went and prayed for them and said, "The Lord kills and brings to life; he brings down to Sheol and raises up' (1 Sam. 2:6)."

We have a striking sequence of proof-texts, serving (1) the cited statement of the Mishnah, A–C, then (2) an opinion of a rabbi in the Tosefta, F–H, then (3) the position of a rabbi, J–K, L–M. The process of providing proof-texts therefore is central, the nature of the passages requiring the proof-texts a matter of indifference. The upshot is simple. We see that the search for appropriate verses of Scripture vastly transcends the purpose of study of the Mishnah and Scripture, exegesis of their rules, or provision of adequate authority for the Mishnah and its laws. In fact, any proposition that is to be taken seriously, whether in the Mishnah, in the Tosefta, or in the mouth of a Talmudic sage himself, will elicit interest in scriptural support.

This quest in Scripture thus extended beyond the interest in supplying the Mishnah's rules with proof-texts. On the contrary, the real issue turns out to have been not the Mishnah at all, nor even the vindication of its diverse sayings, one by one. Once the words of a *sage*—not merely a rule of the Mishnah—are made to refer to

Scripture for proof, it must follow that, in the natural course of things, a rule of the Mishnah or of the Tosefta will likewise be asked to refer to Scripture. The fact that the living sage validated his *own* words through Scripture explains why the sage in the fourth century validated also the words of the then-ancient sages of the Mishnah and Tosefta through verses of Scripture. It is one, undivided phenomenon. Distinctions are not made among media —oral, written, living—of the Torah.

We turn to the way in which the rabbis of the Talmud proposed to resolve differences of opinion. This is important, because the Mishnah presents a mass of disputes. Turning speculation about principles into practical law required resolving them. They handled disputes among themselves in precisely the same way in which talmudic rabbis settled disputes in the Mishnah and so attained a consensus about the law of the Mishnah. The importance of that fact for the present argument is simple. Once more we see that the rabbis of the third and fourth centuries, represented in the Talmuds, treated their own contemporaries exactly as they treated the then-ancient authorities of the Mishnah. In their minds the status accorded to the Mishnah, as a derivative of the Torah, applies equally to the Talmudic sages' teachings. In the following instance we see how the same discourse attached to (1) a Mishnah rule is assigned as well to one in (2) the Tosefta, and, at the end, to differences among (3) the talmudic authorities.

Y. Ketubot 5:1

VI.   A. R. Jacob bar Aha, R. Alexa in the name of Hezekiah: "The law accords with the view of R. Eleazar b. Azariah, who stated, *If she was widowed or divorced at the stage of betrothal, the virgin collects only two hundred zuz and the widow, a maneh. If she was widowed or divorced at the stage of a consummated marriage, she collects the full amount* [M. Ket. 5:1E, D]."

      B. R. Hananiah said, "The law accords with the view of R. Eleazar b. Azariah."

      C. Said Abayye, "They said to R. Hananiah, 'Go and shout [outside whatever opinion you like.' But] R. Jonah, R. Zeira in the name of R. Jonathan said, 'The law accords with the view of R. Eleazar b. Azariah.' [Yet] R. Yosa bar Zeira in the name of R. Jonathan said, 'The law does not accord with the view of R. Eleazar b. Azariah.' [So we do not in fact know the decision.]"

D. Said R. Yose, "We had a mnemonic. Hezekiah and R. Jonathan both say one thing."

E. For it has been taught:

F. *He whose son went abroad, and whom they told, "Your son has died."*

G. *and who went and wrote over all his property to someone else as a gift,*

H. *and whom they afterward informed that his son was yet alive—*

I. *his deed of gift remains valid.*

J. *R. Simeon b. Menassia says, "His deed of gift is not valid, for if he had known that his son was alive, he would never have made such a gift"* [T. Ket. 4:14E–H].

What is important here is that the Talmud makes no distinction whatever when deciding the law of disputes (1) in the Mishnah, (2) in the Tosefta, and (3) among talmudic rabbis. The same already-formed colloquy that is applied at the outset to the Mishnah's dispute is then held equally applicable to the Tosefta's and the sages'. The process of thought is the main thing, without regard to the document to which the process applies.

The sages of the Talmuds in this context recognized no distinction in authority or standing—hence, in status as revelation—between what the Mishnah said and what the written Torah said. And they also used the same processes of validation to demonstrate that what they themselves declared enjoyed the same standing and authority as what they found in the written Torah. So their intent always was to show that in fact there were no gradations in revelation. God spoke in various ways and through diverse media: to prophets and to sages, in writing and in memorizing sayings, to olden times and to the present day. We can discern no systematic effort to distinguish one kind of revelation from another: revelation transmitted in writing, that transmitted orally, revelation to an ancient prophet, an exegesis or a Torah-teaching of contemporary masters. To state matters simply: Either a teaching was true and authoritative, wherever it was found and however it had reached the living age, or a teaching was untrue and not authoritative. Scripture, the Mishnah, the sage—all three spoke with supernatural authority.

Scripture and the Mishnah govern what the sage knows. But it is *the sage* who authoritatively speaks about them. The simple fact is that what sages were willing to do to the Mishnah is precisely what they were prepared to do to Scripture, to impose upon it their own judgment of its meaning. The rabbi speaks with authority about the Mishnah and the Scripture. He therefore has authority deriving from revelation. He himself may participate in the processes of revelation; there is no material difference. The reason, then, is that the rabbi is like Moses, "our rabbi," who received *torah* and wrote the Torah.

To conclude: Since rabbinical documents repeatedly claim that if you want to know the law, you should not only listen to what the rabbi says but also copy what he does, it follows that, in his person, the rabbi represents and embodies the Torah. God in the Torah revealed God's will and purpose for the world. So God had said what the human being should be. The rabbi was the human being in God's image, as revealed in the one whole Torah of Moses, our rabbi. So in the rabbi, the Torah–the word of God– took carnate form and was made flesh. And out of the union of man and Torah, producing the rabbi as Torah incarnate, was born Judaism, the faith of the Torah: the ever-present revelation. For fifteen hundred years, from the time of the writing down of the oral Torah to our own day, the enduring context for the Torah remained the same: encounter with the living God.

8. The Torah, the Dual Torah, and the Oral Torah

After the Mishnah, each of the documents of the oral Torah we have read thus far takes up a position on the definition and meaning of God's revelation to Moses at Mount Sinai. To begin with, the character of the Mishnah, with its general indifference to proof-texts of Scripture, provoked the problem of defining the Mishnah's relationship to Scripture. But in taking up the issue, the successor-writings for the next four centuries broadened and deepened the question. It is important not to miss the heart of matter, to form the erroneous impression that the issue of the oral Torah essentially takes the form of questions about the character of certain books, important then only to intellectuals and now mainly to scholars or pietists.

Nothing could be further from the truth. At issue is the center and heart of the religious life of Judaism: How does God speak here and now? And how shall we learn to listen to God? Why this definitive and fundamental religious reality is at issue here begins with a simple fact. *Torah* means revelation. So when people say that a book falls into the classification of *torah*, or that the Torah encompasses a given piece of writing (or "tradition"), they claim that God speaks through that book or writing. That claim is hardly surprising when we consider the place and authority of Scripture in all forms of Judaism, from the beginning to the present. But the allegation that the Mishnah, or the Sifra, or the Talmud of the Land of Israel, or the sage, all equally carried God's word to Israel bore profound implications.

When the ancient sages, for example, maintained that the Mishnah was part of the Torah, they expressed one of two contradictory positions but agreed on one. One set of sages regarded the Mishnah as a work of tradition, of handing on in memory and orally, autonomous of the written Torah. The other set of sages argued that the Mishnah took up a secondary and derivative position *vis à vis* the written Torah. How so? Statements of the Mishnah required the support of verses of Scripture, so the Mishnah's rules, by themselves, did not stand on their own. Both groups concurred, however, that, alongside Scripture, the Mishnah presented to Israel the laws of life, those rules of reality that God had revealed to Moses at Sinai. So the Mishnah, whether directly or by derivation, stood in line alongside or after Scripture. But the writers of the Mishnah, people whose disciples actually composed the document, were sages remembered as ordinary men. Not prophets, not holy men or wonder-workers (those stories about sages' powers came later); the masters of the Mishnah nonetheless spoke God's message.

That simple claim in behalf of the Mishnah and its authorities meant one thing. God not only spoke to prophets long ago, but continued now through sages to speak to Israel even in the time of the Mishnah. God's message reached Israel even then, long after the age of Moses and the prophets. So the list of authoritative books—the canon of Israel's holy writings—assuredly contained space for new titles. The word "canon," which means authoritative or holy book, comes from the Greek word for "basket." So we may say that the basket of scrolls, the canon of the Torah, remained open. That basket had not been filled to capacity by the written record of God's revelation at Sinai. So what? It followed that, once the Mishnah found its place in the canon, other writings by authorities of the same standing, holy sages, would find room as well. To state matters simply, *the revelation at Sinai had not ceased.* God continued to speak to Israel now, through sages, as before God had spoken through Moses and the prophets. Israel remained God's people not only by reason of the records of the past, but also, and especially, because of the revelation of the present day.

God then speaks here and how. We listen to God when we obey the Torah as the Torah is taught by the sages. That is what is at stake in the oral Torah. When the sages told stories about the wonders some of them did, they stated in that way the deep conviction that God still lived in Israel. So if Israel wishes to know what it means to be "in God's image and after God's likeness," through the Torah and its sages, Israel will find out. And the Torah comes in three media: in writing, in memory and in the incarnate form of the sage.

When, therefore, we follow the unfolding of principal parts of the oral, or memorized, Torah, we pursue the critical issue of Israel's sanctification in the world and salvation at the end of time. How the Mishnah relates to Scripture, a literary problem of no broad concern, turns out to tell us how, in the mind of Judaism, God speaks to Israel. The way in which the Mishnah so troubled the wit and imagination of successor-generations as to frame the program of thought and inquiry for four centuries to come tells us, in a small setting, what was happening on the great stage of Israel's public life. Provoked by the theological problem of scriptural authority (to phrase matters in our own terms), the sages who received the Mishnah generated a conception and a system of the religious life so broad and encompassing as to comprehend the life of Israel, the Jewish people, from that time to this. Through the Torah Israel learns God's will and word every day. So the Torah in two parts, written and oral, embodied in three media—books, memories, men (and today, women as well)—remained ever present. Why? Because God spoke, and continued to speak, and speaks today, to Israel; the Torah conveys God's word and will. So the issues take the form of the study of literature and its history, but at stake is the enduring life of Israel in the image and likeness of God.

Let me then summarize our findings, as we proceed to the final question of this book, which is this: Exactly where and how do the writings at hand make explicit the claim that at Sinai God revealed the Torah through two media? Since, we know, that claim does not come to expression in the Mishnah or in tractate Avot, we wonder when it surfaced and how it found full and clear realization.

The oral Torah—the books written by the sages of late antiquity in the Land of Israel and in Babylonia from ca. 200 to ca. 600 C.E.—lays down three claims. First, the books at hand fall into the classification of *torah,* God's revelation, and are part of the Torah. Second, in addition to Scripture, these books, by their nature, indicate that there *is* another form of the Torah. Hence the Torah is in two media, Scripture and some other. Third, that other medium for the Torah is oral, meaning transmission not in writing but in the form of oral communication of memorized sayings. So we take up these three matters. What is the Torah? How do the sages represent their views of the dual media for the Torah—hence dual Torah? And what, in particular, do they mean when they speak of the oral Torah, that part of the Torah that reaches the people through the memory of sages?

THE TORAH

What conception of the Torah had long been established, and what did the sages from the Mishnah through the Bavli contribute? The Torah of Moses clearly occupied a critical place in all systems of Judaism from the closure of the Torah-book, the Pentateuch, in the time of Ezra, ca. 450 B.C.E., onward. But in late antiquity, the first seven centuries of the Common Era, for one group alone the book developed into an abstract and encompassing symbol. In the Judaism that took shape in that formative age everything was contained in that one thing, that Torah. How so? When the word *torah* is used in rabbinical liberature of late antiquity, it no longer means particular book (e.g., a scroll, on the one side, or the contents of such a book, such as the Mosaic law, on the other). Instead, the word connotes a broad range of clearly distinct categories of both nouns and verbs, concrete facts and abstract relationships alike.

In the writings of the ancient rabbis, "Torah" stands first, for a kind of human being. It connotes, second, a social status and a sort of social group. It refers, third, to a type of social relationship. It further denotes a legal status and differentiates among legal norms signifying the more important from the less important. As symbolic abstraction, fifth, the word encompasses things and persons, actions and status, points of social differentiation and legal and normative standing, as well as "revealed truth."

In all, the main points of insistence of the whole of Israel's life and history in sages' writings come to full symbolic expression in that single word. If people wanted to explain how they would be saved, they used the word Torah. If they wished to sort out their parlous relationships with gentiles, they referred to the word Torah. Torah stood for salvation and accounted for Israel's this-worldly condition and the hope, for both individual and nation alike, of life in the world to come. For the kind of Judaism under discussion, therefore, the word Torah stood for everything; and so it does today. The Torah symbolizes the whole, at once and entire.

Accordingly, the way of life and worldview propagated by the Judaism represented by the principal documents of the formative age, which were closed from early third century through the seventh, stand alone in their focus upon the Torah. Other Judaisms—Judaic ways of life and worldviews—built as their principal construction synagogues in which the Torah had its place as an element of divine service. But not the sages. The framers of the sort of Judaism at hand, called "rabbinic," from the honorific accorded its principal heroes, or "talmudic," from the title of its main literary record, or "classical" and "normative," by reference to the theological evaluation later accorded to it, built master-disciple Torah-study circles. They went to synagogues, yes. But they built Torah-relationships and lived life as the Torah taught. Others merely revered the Torah.

The religious movement at hand took over the Torah and rewrote it in far broader terms than anyone else had ever imagined. Many kinds of Judaism believed in life after death and a world to come. But this distinctive sort of Judaism taught that, after death and in heaven, the Jews will study Torah under the direction of

Moses and of God. For ordinary Israelites, the biological father was the natural father and God in heaven the supernatural one. For this special sector of Israel, the master—the teacher, the rabbi—served as a supernatural father, taking priority over the this-worldy, natural one.

So, as is clear, every detail of the religious system at hand exhibits essentially the same point of insistence, captured in the simple notion of the Torah as the generative symbol, the total, exhaustive expression of the system as a whole. That is why the definitive ritual consisted in studying the Torah through the rites of discipleship. The definitive myth explained that one who studied Torah would become holy, like Moses "our rabbi," and like God, in whose image humanity was made, and whose Torah provided the plan and the model for what God wanted of a humanity created in his image. As Christians saw in Christ God made flesh, so the framers of the system of Judaism at hand found in the Torah that image of God to which Israel should aspire, and to which the sage in fact conformed, a point central to Chapter 7 of this book.

Accordingly, Judaism as we know it at the end of late antiquity reached its now-familiar definition when "the Torah" lost its capital letter and definite article and ultimately became "torah," an abstract classification serving many concrete things. What for nearly a millennium had been a particular scroll of book came to serve as a symbol of an entire system. When a rabbi spoke of torah, he no longer meant only a particular object, a scroll and its contents. Now he used the word to encompass a distinctive and well-defined worldview and way of life. Torah stood for something one does, and knowledge of the Torah promised not merely information about what people were supposed to do, but ultimate redemption or salvation. The shift in the use of the word, accomplished in a particular set of writings out of Judaism in late antiquity, appears dramatically in the following tale:

R. Kahana [a disciple] went and hid under Rab's [his master's] bed. Hearing Rab "discoursing" and joking with his wife. . . . , [Kahana] said to [Rab], "You would think that Abba's [Rab's] mouth had never before tasted the dish." [Rab] said to [Kahana], "Kahana, are you here? Get out! This is disgraceful!" [Kahana] replied, "My lord, it is a matter of *torah*, and I have the need to learn" (B. Ber. 62B).

As soon as we ask ourselves what the word *torah* means in such a context, we recognize the shift captured by the story. For—to state the obvious—to study "the Torah," meaning the Scriptures, one need not practice cultic voyeurism.

Torah thus constitutes the symbol that stands for the kind of Judaism presented by the Talmuds and related literature, defined by the authority of the rabbis who stand behind those documents, and best described as "the way of Torah." So far as outsiders supply the name of a religion, the one at hand may be called "rabbinic Judaism" or "talmudic Judaism," for its principal authority figure or authoritative document; or "normative Judaism," for the definitive theological status of the formulation at hand in the life of the Jewish people. But so far as insiders find language to capture and encompass the whole of what they do and believe, it is, as Kahana's statement tells us, *"torah"*—"and I need to learn . . ."

THE DUAL TORAH

The novelty of the symbolic system of a Judaism expressed through new uses of the word Torah, the cultic activity of Torah-study, and the supernatural relationship of disciple to master of the Torah, attracts our attention. Judaism as sages framed it while absorbing much from its predecessors, was hardly congruent to anything that had gone before. Like earlier systems in some ways, unlike them in others, the talmudic-rabbinic-classical Judaism used the old in new ways and presented the whole fresh, an unprecedented system and structure.

Clearly, the conception of "torah" in Judaism, the religion of the Torah, bears several equally valid meanings, each in context, all homogeneous. What makes Judaism different from Christianity and Islam, the two other religious traditions that refer to the Hebrew Scriptures, is this set of coherent meanings. The other Torah is the one that only Israel, the Jewish people, possesses. The dual Torah of Sinai marks Judaism as unique.

Quite obviously, therefore, just as Christians read the Old Testament through the completion and climax of the New Testament, unique to Christianity, so Judaists read the written Torah through the complement and conclusion of the oral Torah. Just as, for all forms of Christianity, the religious meaning of the Old Testament derives from the life and teachings of Christ, so for all forms of the Judaism of the Torah, classical and contemporary alike, Judaists refer to the documents of the oral Torah when they are in quest of the meaning of the written Torah.

Self-evidently, Judaists and Christians commonly recognize in addition to the religious and theological aspect yet other dimensions of meaning, aspects of facticity, in the Hebrew Scriptures. After all, the entire critical study of the history of ancient Israel derives from Judaists and Christians engaged by conviction to Scripture. The total tradition of analytical exegesis that requires us to read the Hebrew Scriptures not only through the vision of Judaic or Christian faith, but also through the perception and sight of historical inquiry, speaks to substantial sectors of synagogue and church alike. Yet "the one whole Torah of Moses our rabbi," like the Christ of Old Testament prophecy, endures as the definitive aspect of Judaism. That is why if we wish to understand the religion at hand, we must define Judaism in one way. It is the faith that God gave the Torah to Moses at Sinai, and that the Torah was given in two media, part in writing and part in memory or orally.

THE ORAL TORAH

So much for the Torah in general, the meanings imputed to the Torah in Judaism from its formative age in late antiquity to our own day. Let us now turn to the matter of the Torah as Judaism alone has always protrayed it: What exactly is the oral Torah? Let me answer this question as Judaic theology always has and, in its classical form, always will.

The Torah is God's will for Israel and humanity, revealed by

God to Moses at Sinai, written down originally in the Five Books of Moses, later encompassing the entirety of the Hebrew Scriptures. Long before the advent of the founders of the system that came to first expression in the Mishnah, the Hebrew Scriptures had come to nearly full definition. Most Israelites accepted the status, as part of divine revelation, not only of the five books of Moses (the Pentateuch—Genesis, Exodus, Leviticus, Numbers, and Deuteronomy), but also of the prophets (Joshua, Judges, Samuel, Kings, Isaiah, Jeremiah, Ezekiel, and the twelve minor prophets), and most of the writings (Psalms, Proverbs, Job, and the like). Disagreement about some minor matters (the standing of the Song of Songs, for example) should not obscure the broad agreement on nearly the whole of what we know today as the Hebrew Scriptures (Tanakh, for Jews, Old Testament, for Christians). So when we speak of "the written Torah," we refer to writings most people in ancient times recognized as the record of God's will to Israel.

We come now to the question, Precisely how did sages portray the process of the formulation and transmission of the other Torah, the oral one? The medium for the oral Torah was memory. What did this mean? Words were formulated to be memorized, then the formula was repeated to Moses. Moses repeated the formula to Joshua, Joshua handed it on to his disciples, and so through the ages. Through the medium of memory, the other part of the Torah of Sinai, the one that was not written, comes down through the ages. Here is how the Talmud of Babylonia portrays the process of oral formulation and oral transmission of the Torah.

Moses learned from the mouth of the Almighty. Aaron entered, and Moses repeated to him his [Aaron's] lesson. Aaron departed and sat at the left hand of Moses.

His sons entered and Moses repeated to them their lesson. His sons departed. Eleazar sat at the right hand of Moses and Itamar at the left of Aaron.

R. Judah says, "Aaron surely sat at the right hand of Moses."

Again the elders entered, and Moses taught them their lesson. The elders departed, and all the people entered, and Moses taught them their lesson.

So it came out that in the hand of Aaron [were] four, in the hand of his sons three, and in the hand of the elders two, and in the hand of the whole people one.

His sons taught them their lesson. His sons departed. The sages taught them their lesson.

So it came about that in everyone's hand were four.

On this basis R. Eliezer said, "A man is required to repeat a lesson to his disciple four times . . ."

R. Aqiba says, "How do we know that a man is liable to teach his disciple the lesson until he learns it? As it is said . . ." (B. Erubin 54b)

The basic picture then is clear. God speaks to Moses, who repeats and memorizes God's teaching to him. Moses repeats the statement to Aaron, who memorizes it. Aaron's sons, the priests, do the same. Then the elders come and memorize their sayings, and, finally, the people do the same. Each authority learns what God has told Moses and memorizes that saying. Some repeat matters more than others, four, three, two times or only one time, and so the priests are more authoritative than the elders and so on down. The main point for our purposes is simple. The sages of the Talmud of Babylonia clearly maintain that the oral Torah, as much as the written Torah, derives directly from God. The oral Torah comes in the medium of oral formulation and oral transmission through the memory of the authorities and people of Israel.

Since the mode by which God taught Moses clearly corresponds to the mode by which the contemporary sage taught his disciples, the picture emerges clearly. The story fairly claims that the encounter with God, through the Torah, takes place in the charmed circle formed by the master teaching his disciples. The master is like God. The disciples are like Moses. The transaction between them engages not solely the intellect but the soul, and at issue, in the study of the Torah, is sanctification: becoming like God. So when we confront the oral Torah, we deal not with books of law or of explanation of the Mishnah or of Scripture. As I said at the beginning, we take up the critical religious documents of an enduring religious faith. We investigate the expression in writing, the literary expression, of profound religious experience. So far as people can write down what happens to them, what they feel in their hearts and think in their minds when they confront Almighty God, for Judaism the writings of encounter with transcendence take form in the Hebrew Scriptures, the written Torah, and the writings of the sages of late antiquity (and beyond that point), the oral Torah.

The issues are not trivial, nor merely historical, nor mostly literary. In the sages' view, when God speaks to Israel, God speaks through the Torah. When sages speak words of Torah, they speak like God. When they do the things the Torah teaches, they carry out God-like actions. When, above all, they take up transactions with their disciples, they embody in the interstices of human relationships the encounter, indeed the confrontation, between God and man.

In the Judaism of the sages of the Talmud, the oral Torah encompasses all authentic expressions of the Torah that are not recorded in the written Torah. Thus all teachings deemed by Israel's sages to be authoritative and holy enter the category of the oral Torah. Into the classification of oral Torah, therefore, fall many writings, both in ancient and in medieval and modern times. The process of revelation of the Torah goes on and on. But to begin with a particular set of books that reached written form from the late second through the late sixth centuries constituted the oral Torah in its first fully worked out statement.

Where and how in the oral Torah does the story of the oral Torah, the dual Torah, emerge? The answer places into context how the several parts of the oral Torah before us all together comprise this oral Torah. The earliest formulation, in writing, of the conception that God revealed a tradition *in addition* to the one in writing finds exemplification in a saying assigned in the Mishnah (ca. 200 C.E.)' to Joshua b. Hananiah (ca. 100 C.E.), who imputes the saying to Yohanan b. Zakkai, his teacher, who flourished from ca. 10 to ca. 90 C.E.

R. Joshua said, "I have received as a tradition from Rabban Yohanan b. Zakkai, who heard from his teacher, and his teacher from his teacher, as a *halakhah* (law) given to Moses from Sinai, that Elijah will not come to declare unclean or clean, to remove afar or to bring nigh, but to remove afar those that were brought near by violence, and to bring near those that were removed by violence." (M. Eduyyot 8:7)

Guided by this statement alone, we should not have reached the conclusion that people believed that God revealed revealed a dual Torah. What we have in hand is a statement that God revealed traditions over and above those that are written down in Torah. That is a commonplace among the Judaisms of ancient times. Every group of Jews with a distinctive viewpoint on Israel's life took the position that its teachings in particular formed part of God's revelation to Moses at Sinai. Over and above Scripture, therefore, each group pointed to a further revelation, handed on in tradition. The very distinctive formulation of this prevailing conviction is what is important to distinguishing the Judaism of the sages of the talmudic literature, that is, "the one whole Torah of Moses, our rabbi," from all other Judaisms of the age and prior times.

The mere allegation that in addition to Scripture there was tradition will not have surprised anybody. Exactly what this tradition was, in the framing of the oral Torah, and how this tradition was handed on, turned out to be questions that continued to attract attention for a long time. For example, in another pertinent passage, the conception a dual Torah, one of the parts in the medium of human memory, competes with a different conception. In the one to follow, the unwritten tradition of Sinai was not a public *torah*. It was not a revelation generally known. More important, the exact wording of God's revelation at Sinai is not claimed to be available in its original form in the following theory of the oral Torah. In this passage, Eliezer's assertion, in the same words as the decision, gives evidence that to Yohanan were attributed orally formulated and orally transmitted traditions. Those traditions were alleged to have derived from Sinai.

On that day . . . they voted and decided that Ammon and Moab should give Poorman's Tithe in the Sabbatical Year.

And when R. Yose, the son of the Damascene, came to R. Eliezer in Lydda, he said to him, "What new thing did you have in the house of study today?"

He said to him, "They voted and decided that Ammon and Moab give Poorman's Tithe in the Sabbatical Year."

R. Eliezer wept and said, *"The secret of the Lord is with them that fear him, and he will show them his covenant* (Ps. 25:14). Go and tell them, 'Be not anxious by reason of your voting, for I have received a tradition from Rabban Yohanan b. Zakkai, who heard it from his teacher, and his teacher from his teacher, as a *halakhah* given to Moses at Sinai, that Ammon and Moab give Poorman's Tithe in the Sabbatical Year.' "

In this passage, we see, the very sayings of Moses through Yohanan never survived in their original form. We should not have known them had not Eliezer quoted them. So if Yohanan's saying had earlier been given fixed form, and if this was done orally, and if it was thereupon taught to Eliezer for memorization and oral transmission, then that saying nonetheless was not published. For only Eliezer knew about it. The others were in the dark, so they had to vote. This pericope hardly conforms to the picture of the oral formulation and transmission of a *public* tradition, the oral Torah.

We have therefore to ask for a clear and unequivocal statement of the belief that when God revealed the Torah to Moses at Sinai, God revealed the Torah in two media: one in writing, the other in memory. That theory of the oral Torah reaches us, appropriately, in the two great commentaries to the Mishnah, the Talmud of the Land of Israel and the Talmud of Babylonia. The aptness of the origin of the story at hand in the two Talmuds is because of one simple fact. Both Talmuds explain the Mishnah, and the Mishnah is the first, and the most important, document of the oral Torah. The story comes in two versions. The first is the Yerushalmi (ca. 400 C.E.), the second in the Bavli (ca. 500–600 C.E.). In the former, we find nearly every important component of the basic story of the oral Torah, and in the latter we find the critical details omitted earlier. Let us take up the Yerushalmi's statement first.

In the Yerushalmi, we find the first glimmerings of an effort to

theorize in general, not merely in detail, about how specific teachings of Mishnah related to specific teachings of Scripture. What
conception of the Torah underlies such initiatives, and how do
Yerushalmi sages propose to explain the phenomenon of the
Mishnah as a whole? The following passage gives us one statement. It refers to the assertion at M. Hag. 1:8D that the laws on
cultic cleanness presented in the Mishnah rest on deep and solid
foundation in the Scripture.

> A. *The laws of the Sabbath* [M:8B]. . . .
> B. *R. Zeira in the name of R. Yohanan: "If a law comes to hand and you
> do not know its nature, do not discard it for another one, for lo, many
> laws were stated to Moses at Sinai, and all of them have been embedded
> in the Mishnah."*
>
> **Y. Hag. 1:7.V**

The assertion at B is truly striking. The Mishnah now is claimed
to contain statements made by God to Moses. Just how these
statements found their way into the Mishnah, and which passages
of the Mishnah contain them, we do not know. That is hardly
important, given the fundamental assertion at hand. The passage
proceeds to a further, and far more consequential, proposition. It
asserts that part of the Torah was written down, and part was
preserved in memory and transmitted orally. In context, moreover, that distinction must encompass the Mishnah. Thus the
Mishnah's origin as part of the Torah is explained.

Here then is a clear and unmistakable expression of the distinction between two forms in which a single Torah was revealed and
handed on at Mount Sinai, part in writing, part orally. While the
next passage does not make use of the language, Torah-in-writing
and Torah-by-memory, it does refer to "the written" and "the
oral." I believe myself fully justified in supplying the word
"Torah" in square brackets. The reader will note, however, that
the word Torah likewise does not occur at K, L. Only when the
passage reaches its climax, at M, does it break down into a number
of categories—Scripture, Mishnah, Talmud, laws, lore. It there

makes the additional point that *everything* comes from Moses at Sinai. So the fully articulated theory of *two Torahs* (not merely one Torah in two forms) does not reach final expression in this passage. But short of explicit allusion to Torah-in-writing and Torah-by-memory, which (so far as I am able to discern) we find principally in the Talmud of Babylonia, the ultimate theory of Torah of formative Judaism is at hand in what follows.

D. R. Zeirah in the name of R. Eleazar: " 'Were I to write for him my laws by ten thousands, they would be regarded as a strange thing' (Hos. 8:12). Now is the greater part of the Torah written down? [Surely not. The oral part is much greater.] But more abundant are the matters which are derived by exegesis from the written [Torah] than those derived by exergesis from the oral [Torah]."

E. And is that so?

F. But more cherished are those matters which rest upon the written [Torah] then those which rest upon the oral [Torah].

J. R. Haggai in the name of R. Samuel bar Nahman, "Some teachings were handed on orally, and some things were handed on in writing, and we do not know which of them is the more precious. But on the basis of that which is written, 'And the Lord said to Moses, Write these words; in accordance with these words ['L PY] I have made a covenant with you and with Israel' (Ex 34:27), [we conclude] that the ones which are handed on orally ['L PH] are the more precious." [The play on words 'L PY and 'L PH yields the proof.]

K. R. Yohanan and R. Yudan b. R. Simeon—One said, "If you have kept what is preserved orally and also kept what is in writing, I shall make a covenant with you, and if not, I shall not make a covenant with you."

L. The other said, "If you have kept what is preserved orally and you have kept what is preserved in writing, you shall receive a reward, and if not, you shall not receive a reward."

M. [With reference to Deut. 9:10: "And on them was written according to all the words which the Lord spoke with you in the mount,"] said R. Joshua b. Levi, "He could have written, 'On them,' but wrote, 'And on them.' " He could have written,

'All,' but wrote, 'According to all.' He could have written, 'Words,' but wrote, 'The words.' [These then serve as three encompassing clauses, serving to include] Scriptures, Mishnah, Talmud, laws, and lore. Even what an experienced student in the future is going to teach before his master already has been stated to Moses at Sinai."

N. What is the Scriptural basis for this view?

O. "There is no remembrance of former things, nor will there be any remembrance of later things yet to happen among those who come after" (Qoh. 1:11).

P. If someone says, "See, this is a new thing," his fellow will answer him, saying to him, "This has been around before us for a long time."

Y. Hagigah 1:7.V

Here we have absolutely explicit evidence that people believed part of the Torah had been preserved not in writing, but orally. Linking that part to the Mishnah remains a matter of implication. But it surely comes fairly close to the surface, when we are told that the Mishnah contains Torah-traditions revealed at Sinai. From that view it requires only a small step to the allegation that the Mishnah is part of the Torah, the oral part.

The Talmud of Babylonia, or Bavli, finally, took that step. A simple story brings to full and complete articulation the belief in the two media of revelation. Here at the end we find these conceptions: A tradition, in addition to the written Torah, came down from Sinai; the unwritten tradition revealed at Sinai was in fact memorized; this other, oral instruction constituted the oral Torah, bearing exactly that name; and, most important, the sage or rabbi is the master of the oral Torah.

Our Rabbis taught: A certain heathen once came before Shammai and asked him, 'How many Torahs have you?'

"Two," he replied: "the Written Orah and the Oral Torah."

"I believe you with respect to the Written, but not with respect to the Oral Torah; make me a proselyte on condition that you teach me the Written Torah [only]." [But] he scolded and repulsed him in anger.

When he went before Hillel, he accepted him as a proselyte. On the first day he taught him, *Alef, beth, gimmel, daleth* [= A, B, C, D]; the following day he reversed [them] to him.

"But yesterday you did not teach them to me thus," he protested.

"Must you then not rely upon me? Then rely upon me with respect to the Oral [Torah] too." (B. Shabbat 31a)*

So much for the theory of the Torah, the dual Torah, and the oral Torah: It all depends upon the sage. How so? It is in the person of the sages that the two Torahs become one. There are two meanings to the Hebrew words we translate as "oral." One is, "what is transmitted by mouth"; and the other is, "what is memorized." The other half of the one whole Torah of Moses, our rabbi, lives today in the speech and in the memory of those sages of Israel, the Jewish people, who in the model of Moses stand for the Torah. But—let it be said at the end—God alone knows who these are. It is up to us ordinary folk to learn and to teach, to keep and to carry out, the teachings of the Torah, as best we can.

---

*Translated by H. Freedman, pp. 139–140.

Appendix
The Contents of the Oral
Torah: A Topical Outline of
the Mishnah

This account of the oral Torah would be incomplete without a detailed statement of exactly what we find in that part of the Torah. The following outline of the Mishnah presents a picture of the topics of the tractates of the Mishnah and the questions they answer in connection with those themes. It shows precisely what each of the two great Talmuds covers, as well as what topics make their appearance only in the Mishnah and its supplement, the Tosefta. To state matters simply: The Bavli covers the second, third, fourth, and fifth divisions, on Appointed Times, Women, Damages, and Holy Things. The Yerushalmi drops the fifth division, Holy Things, but covers the first division, Agriculture. The sixth division's topical program occurs only in the Mishnah and the Tosefta.

1. *The Topics of the Oral Torah Taken Up in the Talmud of Babylonia*

The Division of Appointed Times

Appointed Times and the Village

Shabbat

I.   General principles of Sabbath observance. 1:1–11
II.   Preparing for the Sabbath: Light, food, clothing. 2:1–6:11
      A. The Sabbath lamp. 2:1–7
      B. Food for the Sabbath. 3:1–4:2
      C. Ornaments for animals, clothing for persons, on the Sabbath. 5:1–6:10
III. Prohibited acts of labor on the Sabbath. 7:1–15:3

A. Generalizations: Prohibited acts of labor. 7:1–2
B. Transporting an object from one domain to another. 7:3–9:7
C. Fundamental principles on carrying from one domain to another. 10:1–5 (+ 6)
D. Transporting an object. Throwing something from one domain to another. 11:1–6
E. Other prohibited acts of labor. 12:1–14:2
F. Healing on the Sabbath. 14:3–4
G. Knot-tying. Clothing and beds. 15:1–3
IV. Other Sabbath taboos. 16:1–24:5
A. Saving objects from a fire on the Sabbath. The taboo against using or handling fire. 16:1–8
B. Handling diverse objects in private domain, so long as the purpose for which the objects is handled is allowed on the Sabbath. 17:1–18:3
C. Circumcision on the Sabbath. 19:1–6
D. Preparing food for humans and beasts. Permitted procedures. 20:1–22:6
E. Seemly behavior on the Sabbath. Permitted and prohibited deeds. 23:1–24:5

Erubin

I. The delineation of a limited domain. 1:1–2:5
A. Forming an alleyway into a single domain. 1:1–7
B. Forming an area occupied by a caravan at rest for the Sabbath into a single domain. 1:8–10
C. A well in public domain. 2:1–4
D. A large field. 2:5
II. The *erub* and the Sabbath limit of a town. 3:1–5:9
A. The *erub:* A symbolic meal for establishing joint ownership of a courtyard or for establishing symbolic residence for purposes of legitimate travel on the Sabbath. 3:1–9
B. The *erub* and violating the Sabbath limit. 4:1–11
C. Defining the Sabbath limit of a town. 5:1–9
III. The *erub* and commingling ownership of a courtyard or alleyway. 6:1–9:4
A. The *erub* and the courtyard. 6:1–10
B. Areas which may be deemed either distinct from one another or as a commingled domain, so that residents have the choice of preparing a joint *erub* or two separate ones. 7:1–5
C. The *shittuf* (also a symbolic joint meal) and the alleyway. 7:6–8:2

D. Neglecting the *erub* for a courtyard and the consequences thereof. 8:3–5

E. An *erub* for more than one courtyard. 8:6–8:11

F. An *erub* and the area of roofs. 9:1–4

IV. The public domain in general. 10:1–10 (+ 11–15)

Besah

I. The Houses and other authorities. 1:1–3:1

II. Designating food before the festival for use on the festival. 3:2–8

III. Doing actions connected with preparing food on a festival day in a manner different from ordinary days. Other restrictions. 4:1–5:2

IV. Appendix. 5:3–7

Moed Qatan

I. Labor on the intermediate days of a festival. 1:1–10, 2:1–3

A. In the fields. 1:1–4

B. Miscellanies. 1:5–7

C. Cases of emergency and grievous loss of property. 2:1–3

II. Commerce on the intermediate days of a festival. 2:3–3:4

III. Burial of the dead and mourning on the intermediate days of a festival. 3:5–9

Appointed Times and the Cult

Pesahim

I. Preparation for Passover. 1:1–4:8

A. Removing leaven. 1:1–2:4

B. Removing and avoiding what ferments. 2:5–3:8

C. Other requirements for 14 Nissan. 4:1–8

II. The Passover offering on the night of 14 Nissan. Slaying and eating it. 5:1–9:11

A. General rules on slaughtering the Passover offering. 5:1–10

B. Special rules for the Sabbath which coincides with 14 Nissan. 6:1–6

C. Roasting and eating the Passover offerings. 7:1–4

D. Special rules for the Passover offering. 7:5–9:5

1. Uncleanness. 7:5–10

2. Not breaking the bone of the Passover offerings. 7:11–12

3. Eating the offering in a group. 7:13–8:8

4. The second Passover. 9:1–5

E. A special case: An animal designated for use for a Passover offering which was lost, or for which a substitute was designated, and how one deals with such cases. 9:6–11

III.   The Passover *seder*. 10:1–9

Sheqalim

I.   Collecting the *sheqel*. 1:1–2:5
       A. Imposing the obligation to pay. 1:1–7
       B. Transporting the *sheqel*. Sacrilege. 2:1–5
II.   Using the *sheqel* for Temple offerings for the altar. 3:1–4:9
       A. Taking up the *sheqel* for the public offerings. 3:1–4
       B. Disposing of the *sheqel* for various offerings. 4:1–9
III.   The Temple administration and its procedures. 5:1–8:8
       A. The administration. 5:1–2
       B. Procedures for selling drink offerings. 5:3–6
       C. Collecting other funds in the Temple. 5:6–8:8
       D. Disposing of money and objects found in the Temple and in Jerusalem. 7:1–8:3
       E. Miscellanies. 8:4–8

Yoma

I.   The conduct of the Temple rites on the Day of Atonement. 1:1–7:5
       A. Preparing the high priest for the Day of Atonement. 1:1–7
       B. Clearing the ashes off the altar. 1:8–2:6
       C. The narrative resumes: The daily whole offering on the Day of Atonement. 2:5–3:4
       D. The narrative continues: The high priest's personal offering for the Day of Atonement. 3:6–8
       E. The narrative continues: The two goats and other offerings on the Day of Atonement. 3:9–5:7
       F. The scapegoat and its rule. 6:1–8
       G. The rite concludes with Torah reading and prayer. 7:1–5
II.   The laws of the Day of Atonement. 8:1–9
       A. Not eating, not drinking. 8:1–7
       B. Atonement. 8:8–9

Sukkah

I.   Objects used in celebrating the Festival. 1:1–3:15
       A. The *sukkah* and its roof. 1:1–2:3
       B. Dwelling in the *sukkah*. 2:4–9
       C. The *lulab* and the *etrog*. 3:1–15

II.   The rites and offerings of the Festival. 4:1–5:8
        A. The Festival rites carried out on the successive festival days. 4:1–5:4
        B. The offerings on the altar. 5:5–8

Rosh Hashshanah

I.   The designation of the new month through the year. 1:1–3:1
        A. Prologue: The four new years. 1:1–2
        B. The new moon. Receiving testimony of the appearance of the new month. 1:3–3:1
II.   The *shofar*. 3:2–4:9
        A. Rules of the *shofar*. 3:2–4:4
        B. The liturgy of the New Year. 4:5–6
        C. Sounding the *shofar* in the liturgy. 4:7–9

Taanit

I.   Fasts called in order to bring rain. 1:1–2:10, 3:1–9
        A. The sequence of fasts for rain. 1:1–7
        B. The liturgy of the community for a fast day. 2:1–5
        C. Other rules about public fasts. 2:8–10
        D. Other uses of the *shofar* as an alarm, besides for fasts. 3:1–9
II.   The delegation *(ma'amad):* Israelite participation in the cult. Various special occasions. 4:1–8
        A. The delegation. 4:1–4
        B. Other occasions. 4:5
        C. Sad days. 4:6–8

Megillah

I.   The rules of reading the Scroll of Esther. 1:1–2:6
II.   The laws of synagogue property and liturgy. 3:1–4:9
        A. Disposition of synagogue property. 3:1–3
        B. Rules for reading the Scriptures in synagogue worship. 4:1–5
        C. Conduct in the synagogue: Reading the Torah, blessing the congregation, leading the prayers. 4:6–8

Hagigah

I.   The appearance offering festal offering, and peace offering or rejoicing. 1:1–2:4
        A. Liability to these offerings. The cost of them. 1:1–2:1
        B. The festal offering and the Sabbath. 2:2–4
II.   The rules of uncleanness as they affect ordinary folk and holy things of the cult or festivals. 2:5–3:8

A. Gradations of strictness of rules of uncleanness, with the strictest rules affecting the cult. 2:5–3:3

B. Holy things and the festival. 3:4–8

The Division of Women

The Beginning of Marriage

Qiddushin

I. Betrothals. 1:1–3:11
  A. Rules of acquisition. 1:1–10
  B. Procedures of betrothal: Agency, value, stipulations. 2:1–5
  C. Impaired betrothal. 2:6–3:1
  D. Stipulations. 3:2–6
  E. Doubts. 3:7–11
II. Castes for the purposes of marriage. 3:12–4:11
  A. The status of the offspring of impaired marriages. 3:12–13
  B. Castes and intermarriage. 4:1–7
  C. Miscellany. 4:8–11
III. Homiletical conclusion. 4:12–14

Ketubot

I. Formation of the marriage: The material rights of the parties to the marital union. 1:1–5:1
  A. The wife. 1:1–2:10
    1. The virgin and her marriage contract. 1:1–4
    2. Conflicting claims for a marriage contract for a virgin. 1:5–2:3
    3. Miscellanies or testimony. 2:3–2:10
  B. The father and the husband (cf. Deut. 22:15–29), 3:1–5:1
    1. The fine paid to the father (Deut. 21:22) for rape or seduction. 3:1–4:1
    2. The father. 4:2 (+ 3)
    3. The father and the husband. 4:4–6
    4. The husband. 4:7–5:1
II. The duration of the marriage: Reciprocal responsibilities and rights of husband and wife. 5:2–9:1
  A. The wife's duties to the husband. 5:2–5
  B. The husband's marital rights and duties to the wife. 5:6–6:1
  C. The dowry. 6:2–7
  D. The marital rights and duties of the wife. 7:1–10
  E. The property rights of the wife. 8:1–9:1

III.   Cessation of the marriage: the collection of the marriage contract.
       9:2–12:4 (+ 13:1–9)
       A. Imposing an oath. 9:2–9
       B. Multiple claims on an estate. 10:1–6
       C. Support of the widow. 11:1–5
       D. Rights to and collection of a marriage contract: Special cases.
          11:6–12:4
       E. Two casebooks. 13:1–9
IV.   Conclusion. 13:10–11

The Duration of the Marriage

Nedarim

I.   The language of vows. 1:1–3:11
       A. Euphemisms. 1:1–2:5
       B. Language of no effect. 3:1–4 (+ 5)
       C. Language of limited effect. 3:6–11
II.   The binding effects of vows. 4:1–8:6
       A. Vows not to derive benefits. 4:1–5:6
       B. Vows not to eat certain food. 6:1–7:2
       C. Vows not to use certain objects. 7:3–5
       D. The temporal limitation in vows. 7:6–8:6
III.   The absolution of vows. 8:6–11:12
       A. Grounds for the absolution of vows. 8:6–9:10
       B. The annulment of the vows of a daughter. 10:1–4
       C. The annulment of the vows of a wife. 10:5–8
       D. The husband's power to annul the wife's vows: Special rules.
          11:1–1:8
       E. Vows of a woman not subject to abrogation. 11:9–10
       F. Redactional conclusion. 11:12

Nazir

I.   Becoming a Nazirite: The vow. 1:1–4:3
       A. The language of the vow to be a Nazirite. 1:1–7
       B. Stipulations and the Nazirite vow. 2:1–10
       C. The duration of the vow. 3:1–7
       D. Annulling the vow. 4:1–3
II.   The Nazirite's offerings. 4:4–5:7
       A. Designation and disposition of the offerings. 4:4–5:4
       B. Concluding conundrum. 5:5–7
III.   Restrictions on the Nazirite. 6:1–8:2 (+ 9:1–5)
       A. The grape. 6:1–4
       B. Transition. 6:5

C. Cutting hair. 6:6–11
D. Corpse uncleanness. 7:1–4
E. Doubt in the case of the Nazir. 8:1–9:2 (+ 3–5)

Sotah

I.   Invoking the ordeal. 1:1–3
II.   Narrative of the ordeal. 1:4–3:5 (+ 3:6–8)
III. Rules of the ordeal. 4:1–6:4
      A. Exemptions and applicability. 4:1–5:1 (+ 2–5)
      B. Testimony and exemptions from the ordeal. 6:1–4
IV.   Rites conducted in Hebrew. 7:1–9:15
      A. A catalogue. 7:1–8
      B. The anointed for battle and the draft exemptions (cf. Deut. 20:1–9). 8:1–7
      C. The rite of the heifer (cf. Deut. 21:1–9). 9:1–9 (+ 10–15)

The End of a Marriage

Yebamot

I.   Establishing and severing the marital bond. 1:1–5:6
      A. Neither levirate marriage nor *ḥaliṣah:* Consanguinity. 1:1–2:10
      B. *Ḥaliṣah* but no levirate marriage. 3:1–3:10
      C. Levirate marriage. 4:1–4:13
      D. Reprise: Marriage, divorce, levirate marriage. *Ḥaliṣah.* 5:1–6
II.   The special marital bond: Marriage into the priesthood. 6:1–9:6
      A. When a woman may eat heave offering. 6:1–6
      B. Who may eat heave offering. 7:1–8:2
      C. Miscellany. 8:3
      D. The eunuch. 8:4–6
      E. Concluding construction for units I and II. 9:1–6
III. Severing the marital bond. 10:1–16:7
      A. Marital ties subject to doubt. 10:1–11:7
      B. Severing the marital bond of the deceased childless brother's widow. The rite of *ḥaliṣah* and how it is performed. 12:1–6
      C. Severing the marital bond of the minor. Exercising the right of refusal. 13:1–13
      D. The infirm marital bond of the deaf mute. 14:1–4
      E. Severing the marital bond through the death of the husband. 15:1–16:7
         1. The woman's testimony. 15:1–16:2
         2. Identifying a corpse. 16:3–7

Gittin

I. Delivering and preparing a writ of divorce. 1:1–3:8
    A. Delivering a writ of divorce. 1:1–2:1
    B. Preparing a writ of divorce. 2:2–3:3
    C. Confirming the prevailing supposition. 3:4–8
II. Fifteen rulings made for the good order of the world. 4:1–5:9
III. The law of agency in writs of divorce. 6:1–7:2
    A. Receiving the writ of divorce. 6:1–4
    B. Appointing agents to prepare and deliver a writ of divorce. 6:5–
       7:2
IV. Stipulations in writs of divorce. 7:3–7:9
V. Invalid writs of divorce. 8:1–9:10
    A. Improper delivery. 8:4–10
    B. Improper preparation of the writ. 8:4–10
    C. Improper stipulations. 9:1–2
    D. Improper witnesses. 9:4–9:8
    E. Conclusion. 9:9–10

The Division of Damages

Civil Law

Baba Qamma

I. Damages done by chattels. 1:1–6:6
    A. The fundamental rules of assessing damages when the cause is
       one's property, animate and inanimate. The ox. 1:1–2:6
    B. Damages done in the public domain. 3:1–7
    C. Exercises and illustrations on the ox. 3:8–4:4
    D. The ransom and the death penalty for the ox. 4:5–5:4
    E. Damages done by the pit (M. 1:1). 5:5–7
    F. Crop-destroying beast (M. 1:1). 6:1–3
    G. Damages done by fire (M. 1:1). 6:4–6
II. Damages done by persons. Theft. 7:1–10:10
    A. Penalties for the theft of an ox or a sheep (df. Ex. 22:1–4). 7:1–7
    B. Penalties for assault. 8:1–7
    C. Penalties for damages to property. Restoring what is stolen. 9:1–
       10:10

Baba Mesia

III. The disposition of other people's possessions. 1:1–3:12
    A. Conflicting claims on lost objects. 1:1–4

Baba Batra

Abodah Zarah

II.   Idols. 3:1–4:7
    A. General principles. 3:1–6
    B. The *asherah*. 3:7–10
    C. The *Merkolis*. 4:1–2
    D. Nullifying an idol. 4:3–7
III.   Libation wine. 4:8–5:12

The Courts and Administration

Sanhedrin

I.   The court system. 1:1–5:5
    A. Various kinds of courts and their jurisdiction: Civil, criminal, and political. 1:1–6
    B. Heads of the Israelite nation and court system. High priest and king. 2:1–5
    C. Procedures of the court system. 3:1–5:5
        1. Commercial cases. 3:1–8
        2. Capital cases. 4:1–5:5
II.   The death penalty. 6:1–11:6
    A. Stoning. 6:1–6
    B. Four modes of execution and how they are administered. 7:1–3
    C. Those put to death by stoning. 7:4–8:7
    D. Those put to death by burning or decapitation. 9:1–10:6
    E. Those put to death through strangulation. 1:1–6

Makkot

III.   Perjury and its penalties. 1:1–10
IV.   The penalty of exile (banishment). 2:1–8
    A. Those subjected to banishment. 2:1–3
    B. The cities of banishment. 2:4–8
V.   The penalty of flogging. 3:1–14
    A. Those subjected to flogging. 3:1–9
    B. The procedure of flogging. 3:10–14
VI.   Concluding homilies. 3:15–16

Shebuot

I.   Uncleanness of the cult and its holy things and the guilt offering. 1:1–2:5
    A. General introduction. 1:1
    B. Uncleanness and the cult. 1:2–2:5

II.   Oaths. 3:1–8:6

     A. Oaths in general. 3:1–6

     B. The rash oath. The vain oath. 3:7–11

     C. The oath of testimony. 4:1–13

     D. The oath of bailment, 5:1–5

     E. The oath imposed by judges. 6:1–7:8

     F. Oaths and bailments. Concluding exercise. 8:1–6

Horayot

I.   The offering brought because of an erroneous decision by a court. 1:1–5

II.   The offering brought by the high priest who has unwittingly done what is contrary to the commandments of the Torah. The ruler. 2:1–5

III.   The individual, anointed priest, and community. 2:5–3:8

The Division of Holy Things

Rules of the Cult

Zebahim

I.   Improper intention and invalidating the act of sacrifice. 1:1–4:6

II.   The rules for sacrifice of animals and fowl. 5:1–7:6

     A. Animals. 5:1–6:1

     B. Fowl. 6:2–7:6

III.   Rules of the altar. 8:1–12:4

     A. Rules for disposing of sacrificial portions or blood which derive from diverse sacrifices and have been confused. 8:1–12

     B. The altar sanctifies what is appropriate to it. 9:1–7

     C. Precedence in use of the altar. 10:1–7 + 8

     D. Blood of a sin offering which spurts onto a garment (Exposition of Lev. 6:27–28). 11:1–8

     E. The division of the meat and hides of sacrificial animals among the eligible priests. 12:1–4 (+ 5–6)

IV.   The proper location of the altar and the act of sacrifice. 13:1–14:10

Menahot

I.   Reprise for meal offerings of the principles of animal offerings of M. Zebahim. Improper intention and invalidating the meal offerings. 1:1–4:5

     A. Reprise of Zebahim. 1:1–3:1

     B. Other rules of invalidation. 3:2–4:5

II.   The proper preparation of meal offerings. 5:1–9:9
      A. General rules. 5:1–6:7
      B. The meal offering accompanying the thank offering. 7:1–6
      C. Source of flour, oil, and wine used for the offering. 8:1–7
      D. Measuring the materials used for the offering. 9:1–5
      E. Conclusion. General rules. 9:6–9
III. Special meal offerings. 10:1–11:9
      A. The 'omer. 10:1–9
      B. The two loaves of Pentecost and the show bread. 11:1–9
IV.   Vows in connection with meal offerings. 12:1–13:10

Hullin

I.   Rules of slaughtering unconsecrated animals for use at home or in
      the Temple. 1:1–4:7
      A. General rules. 1:1–4 (+ 5–7)
      B. Specific regulations. *Terefah* rules. 2:1–6
      C. Slaughter and illicit sacrifice. 2:7–10
      D. *Terefah* and valid carcasses. 3:1–7
      E. The effect of valid slaughter on the parts of a beast's body, e.g.,
         on the fetus. 4:1–7
II.   Other rules on the preparation of food, principally for use at home.
      5:1–12:5
      A. *It and its young* (Lev. 22:28). 5:1–5
      B. The requirement to cover up the blood (Lev. 17:13–14). 6:1–7
      C. The prohibition of the sciatic nerve (Gen. 32:32). 7:1–6
      D. Milk and meat (Ex. 23:19, 34:26; Deut. 12:21). 8:1–6
      E. Connection. 9:1–8
      F. The shoulder, two cheeks, and maw, which are given to the
         priest (Deut. 18:4). 10:1–4
      G. First fleece goes to the priest (Deut. 18:4). 11:1–2
      H. The law of letting the dam go from the nest when taking the
         young (Deut. 22:6–7) 12:1–5

Keritot

I.   The sin offering (Lev. 5:17–19). 1:1–2:2
II.   A single sin offering and multiple sins. 2:3–3:10
III. The suspensive guilt offering. 4:1–6:8

Tamid

I.   The priests arise in the morning. Clearing the altar of ashes. 1:1–4,
      2:1–5

II.   Selecting the lamb for the daily burnt offering. 3:1–5
III.   Clearing the ashes. 3:6–9
IV.   Slaughtering the lamb. 4:1–3
V.   The priests bless the congregation. The lambs are brought to the altar. 5:1–4
VI.   Clearing the ashes. 5:5–6:2 (+ 3)
VII.   Conclusion of rite. The limbs are tossed on the altar.

Qinnim

These exercises are summarized, not outlined, as follows:

1:1   The blood of the sin offering of fowl is sprinkled below, that of the beast, above, the red line. The blood of burnt offering of fowl is sprinkled above, of beast, below. The proper rite of a pair of birds: a pair brought in fulfillment of an obligation is deemed to include one as a sin offering and one as a burnt offering: a pair brought as a vow or freewill offering is deemed to be only burnt offerings.

1:2   A sin offering which was confused with a burnt offering or a burnt offering with a sin offering. A bird designated as a sin offering confused with birds which were not designated but brought in fulfillment of an obligation.

1:3   Under what circumstances [do the rules of 1:1–2 apply]? In the case of confusion of an offering brought in fulfillment of an obligation with one designated as a freewill offering.

1:4   Continuation of 1:3

2:1   An unassigned pair of birds from which one flew off into the air—let the owner purchase a mate for the second.

2:2   Continuation of 2:1

2:3   Continuation of 2:1

2:4   A pair of birds which had not been designated and a pair of birds which had been designated—a bird flew from one to the other. Continuation of 2:1

2:5   A pair of birds for a sin offering at one side, a pair for a burnt offering at the other, and an unassigned pair in the middle—if one of the unassigned ones flew from the middle to the sides, it has caused no loss. Completion of 2:4

3:1–2   Under what circumstances [do the rules of 1:1–2 apply]? In the case of a priest who makes an inquiry. But if he does not, so that a *post facto* decision is required—1:3 now cited and spelled out.

3:3–5   1:2 cited and spelled out, once more for a *post facto* decision.

3:6   A woman who said, "Lo, I pledge myself to bring a pair of birds if I bear a male child," if she has a boy, brings two pairs, one for the vow, one for the obligation. Reconsideration of the problem of 2:51–N.

Rules for Providing Animals for Daily Sacrifices and for the Upkeep of the Altar and Temple Buildings and Support of the Priestly Staff

Bekhorot

I.   The firstborn of animals. General rules. 1:1–4:2
      A. The firstborn of the ass. 1:1–7
      B. The firstborn of the cow. Reprise of M. Bekh. 1 2:1–8
      C. Further matters of doubt. 2:9–3:2
      D. Not shearing the firstling (Deut. 15:19). 3:3–4
      E. The requirement to tend to the firstling before handing it over to the priest. 4:1–2
II.   Slaughtering a firstling by reason of blemishes. 4:3–6:12
      A. Examining a firstling to see whether or not it is blemished. 4:3–10
      B. Further rules of slaughtering the firstling. 5:1–6
      C. Blemishes. 6:1–7:7
         1. In animals. 6:1–6:12
         2. In priests. 7:1–7
III. Firstborn of man. 8:1–9
IV.   The tithe of cattle. 9:1–8

Arakhin

I.   Valuations and vows for the benefit of the Temple. (Lev. 27:1–8). 1:1–6:5
      A. Basic rules. 1:1–4
      B. Two formal constructions. 2:1–6, 3:1–5
      C. Ability to pay in vows. 4:1–4
      D. The difference between pledging a valuation and vowing the worth, or price, of someone or something. 5:1–5
      E. Collecting valuations. 5:6–6:5
II.   The dedication and redemption of a field which is received as an inheritance (Lev. 27:16–25). 7:1–8:3
III. The devoted thing *[herem]* (Lev. 27:28–29). 8:4–7
IV.   The sale and redemption of a field received as an inheritance and of a dwelling house in a walled city (Lev. 25:25–34). 9:1–8

Temurah

I. The rules of substitution: Who may do so, and to what (Lev. 27:-14). 1:1–2:3
   A. Liability to the law of substitution. 1:1–2
   B. Exemptions from the law of substitution. 1:3–6
   C. Formal appendix. 2:1–3

II. The status of the offspring of substitutes. 3:1–4 (+ 2–4)
   A. Diverse sacrifices and their substitutes and offspring. 3:1–5
   B. Appendix on the supererogatory sin offering. 4:1–4

III. The language used in effecting an act of substitution. 5:5–6 (+ 1–4)
   A. Formal prologue. 5:1–4
   B. The effective formula. 5:5–6

IV. Formal appendix. 6:1–7:6

Meilah

I. Sacrilege of sacrifices in particular (Lev. 5:15–16). 1:1–3:8
   A. When the laws of sacrilege apply to a sacrifice. 1:1–4
   B. Stages in the status of an offering. 2:1–9
   C. Cultic property which is not subject to sacrilege but which also is not to be used for noncultic purposes. 3:1–8

II. Sacrilege of Temple property in general. 4:1–6:6
   A. Sacrilege has been committed only when the value of a *perutah* of Temple property has been used for secular purposes. The joining together of diverse objects for the purpose of reaching the *perutah's* value. (4:1–2 (+ 3–6)
   B. Sacrilege is defined by the one who does it, or by the thing to which it is done. 5:1–2
   C. Sacrilege effects the secularization of sacred property. 5:3–5
   D. Agency in effecting an act of sacrilege. 6:1–5 (+ 6)

Middot

I. Watch posts and gates. 1:1–9
II. The layout of the Temple mount. 2:1–6
III. The altar and porch. 3:1–8
IV. The sanctuary and courtyard. 4:1–7, 5:1–4

2. *The Topics of the Oral Torah Taken Up in the Talmud of the Land of Israel*
   The Talmud of the Land of Israel covers the second, third, and fourth divisions—Appointed Times, Women, Damages. It omits reference to the fifth division, Holy Things. But instead it provides a detailed exegesis of the Mishnah's first division, Seeds or Agriculture.

The Division of Agriculture

Producing Crops in a State of Holiness

Kilayim

I.   Plants: Growing together different kinds of plants. 1:1–7:8
     A. Plants which are or are not considered diverse kinds with one another. 1:1–6
     B. Grafting one kind of plant onto another. 1:7–9D
     C. Sowing together different kinds of crops. 1:9E–3:7
        1. Sowing together different kinds of crops in the same space. 1:9E–2:5
        2. Sowing together different kinds of crops in adjacent spaces. 2:6–3:3
        3. Sowing together different kinds of crops in adjacent spaces. Special case: Trailing plants. 3:4–7
     D. Sowing crops among vines. 4:1–7:8
        1. Permitted sowing of crops in a vineyard. 4:1–5:4
        2. Prohibited sowing of crops in a vineyard. 5:5–8
        3. Permitted sowing of crops near vines: Special cases. 6:1–7:2
        4. Prohibited sowing of crops near vines: Special cases. 7:3–8
II. Animals: Mating or yoking together animals of different kinds. 8:1–6
III. Fibers: Mingling wool and linen. 9:1–10

Shebiit

I.   The sixth year of the sabbatical cycle. 1:1–2:10
     A. Field labor during the sixth year, the effects of which are felt during the sabbatical year. 1:1–2:5
     B. Produce grown during the sixth year, which matures during the sabbatical year. 2:6–10
II. The sabbatical year. 3:1–9:9
     A. Field labor: Permitted and forbidden labors during the sabbatical year. 3:1–6:6
     B. Produce: Permitted and forbidden uses of produce grown during the sabbatical year. 7:1–9:9
III. Appendix: The release of debts at the end of the sabbatical year, and the *prozbul* (i.e., the documents which allows a lender to collect a debt even after the sabbatical year). 10:1–9

Orlah

I. Definition of what constitutes *orlah* fruit. 1:1–9
   A. Fruit tree. 1:1–2
   B. Planting. 1:3–5
   C. Fruit, status of the parts. 1:7–9
II. Mixtures of forbidden and permitted produce. 1:6, 2:1–17
   A. An orchard of permitted and forbidden saplings. 1:6
   B. Procedure for neutralizing forbidden produce in a mixture. 2:1–3
   C. Mixtures not neutralized. 2:4–7
   D. Mixtures of forbidden and permitted leaven in dough. 2:8–9, 11–12
   E. Different seasonings combine in a mixture. 2:10
   F. Vessels greased with clean, then unclean, oil. 2:13
   G. Mixtures with three components. 2:14–17
III. Prohibition of use of *orlah* fruit. 3:1–8
   A. Forbidden dyes and weaving. 3:1–3
   B. Fire made with coals from *orlah* fruit. 3:4–5
   C. Mixtures of items made with *orlah* fruit. 3:6–8
IV. Cases of doubt. 3:9
   A. Fruit in a status of doubt vis-à-vis the *orlah* taboo is prohibited in the Land of Israel, permitted elsewhere.
   B. Application of the prohibitions to land outside of the holy Land.

Disposing of Crops in a State of Holiness

Peah

I. The corner of the field (Lev. 19:9, 23:22), to be left to the poor. 1:1–4:9
   A. The definition of the field liable to the tax. 1:1–3:8
   B. The definition of the produce liable to the tax. 4:1–2
   C. How the poor acquire the produce. 4:3–9
II. Gleanings, to be left to the poor. 4:10–5:6
   A. The definition of gleanings. 4:10–5:6
   B. Who is permitted to receive gleanings and transactions therein. 5:4–6
III. The forgotten sheaf, to be left to the poor. 5:7–7:2
   A. The definition of the forgotten sheaf. 5:7–7.2
IV. Grape gleanings, to be left to the poor (Lev. 19:10). Definition. 7:3
V. Defective grape cluster, to be left to the poor. Definition. 7:4–8
VI. General rules governing gifts to the poor. Poor man's tithe (Deut. 14:28 f.). 8:1–9

A. When the poor glean. 8:1
B. The claims of the poor to produce. 8:2–4
C. The minimum requirement of poor man's tithe. 8:5–9

Demai

I. Items subject/not subject to tithing as *demai;* the handling and use of *demai* produce. 1:1–4, 2:1
II. Commercial and commensal relations between those who are and are not trustworthy in the matter of tithing. 2:2–5, 3:1–6, 4:1–7
    A. Definitions: the trustworthy person and the *haber.* 2:2–3
    B. Situations in which one must/need not tithe produce that leaves one's possession. 2:4–5, 3:1–6
    C. Situations in which one believes those who ordinarily are not deemed trustworthy in the matter of tithing; credibility. 4:1–7
III. Details of tithing procedure; exemplifications of the principle that tithes must not be separated for produce liable to tithing from produce which is exempt, etc. 5:1–11
IV. Appendix. 6:1–12, 7:1–8
    A. Cases of shared ownership: To what extent must one take responsibility for tithing the portion which one gives to the other fellow? 6:1–12
    B. Further details of the tithing procedure; further cases involving the principle that one must not separate tithes for produce which is liable to tithing from produce which is exempt (mixtures). 7:1–8

Terumot

I. How heave offering (priestly ration) is separated. 1:1–4:6
    A. Valid and invalid designations of produce to be heave offering. 1:1–3:4
    B. The rite of the separation of heave offering. 3:5–4:6
II. Heave offering which has been separated, but still is in the hands of the householder. 4:7–10:12
    A. Heave offering which falls back into the batch from which it was separated: Neutralization. 4:7–5:9
    B. Consumption of heave offering by nonpriest. 6:1–8:3
    C. Nonpriest's responsibility to watch over heave offering for priest. 8:4–12
    D. Heave offering which is planted. 9:1–7
    E. Heave offering cooked or prepared with unconsecrated produce. 10:1–12

III. The disposition of heave offering in the hands of the priest. 11:1–10
    A. Proper preparation of food in the status of heave offering. 11:1–3
    B. Refuse from food in the status of heave offering. 11:4–8
    C. Heave offering which has use other than as human food. 11:9–10

Maaserot

I. Conditions under which produce becomes subject to the law. 1:–4
    A. General conditions. 1:1
    B. Specific conditions. 1:2–4
II. Procedures by which harvested produce is rendered liable to the removal of tithes. 1:5–4:5A
    A. Processing and storage of untithed produce. 1:5–8
    B. Acquisition of produce in four modes. 2:1–3:4
        1. Gifts. 2:1–4
        2. Purchases. 2:5–6
        3. Barter. 2:7–3:3
        4. Lost produce. 3:4
    C. Bringing produce into the courtyard or home. 3:5–10
    D. Preparation of produce for use in a meal. 4:1–5A
III. Unmet conditions and incomplete procedures: Cases of doubt 4:5B –5:8
    A. Unmet conditions: Edibility. 4:5B–6
    B. Incomplete procedures: Harvest. 5:1–2
    C. Unmet conditions: Edibility. 5:3–5
    D. Incomplete procedures: Processing. 5:6–7
    E. Unmet conditions. 5:8
        1. The Land of Israel.
        2. Edibility.

Maaser Sheni

I. Eating second tithe in Jerusalem. 1:1–2:4
    A. Other prohibited uses. 1:1–2
    B. Disposition of inedible items. 1:3–7
    C. Proper use of edible items. 2:1–4
II. Transferring the status of second tithe. 2:5–4:12
    A. From coins to coins. 2:5–9
    B. From coins to produce. 2:10–3:4
    C. From produce to coins. 3:5–4:8
    D. Produce and coins, the status of which is in doubt. 4:9–12
III. Special topics. 5:1–15
    A. Produce of a planting's fourth year. 5:1–5

B. The law of removal. 5:6–9
C. The confession. 5:10–15

Hallah

I.   The substrate of dough offering: Definition of bread-dough that is liable. 1:1–2:2
A. Must be capable of being leavened. 1:1–4C
B. Must be prepared in way in which bread normally is prepared. 1:4D–6F
C. Owner, not baker, is obliged to separate offering (an insertion placed here because of formal affinities with surrounding material). 1:6G–7
D. Must be fit for human consumption. 1:8
E. Appendix: Similar degree of consecration of dough offering and heave offering. 1:9
F. Two unusual cases. 2:1–2
II. The process of separating dough offering. 2:3–9
A. Unusual cases. 2:3–5
B. Measurements. 2:6–7
C. A further case concerning uncleanness. 2:9
III. The point at which liability to dough offering takes effect. 3:1–6
IV. Liability to dough offering of various mixtures. 3:7–4:6
V.   Liability of dough outside Israel. 4:7–11

Bikkurim

I.   The obligation to bring first fruits and to make the stated recitation. 1:1–11
A. Those who do not bring first fruits at all. 1:1–3
B. Those who bring first fruits but do not make the recitation. 1:4–9
C. Those who bring and recite. 1:10–11
II. Comparisons between various agricultural gifts and tithes. Human blood and that of a domesticated animal or reptile. A *koy* and a wild or a domesticated animal. 2:1–11
A. A comparison of the laws governing first fruits, heave offering, and second tithe. 2:1–4
B. Ways in which heave offering of the tithe is like first fruits or heave offering. Ways in which the citron tree is like a tree or a vegetable. 2:5–6
C. Other comparisons. 2:7–11
III. The rules of setting first fruits apart and bringing them to Jerusalem. A narrative of the rite. 3:1–12

A. Setting first fruits apart. 3:1
B. Bringing first fruits to Jerusalem. 3:2–4
C. Presenting the first fruits to the priest. 3:5–8
D. Miscellanies. 3:9–12

Berakhot

I. Reciting the *Shema*. 1:1–3:8
  A. The time for saying the *Shema*, evening and morning. 1:1–3
  B. The liturgy of saying the *Shema* and the text of the *Shema* itself. 1:4–2:3
  C. Special cases in which the requirement to say the *Shema* is suspended or does not apply. 2:4–3:8
  D. Additions to the prayer. 5:2–5
II. Reciting the prayer. 4:1–5:5.
  A. The time for reciting the prayer. 4:1–2.
  B. The liturgy of the prayer. 4:3–4.
  C. Special cases in which the requirement to say the prayer is suspended or does not apply. 4:5–5:1.
  D. Additions to the prayer. 5:2–5.
III. Blessings for food and for meals. 6:1–8:8
  A. Categories of foods and saying a blessing before eating them. 6:1–7
  B. The grace after meals and its protocol. 6:8–7:5
  C. Special rules regarding blessings at meals and other rites connected with meals. 8:1–8
IV. Other kinds of blessings and private prayers. 9:1–5

3. *The Topics of the Oral Torah Treated Only in the Mishnah and the Tosefta*

The Mishnah's sixth division, Purities, gains attention in the two Talmuds only at one point, Niddah, the tractate on the uncleanness of a woman in her menstrual period. Otherwise, the topical program of the large and well-articulated division on Purities is worked out only in the Mishnah and its complementary tractates in the Tosefta.

The Division of Purities

Sources of Uncleanness

Ohalot

I. Proems. 1:1–8
II. Modes of imparting uncleanness, sources of uncleanness. 2:1–3:5
  A. Basic definitions. 2:1–5
  B. Dividing sources of uncleanness. 2:6–3:5

III. Tents. 3:6–16:2E

    A. An opening of a squared handbreadth suffices for the passage of uncleanness. 3:6–7

    B. The subdivisions of a tent, if of requisite space, constitute tents on their own. 4:1–3, 5:1–4

    C. Utensils afford protection with the walls of tents. 5:5–7

    D. Men and utensils serve as tents to contaminate but not to afford protection. 6:1–2

    E. Walls serving more than one house and how they are subdivided. 6:3–7:2

    F. Miscellanies. 7:3–6

    G. Substances which interpose and bring uncleanness. 8:1–6

    H. Rules of interposition and overshadowing. 9:1–12:8

        1. The hive. 9:1–14

        2. Further cases. 9:15–16

        3. The hatchway. 10:1–7

        4. Other problems. 11:1–12:8

    I. Apertures through which corpse uncleanness exudes. 13:1–6

    J. Projections which serve to overshadow. 14:1–7

    K. Miscellanies and conclusion. 15:1–16:2E

IV. Sources of uncleanness analogous to corpse matter. 16:2F–18:10

Negaim (Lev. 13–14)

I. The proem. 1:1–6

II. Plagues in general. Miscellanies. 2:1–5, 3:1–2

III. The prologue. 3:3–8

IV. The bright spot. 4:1–8:10

    A. Tokens of uncleanness in the bright spot. 4:1–3

    B. Miscellanies on white hair. 4:4

    C. Fifteen problems involving the bright spot. 4:4–4:11

    D. Doubts in matters of plagues are resolved in favor of cleanness. 5:1–5

    E. Places on the human being which are not susceptible to uncleanness. 6:7–7:2

        1. Because of the appearance of a bright spot containing quick flesh.

        2. Because of the appearance of a bright spot.

        3. Bright spots which are not susceptible to uncleanness no matter where they occur.

    F. Removing the symptoms of uncleanness. 7:3–5

    G. Breaking forth over the entire body. 8:1–10

V. The boil and the burning. 9:1–3

VI.   Scalls. 10:1–9
VII. The baldspot on forehead and temple. 10:10
VIII. Garments. 11:1–12
IX.   Houses. 12:1–7, 13:1–13
X.   Process of purification of the leper. 14:1–13

Niddah

I.   Retroactive contamination. 1:1–2:4
II.   Unclean excretions. 2:5–5:2
   A. The unclean blood. 2:5–7
   B. Status of abortions as to uncleanness. 3:1–7
   C. Samaritans, Sadducees, and gentile women. 4:1–3
   D. Status of blood produced in labor. 4:4–6
   E. Status of blood in *zibah* period. 4:7
   F. Blood produced in birth by Caesarean section. 5:1A–D
   G. Point at which unclean fluid imparts uncleanness. 5:11E–G (+ 5:2)
III. Rules applicable at various ages (and attached apophthegmatic construction). 5:3–6:12
IV. Doubts in connection with unclean excretions. 6:13–9:10
   A. Bloodstains and other matters of doubt. 6:13–14
   B. Blood of menstruating woman, flesh of corpse, etc. 7:1
   C. Doubts about creeping thing, bloodstain. 7:2
   D. Bloodstains (= doubtfully unclean blood) of Israelites, gentiles, and Samaritans. 7:3–5
   E. Doubts about bloodstain and drops of blood. 8:1–9:7
   F. The fixed period. 9:8–10
V.   Concluding miscellanies (Houses). 9:11–10:8
   A. Nature of female excretions. 9:11–10:1
   B. Doubts of cleanness *re failure* to examine. 10:2–3
   C. Uncleanness of *zab*, menstruating woman. 10:4–5
   D. Status of woman in period of purifying after childbirth. 10:6–7
   E. She who sees blood on eleventh day of *zibah* period. 10:8

Makhshirin

I.   Intention: Divisible or indivisible. 1:1–6
II.   Water capable of imparting susceptibility, mixed with water incapable of imparting susceptibility. 2:1–3 (+ 2:4–11)
III. Absorption of water. 3:1–3
IV. Water used for one purpose—status as to a secondary purpose. 3:4–5:8

V.   Stream as connector. 5:9–11I
VI.   Liquids not used intentionally are insusceptible. 5:11J–M, 6:1–3
VII. Liquids which impart susceptibility to uncleanness. 6:4–8

Zabim

I.   Becoming a *zab*. 1:1–6, 2:1–3
II.   Transferring the *zab's* uncleanness. 2:4, 3:1–3, 5:1–12
      A. Pressure. 2:4, 3:1–3
      B. Generalization. 5:1–12

Tebul Yom

I.   Connection in the case of the *tebul yom*. 1:1–3:5
      A. The principle. 1:1–5
      B. Liquids and connection in the case of the *tebul yom*. 2:1–8
      C. Solid food and connection in the case of the *tebul yom*. 3:1–5
II.   The uncleanness of the *tebul yom*. 3:6, 4:1–4 (+ 4:5–7)

What Is Affected by Uncleanness

Kelim

I.   Proems. 1:1–9
II.   Earthenware utensils. 2:1–10:8
      A. Prologue. 2:1
      B. Susceptibility and insusceptibility of earthenware utensils. 2:2–3:4
      C. Connection and materials used for repairing clay utensils. 3:5–4:4
      D. Baking ovens. 5:1–7:6
      E. Contamination of baking ovens. 8:1–9:7
      F. The tightly stopped up cover in the tent of the corpse. 10:1–8
III. Metal utensils. 11:1–14:8
IV.   Other materials (wood, leather, etc.). 15:1–18:2
      A. Proem. 15:1A–E
      B. Wooden utensils and their susceptibility. 15:1F–16:3
      C. Leather utensils. 16:4–8
      D. The measure of breakage to render an object insusceptible. 17:1–12
      E. General traits of utensils as to susceptibility: Materials, receptacles. Miscellanies. 17:13–18:3E
V.   The wooden bed and its ropes. 18:3F–19:6

Modes of Purification From Uncleanness

A. Purification of the priest. 3:1–4

B. Purification rite must be performed with intent specifically for the rite in hand. Preparations for one slaughter do not serve for some other.

C. Intruded detail, the collected ashes of previously burned cows (3:1B) now explained. Who burned cows?

D. Moving cow and priests (3:1–2) from Temple Mount to Mount of Olives

E. Priest then made unclean.

F. The pyre.

G. The slaughter

H. Cedar, hyssop, scarlet wool thrown into cow.

I. Preparation and disposition of ash.

III. The conduct of the rite. Laws. 4:1–4

A. The cow is (or is not) subject to the laws of the sanctuary.

B. It must be burned in its pit.

C. Sprinkling the blood.

D. Burning the cow.

E. Flaying the cow.

F. Slaughter with wrong intention (= A).

G. Acts of extraneous labor. Contamination.

H. General rules on the rite.

I. Reprise of A.

IV. The purity of utensils used in the rite. 5:1–4

A. The utensil must be guarded even from the time before it is susceptible to uncleanness.

B. Immersing a utensil used for the purification rite.

C. The reed used for collecting ashes.

V. Utensils used in the rite. 5:5–9

A. The mixing of ashes into the water takes place in a whole utensil.

B. Trough used for mixing.

VI. Mixing the ash and the water. 6:1–3

A. The mixing of the ash into the water must be intentional.

B. Retrieving ash for further use.

C. Water-and-ash mixture is presumed to enter a narrow-mouthed flask.

VII. Drawing the water. 6:3–8:1

A. Water must come from a utensil, not be squeezed out of a sponge.

B. Water must be drawn by hand into a utensil.

C. Drawing of water followed by mixing of ashes into the water

must not be interrupted by an act of labor extraneous to the rite
(= 4:4). If it is, the water is spoiled.

 D. If the water is guarded by two men, so long as one is a suitable watchman, the water is acceptably guarded.

VIII. Extraneous matter. 8:2–8

 A. The one who mixes ashes into water should not wear a sandal, because if liquid falls on the sandal, the sandal is made unclean and it makes the man unclean.

 B. All seas are like a pool, Meir. Judah: The Mediterranean alone is like a pool. Yose: Seas when running are like springs but cannot be used for the cow.

IX. Water used for the rite. 8:9–11, 9:1–6 + 9:7

 A. Spring water is to be used. It must be sweet, flow regularly, not be mixed.

 B. If unfit water fell into fit water, it can be removed, so Eliezer. Sages: It cannot.

 C. If an insect fell into water and burst or imparted a color to the water, it is unfit.

 D. If an animal left spittle in the water, it is unfit.

 E. An unacceptable intention does (does not) spoil the water.

 F. Unfit water and its disposition.

 G. Protection of water and ash.

 H. Mixture of suitable and unsuitable ash.

Uncleanness and the purification rite. 9:8–9, 10:1–6, 11:1–6

 A. Capacity of unfit water, ash, to convey uncleanness.

 B. What can contact *midras* is regarded as unclean with *maddaf* uncleanness so far as the purification rite is concerned.

 C. The water must be kept in a clean place.

 D. Joshua's view, illustrated in seven cases.

 E. Doubts in cleanness of the purification rite.

 F. Heave offering which fell into purification water.

 G. An extraneous unit.

XI. Hyssop for sprinkling. 11:7–9, 12:1.

 A. What sort of hyssop is used.

 B. What part of hyssop is used in sprinkling.

 C. Uncleanness and the hyssop.

 D. Hyssop defined: three stalks, three buds, etc.

 E. If hyssop is too short to dip into the water.

XII. The rules of sprinkling. 12:2–11

 A. Doubts as to sprinkling are resolved strictly.

 B. Sprinkling requires the proper intent of the one who does the sprinkling.

C. Doubts as to sprinkling in the public domain are solved leniently; in the private domain, strictly
D. Purification water which has carried out its proper function, having been sprinkled, no longer conveys uncleanness.
E. Sprinkling with an unclean hyssop.
F. We do not reckon degrees of uncleanness in the purification rite.
G. Connection for uncleanness and for sprinkling.
H. Who may sprinkle.
I. When sprinkling may take place.

Miqvaot

I. Proem: Six grades of gatherings of water. 1:1–8
II. Doubts about immersion and immersion pools. 2:1–3
III. Diverse sorts of water, 2:4–10, 3:1–4, 4:1–5, 5:1–6.
IV. The union of pools to form the requisite volume of water: 5:6, 6:1–11
V. Miscellanies: Water and wine. Mud. Water in various locales. 7:1–5 (+ 10:6–8), 7:6–7
VI. The use of the pool: Interposition. 8:5, 9:1–7, 10:1–5, 6–8

Yadayim

I. Washing hands. 1:2–4:4
  A. Repertoire of rules. 1:1–2:4
  B. The status and condition of the water, first and second rinsing. 2:1–4
II. The status of uncleanness imputed to hands. 3:1–2
III. The uncleanness of sacred Scriptures. 3:3–5, 4:5–6
IV. Appendix. Traditions on "On that Day." 4:1–4
V. Appendix. Traditions on "We complain against you." 4:7–8

Bibliography

Each of the components of the oral Torah treated in this book has received its share of sustained scholarly study. Bibliographies on the entire rabbinic corpus of writing produced in late antiquity are gathered in J. Neusner, ed., *The Study of Ancient Judaism* (New York: Ktav Publishing House, 1981), vol. I, "Mishnah, Midrash, Siddur" and vol. II, "The Palestinian and Babylonian Talmuds."

A second substantial bibliographical essay is H. L. Strack and G. Stemberger, *Introduction to Talmud and Midrash* (Chico: Scholars Press, 1987) Studies in the Humanities, a planned translation from the German *Einleitung in Talmud und Midrasch,* 7th ed. This translation is being prepared by G. Stemberger and edited by Caroline McCracken-Flesher. Bibliographies on individual items in the present book will, of course, be readily located in the items listed by the authors of *The Study of Ancient Judaism* and of *Introduction to Talmud and Midrash.*

This book rests upon my earlier researches, which are as follows, specified chapter by chapter:

1. **The Oral Torah Written Down:** *The Mishnah*
   A History of the Mishnaic Law of Purities. Leiden: E. J. Brill, 1974–1977.

I.	*Kelim. Chapters One through Eleven.*
II.	*Kelm. Chapters Twelve through Thirty.*
III.	*Kelim. Literary and Historical Problems.*
IV.	*Ohalot. Commentary.*
V.	*Ohalot. Literary and Historical Problems.*
VI.	*Negaim. Mishnah-Tosefta.*
VII.	*Negaim. Sifra.*

II.   *Erubin, Pesahim. Translation and Explanation.*

III.   *Sheqalim, Yoma, Sukkah. Translation and Explanation.*

IV.   *Besah, Rosh Hashshanah, Taanit, Megillah, Moed Qatan, Hagigah. Translation and Explanation.*

V.   *The Mishnaic System of Appointed Times.*

A History of the Mishnaic Law of Damages. Leiden: E. J. Brill, 1983–1985.

I.   *Baba Qamma. Translation and Explanation.*

II.   *Baba Mesia. Translation and Explanation.*

III.   *Baba Batra, Sanhedrin, Makkot. Translation and Explanation.*

IV.   *Shebuot, Eduyyot, Abodah Zarah, Abot, Horayyot. Translation and Explanation.*

V.   *The Mishnaic System of Damages.*

Judaism: The Evidence of the Mishnah (Chicago: University of Chicago Press, 1980).

2. **The Mishnah and The Tosefta**
    My history of the Mishnaic Law presents each passage of the Tosefta in relationship to the counterpart in the Mishnah, with brief comments on the critical issue of how the Tosefta relates to the Mishnah. In addition, a six-volume translation of the Tosefta is in print as *The Tosefta. Translated from the Hebrew* (New York: Ktav Publishing House, 1977–1985) I–VI. I translated volumes II–VI and (with a former student) edited my students' translation of volume I. The Tosefta here is treated with the Mishnah.

3. **The Theory of Tradition of the Oral Torah:** *Pirqe Avot Torah from Our Sages. Pirke Avot. A New American Translation and Explanation* (Chappaqua, New York: Rossel, 1984).

4. **Explaining the Oral Torah:** *The Sifra and the Yerushalmi A History of the Mishnaic Law of Purities* (Leiden, 1975). VII. *Negaim. Sifra.*
    The Talmud of the Land of Israel: *The Talmud of the Land of Israel. A Preliminary Translation and Explanation* (Chicago: University of Chicago Press, 1982–1988) I–XXXIV; *The Talmud of the Land of Israel* (1983) XXXV. *Introduction. Taxonomy;*

Judaism in Society: The Evidence of the Yerushalmi (Chicago: University of Chicago Press, 1984); and *Our Sages God, and Israel, An Anthology* (Chappaqua, New York: Rossel, 1984). For my discussion of the nature of *midrash* in relationship to the Mishnah and the Yerushalmi in Chapter Four see *Midrash in Context. Exegesis in Formative Judaism.*

5. **Recasting the Written Torah as Oral Torah:** *Leviticus Rabbah Judaism and Scripture. The Evidence of Leviticus Rabbah* (Chicago: University of Chicago Press, 1985). *The Integrity of Leviticus Rabbah* (Chicago: Scholars Press, 1985). *Genesis Rabbah:* I deal with the taxonomic relationship between Genesis Rabbah and the Yerushalmi in my *Midrash in Context. Exegesis in Formative Judaism* (Philadelphia: Fortress Press, 1983). My work on Genesis Rabbah in addition to *Midrash in Context* includes the following: *Genesis Rabbah. The Judaic Commentary on Genesis. A New American Translation.* Atlanta, GA: Scholars Press for Brown Judaic Studies, 1985: I. *Parashiyyot* One through Thirty-Three. Genesis 1:1–8:14. II *Parashiyyot* Thirty-Four through Sixty-Seven. Genesis 8:15–28:9. III. *Parashiyyot* Sixty-Eight through One Hundred. Genesis 28:10–50:26; *Comparative Midrash: Genesis Rabbah and Leviticus Rabbah.* Atlanta, GA: Scholars Press for Brown Judaic Studies, 1985; *Reading Scriptures: An Introduction to Rabbinic Midrash. With special reference to Genesis Rabbah* Chappaqua, NY: Rossel, 1986. The translation of *Parashah* 1 of Leviticus Rabbah is based on the critical text and commentary of M. Margulies, *Midrash Wayyikra Rabbah. A Critical Edition Based on Manuscripts and Genizah Fragments, with Variants and Notes* (Jerusalem, 1953).

6. **The Written Torah and the Oral Torah in Conclusion:** *The Bavli The Talmud of Babylonia. A New American Translation* (Chico: Scholars Press for Brown Judaic Studies, 1984) I. My parts, all in print are as follows: I. *Berakhot;* VI. *Sukkah;* XIV. *Sotah;* XXIII. *Sanhedrin* (in three volumes); XXXII. *Arakhin.* I refer also to my *A History of the Jews in Babylonia* (Leiden, 1965–1970) I–V and *Judaism in Conclusion. The Evi-*

dence of the Bavli (Chicago: University of Chicago Press, 1986).

7. **Our Sages of Blessed Memory:** *Torah in the Flesh*
   I have dealt with the figure of the rabbi as Torah incarnate in my *History of the Jews in Babylonia, Midrash in Context,* and *Torah: From Scroll to Symbol in Formative Judaism* (Philadelphia: Fortress Press, 1983, 1985), part of my trilogy, *The Foundations of Judaism: Method, Teleology, Symbol.*

8. **The Torah, The Dual Torah, and The Oral Torah**
   I also have drawn, for my discussion of the symbol of Torah, on *Torah: From Scroll to Symbol in Formative Judaism* (Philadelphia: Fortress Press, 1985).
   I should have gladly included a chapter on Sifre to Deuteronomy. Since a colleague was at work on a translation and introduction to that interesting document, I did not undertake a study of my own. The work went to press while this book was underway. I requested the right to read the manuscript and quote from the translation and introduction for the purposes of the present work. That request was not granted before this book went to the printer. Accordingly, readers interested in how Sifre to Deuteronomy fits into the larger canonical picture portrayed here will have to see how the issue is treated, if at all, in Robert Hammer, trans., *Sifre to Deuteronomy* (New Haven and London: Yale University Press, 1986).

Glossary

Bar Kokhba. General who led a war against Rome in the Land of Israel from 132 to 135 A.D. The war briefly succeeded but ended in disaster, with Jewish settlement in the southern half of the Land of Israel wiped out.

Bavli. The Talmud of Babylonia (present-day Iraq), completed about 600 A.D.

eschaton. The end of time. Eschatology is the theory of the end of time; what happens at the conclusion of history.

Essene library at Qumran. The Dead Sea Scrolls, a library found at a site known today as Qumran and representative of a group known in the writings of Josephus as Essenes. The scrolls constitute a library of known and newly discovered writings.

exegesis. Interpretation, explanation, the unpacking and spelling out of the meaning of a statement. Usually the exegete, or the one who does the explaining, works out the meaning of a given statement by finding in it points important to a larger conception or argument he or she has in mind.

Galilean sages. Sages located in the region of the Land of Israel called Galilee, in the northern part of the country.

Genesis Rabbah. A collection of rabbinic comments on the book of Genesis, generally thought to have been concluded ca. A.D. 400–450, in the land of Israel.

Judah the Patriarch. Head of the Jewish government in the Land of Israel ca. A.D. 200, responsible for the closure and promulgation of the Mishnah as the governing document for the Jewish administration set up by the Romans after the Bar Kokhba War.

Land of Israel. Judaism claims the land known to Arabs as Palestine and to Christians as the Holy Land as the Land of Israel; that is, the land promised by God to the founders of the Jewish people, Abraham, Issac, and Jacob. Today the state of Israel occupies and governs the Land of Israel in the name of the Jewish people.

levirate. Brother-in-law, referring to the marriage between a deceased childless brother's widow and a surviving brother-in-law, such as is required by Deut. 25:5–10.

Levite. A member of the caste of Levites, Temple officials, and ritual authorities.

Leviticus Rabbah. A rabbinical commentary to the book of Leviticus, generally thought to have been closed ca. A.D. 400–450.

midrash. An explanation of a verse of the Hebrew Scriptures deriving from a rabbinical sage.

min. A heretic. An Israelite who believes propositions rejected by the sages of the Torah.

Mishnah. A code of laws describing a utopian Israelite world, promulgated by Judah the Patriarch ca. A.D. 200. When relevant, it guides the administration of the lives of the Jews of the Land of Israel. The Mishnah became the foundation of the two Talmuds and the basis for Judaism.

Nazir. One who has taken a vow to abstain from wine and other matters, covered in Numbers 6:1–21.

oral Torah. The part of God's revelation at Mount Sinai that was handed on not in writing but in the medium of memorization, hence orally. It is now contained in the Mishnah and in documents that succeeded and carried on the teachings of the Mishnah, as well as in documents that explained Scripture produced by the sages of the Mishnah and their heirs.

pericope. A passage, a completed argument or unit of thought, with a fully worked out proposition, story, or argument.

Pirqe Avot. Sayings of the Founders, a tractate of the Mishnah, produced about a generation after the rest of the Mishnah had been completed that explains the origin of the Oral Torah at Mount Sinai.

pseudepigraphic. A writing attributed to someone other than the actual author, for example, a book written in the first century of the Common Era but attributed to the biblical author Ezra or Jeremiah or Baruch, Jeremiah's secretary.

redaction. The organization and completion of a piece of writing: editing and closure of a book.

Sifra. The rabbinic commentary to the book of Leviticus, attributed to the same authorities who produced the Mishnah.

Sifre. The rabbinic commentaries to the books of Numbers and Deuteronomy. There are hence two such documents, Sifre to Numbers, and Sifre to Deuteronomy (to be compared to "my brother, Darrell, and my other brother, Darrell"), containing sayings of authorities who produced the Mishnah.

stich. A passage, a line or part of a line of a larger composition.

Temple in Jerusalem. Center for sacrifice and prayer, originally constructed by King Solomon, destroyed in 586 B.C., rebuilt about three generations later, and kept in service until finally destroyed by the Romans in 70. At that time animal sacrifice ended in Judaism.

Torah. The revelation of God to Moses at Mount Sinai. A teaching in the status of divine revelation.

torah. A teaching in the status of divine revelation.

Tosefta. A collection of supplements to the Mishnah.

written Torah. That part of the torah of Sinai that was transmitted in writing that is known to Christians as the Old Testament. Jews know it as Tanakh, and it appears in three components: Torah, the Pentateuch, Prophets; the books from Joshua through Ezekiel and the twelve minor prophets; and the Writings, such as Psalms, Proverbs, and Job.

Yerushalmi. The Talmud of the Land of Israel, an amplification and expansion of the Mishnah, generally thought to have been completed ca. A.D. 400.

Index to Biblical and Talmudic References

General Index